For Cheryl
my good ...
and confident
May I know Many
more like you
having Your
grace + talent

## The Complete
## Job-Search Handbook

Books by Howard Figler

PATH: A Career Exploration Workbook for Liberal Arts Students
Outreach in Counseling (with David J. Drum)

# The Complete Job-Search Handbook

All the Skills You Need to Get Any Job
and Have a Good Time Doing It

## Howard Figler

Holt, Rinehart and Winston
NEW YORK

Published by Holt, Rinehart and Winston, 383 Madison Avenue, New York, New York 10017.

Published simultaneously in Canada by Holt, Rinehart and Winston of Canada, Limited.

**Library of Congress Cataloging in Publication Data**
Figler, Howard.
    The complete job-search handbook

    Bibliography: p. 269.
    Includes index.
      1. Applications for positions.    2. Vocational guidance.    3. Employment
interviewing.    I. Title.
HF5383.F52       650'.14       79-4153
ISBN Hardbound: 0-03-044121-8
ISBN Paperback: 0-03-044126-9

First Edition

Designer: Lana Giganti
Printed in the United States of America
10  9  8  7  6  5  4  3  2  1

The author is grateful to the following publisher for permission to reprint previously
copyrighted material:

From *PATH: A Career Workbook for Liberal Arts Students* by Howard E. Figler; copyright
© 1975 by Howard E. Figler. Reprinted by permission of the Carroll Press, Cranston,
Rhode Island.

To my mother and father

# Contents

Acknowledgments ..............................ix
Introduction ....................................1

## Part 1 • Self-Assessment Skills

1 Values ..........................................41
2 Feelings .......................................55
3 Skills ...........................................60
4 Creativity ......................................80
5 Risking .........................................92
6 Goal Setting ...................................98

## Part 2 • Detective Skills

7 Introduction ................................107
8 Prospect List ...............................113
9 Personal Referral Network ..................120

## Part 3 • Research Skills

10 Introduction ...............................133
11 Printed Materials ..........................137
12 Inquiring Reporter .........................143
13 Participant Observation ...................154

## Part 4 • Communication Skills

14 Introduction ...............................163
15 Listening ...................................170
16 Questioning ................................180
17 Assertiveness ..............................188
18 Self-Disclosure ............................198
19 Writing .....................................206

# Part 5 • Transition Skills

20 **Support Group** .............................. 221
21 **Self-Marketing** ............................. 230
22 **Remote Control** ............................ 237
23 **Interim Jobs** .............................. 243

# Part 6 • Other Perspectives

24 **For Shy People** ............................ 251
25 **Zen of the Career Search** ................... 257

**Notes** ...................................... 266

**Selected Annotated Bibliography** ............ 269

**Index** ..................................... 275

# Acknowledgments

The twenty-skills format of this book was inspired by Allen Ivey and his book *Microcounseling* (Chas. C Thomas, Springfield, Ill., 1971). I am indebted to Ivey for enabling me to understand that career search skills can be isolated, practiced, and taught to others.

My good friend and advisor, Bob Entwistle, gave this manuscript its first push and then gently nudged it to completion. Bob had faith in these ideas when no one else did and applied them to his own emerging career.

Once I had written the manuscript, Dave Drum, Bob Calvert, and Bob Babcock reviewed it and offered numerous suggestions that resulted in major changes. I am grateful to have colleagues with their wisdom and unselfishness.

As the manuscript neared its final revision, I was aided gently by my colleagues at Dickinson College— Diane Ronningen, Dottie Wolfe, and all the career assistants who were trained with the ideas in this book. My co-workers put the skills of the career search into action and provided indelible proof that we are on the right track.

Finally, Natalie Chapman, my editor at Holt, Rinehart and Winston, shaped the final version of this book with such keen judgment that I could award her an honorary degree in career counseling. I am also indebted to Natalie for her forthrightness and unfailing good cheer.

The invisible army behind this book is the legions of career counselors who are proving that they are not job brokers or witch doctors paid to divine career futures, but a new breed of professional, teaching people how to seek career goals in ways that are enjoyable, productive, and in tune with the natural rhythms of the seekers' lives.

# The Complete
# Job-Search Handbook

# ✌ Introduction ✌

*People are always blaming their circumstances for what they are. I don't believe in circumstances. The people who get on in this world are the people who get up and look for the circumstances they want, and if they can't find them—make them.* • George Bernard Shaw
*Mrs. Warren's Profession*

There are some people in this world who can advance their careers simply by declaring they are available. Like blaring trumpets, their credentials speak for themselves, announcing the presence of persons who are obviously suited to perform particular jobs. Such people are renowned for certain public achievements, or possess advanced degrees that automatically qualify them for certain work, or have rare or outstanding talents, or can measure their previous accomplishments on dollar scales that preclude the need for further investigation to certify competence. These individuals need not read this book because career opportunities drop into their laps. Top-drawer people can make it on their own; the rest of us need all the help we can get.

Let's suppose you are seeking better work, but have no single outstanding credential you can use in marketing yourself. You have done very competent and dedicated work for many years and have been appreciated by your peers and superiors. The trouble is, you have no highly visible way to call attention to the work you have done. You know you are good at what you do, but cannot translate this into words, numbers, or other marketable symbols. Every time you proceed to look for an improvement in your career, it's as though you're starting all over again. No one outside your present colleagues knows what you are capable of doing. Applying for a new job becomes a trial of persuading yourself and others that you are not faking, stepping out of your

1

league, or otherwise misrepresenting yourself. This predicament describes 98 percent of us at one time or another. We are struggling to be noticed, searching for the key phrases that will tell a prospective employer everything we are capable of doing without seeming pretentious or overbearing.

If you have not won awards for your past work performance, are not famous or known to the general public in some respect, cannot announce your potency in terms of dollar sales, you are a mere mortal in the career search process. There is no magic available for you. The success of your search will depend on how well you understand the process of finding better work and the things people do to convey their abilities to a new market.

Many readers have been tantalized by reports of the hidden job market. Philosophers of the career search have encouraged people to seek new opportunities by using take-charge methods that uncover unadvertised jobs. Once having tried these methods, many are frustrated by their apparent inability to acquire these unseen career opportunities. They are unsuccessful because they lack many of the skills to put a take-charge attitude into action.

You-can-do-it philosophies invest you with courage, but courage is not enough. You must have the tools to accompany your firm resolve—the skills of self-assessment, detective work, researching, interpersonal communication, and managing a career transition. Take-charge philosophies assume that the individual is already quite powerful and self-confident in the approach to the marketplace. I doubt that many readers feel so powerful, even after absorbing the philosophy of a self-initiated career search.

Recently several authors have laid a strong foundation for understanding how to conduct a self-directed career search by explaining how job markets function and why passive approaches are far less effective than methods in which you actually control the search. They even offer detailed procedures you can use and describe the best ways to approach employers directly.

These methods are designed to inspire you and give you a clear picture of how the most successful job seekers operate.

The trouble starts when the newly optimistic job seeker tries to put take-charge methods into practice, then quickly realizes that a new awareness and a positive attitude are not enough to ensure success in the search. In short, she or he lacks many of the skills necessary to make the new strategies work.

The advocates of the self-directed career search have done an admirable job of outlining the most successful strategies, but they have not been clear enough about the specific skills that are prerequisite to these strategies. They have implied what these skills are, but have not defined them sufficiently and have not made it clear that a person must learn and practice these skills in the daily routine before tackling the target employers.

Richard Bolles (author of *What Color Is Your Parachute?* and *Newsletter about Life/Work Planning*) has made the most significant contribution to date toward defining the essential career skills and how they can be learned. The purpose of this book is to expand the ideas proposed by Bolles and others into a comprehensive model of career skills. Such a model can be used by individuals, career counselors, and others who want to learn all the elements that constitute a career search.

Career skills are like wilderness skills. When you are lost deep in the woods of an unknown territory, you have no clues to how to get out of the predicament, but you know you will manage to survive and prosper because you understand the land and how to use its resources. You can be lost anywhere, and yet make a successful recovery. Similarly, you want to be able to survive in new career landscapes without resorting to magical assistance from other sources.

## Everyone Needs Career Skills

Perhaps at times you have felt you have certain advantages that allow you to be casual, even lazy, about looking for better work. Consider yourself among the 2 percent in the privileged class of job seekers if you are in the top 10 percent of your college class, your IQ is above 135, you are a former athlete or other visible public figure, you are extraordinarily beautiful or six-foot three and handsome, you are a graduate of an Ivy League or other prestigious university, or you are naturally gifted as a salesperson for yourself. If any of these is true of you, you may not be sure whether you need this book. Be assured, however, that relying on a single great talent or personal characteristic can be dangerous over the long haul. Beauty fades, talent wanes, and circumstances change unexpectedly. In the long run, nothing can substitute for a knowledge of how to develop and use career skills.

For most ordinary folk, comfort, peace of mind, and self-assurance in the career search derive not from knowing that you possess one great talent to depend on, but from knowing you possess the appropriate skills to find other work if this talent should dissipate or lose its natural market.

Those 98 percent who are plain looking, possess average college grades, have no great accomplishments, graduated from nonprestigious universities, receive little recognition on the job, have checkered career patterns, or are otherwise inheritors of ordinariness actually can, and do, turn the tables on the privileged by learning to acquire career skills from the very start. By having to survive, they learn to be superior survivors. The ordinary folk become stronger; the inheritors of great career wealth lose their potency when they can no longer receive automatic appointments based on their appearance, credentials, or birthright.

Fear not the burden of being ordinary. I know the hordes of job competitors you imagine make you highly anxious, but you can turn this anxiety to your advantage. So many talented and untalented people depend on luck, magic formulas, handouts from family or friends, or whims of the marketplace that a little initiative and focused effort can yield a greater gain. While they are wasting their energies looking for handouts, your knowledge of the secrets of the career search process will pay off.

## You Have Been Told to Work Too Hard

Despite the value of career skills, many in the vast middle class of job hunting are discouraged by well-intentioned friends or counselors who say: "Job hunting is hard work, so push yourself, make an all-out effort"; or "Know *exactly* what you want before making an application"; or "Get out there and take control of the process, take charge!" (as though you were a football quarterback being exhorted by the fiery coach).

These are empty messages. They serve more to frustrate you than stir you to action. Admonished to work hard, work harder, know thyself, drive, drive, drive, you wonder what you are supposed to do first.

Most of all, you do not want to work hard. You do not want to embrace a philosophy of career seeking that sounds as if it were written for Superman. You want a career search strategy that will not rip your life apart or double your anxiety level in one swift stroke.

In all likelihood, you have already devised a homemade strategy for your career search and have built it into your daily routine. You are making some progress on your wits and common sense, without having to quit your present work, spend a fortune on career consultants, or have your palm read for further clues. In short, you are doing a decent job of job hunting on your own. However, you need a few hints about what you are doing wrong. These clues should suggest where you can make adjustments in your search while not disturbing the life routine to which you have become accustomed.

It has been said that getting a job is harder than any job you will ever do. Don't let that scare you. Landing a job is easier than you may believe. You can use the model of twenty career skills in this book to decide which skills you have been neglecting. You will see that you are already using many career skills very effectively and will be encouraged to perfect your own methods.

---

# The Blessings of the Career Search

---

While you are pleased to know there is hope for ordinary folk who seek better work, there is another part of you that says the career search is the curse of the employment misfit, or your penalty for being so untalented that no one notices you, or simply a bigger pain than anything else imaginable. It is a mistake to believe that a career search is a punishment for past failures. What may appear to be the curses of an extended exploration for better work are truly blessings in disguise:

- The curse of having to make the rounds of many employers, endure many interviews, and read numerous career materials before you decide becomes the blessing of reaching a large number of professional people who are acquainted with you and your work and can thus serve as your present and future contacts.
- The curse of struggling to identify your hidden talents—your subtle, not easily labeled abilities—becomes the blessing of discovering that you have many qualifications and skills that are marketable in a wide variety of employment contexts.
- The curse of not knowing exactly what your future will be, of living with unknown options and uncertain timetables, becomes the blessing of being secure enough so you don't jump at the first job opportunity; you enjoy playing with the many creative possibilities on your career landscape and trust that the mysterious plot in your career story will be resolved in your favor.
- The curse of having to ask many people a lot of

questions, probe their psyches, and intrude upon their valuable time becomes the blessing of learning interview skills so you can elicit information and attitudes from anyone with ease in a way that makes the interview even more pleasing to the other people than to yourself.

- The curse of having to explain yourself to everyone, justify your reasons for even wanting to talk about career matters, becomes the blessing of having the skills to portray yourself clearly, creatively, and in terms that are marketable without being pretentious or self-conscious.

- And the curse of taking on a task that seems to be a job in itself becomes the blessing of learning that most elements of the career search are already entwined in your daily routine of work and play and need only be improved or emphasized by a more conscious and focused effort on your part.

Perhaps the greatest blessing of career skills is that they can be used long before you are interviewed for your next job. You begin your search for your next position the very day you are hired in your present one.

There is a prevailing myth that all judgments of you as a job candidate are held in suspense until you arrive for the formal interview. That is why so many interviewees practice trying on new clothes and muttering magic phrases they hope will capture the interviewer's attention. This sort of preparation is self-defeating; if you believe that key words, manner of dress, or significant glances during a job interview will make the difference, you will find it extremely difficult to be your natural self. You will be one more victim of interview psychosis.

But if you take advantage of career skills long before the formal interviews, you will already know a lot about your target employer, who will also know a lot about you. As you will see in the forthcoming chapters, you can assess yourself, detect the available jobs, become expert about prospective employers, practice your communication skills, establish a network of helpers, and spend many hours with the people for whom you would like to work long before you decide to announce your intentions. The courtship is what counts; the wedding ceremony is a mere formality.

## Who and What This Book Is For

This book is for college graduates, career changers, returning workers, midlife-crisis and second-career people, and any others who feel they deserve better careers than they currently have. I assume you have opened this book not for casual reasons, but because you need some immediate help with your special career predicament. Career decisions probably are not new to you; I suspect you believe you already know a lot about the subject. You may already have tried several systems that disappointed you and may be curious to see if anything new can be said. You are open to a new approach, anything that will dislodge you from your present rut.

If you are like most people, you prefer not to read a whole book to extract the information you need. To accommodate your desire to get information quickly, I have organized this volume so you can see what topics are covered at a glance. Like a patient who prefers a quick diagnosis to having the entire body examined, you prefer the shortest of shortcuts possible to obtain relief. You can skip around in this book, read the parts you like best or need most. I wrote it to be used that way because you are probably already doing many things right in the career search. You are also doing a few things wrong and want to know what they are and how to correct yourself quickly.

How is this book different from other books on career guidance? First of all, it does its best to illuminate the entire *process* that occurs when a person seeks better work. This process consists of using skills career advisors have heretofore taken for granted or ignored. The book spells out every skill you need to conduct a successful career search. I propose that these career skills will come more naturally to you than "job hunting techniques" and that you will not need to depend on "placement" help once you become familiar with these skills.

I call these essential processes *career skills*; I maintain that you can enhance and improve every one of them with ordinary effort, simply by using them routinely in your career search.

Second, I propose that most of your career search activity can and ought to be initiated long before the formalities of résumé preparation and job interviews. If you wait until you *must* have a new job or career next month, you will have allowed most of your opportunities to pass you by. You can and should do career exploration every day of your life.

Third, most career processes or skills have not been clarified before because they are connected to certain generic life skills that you already use to solve other life problems. You have been using career skills every day, probably unconsciously. The purpose here is to make sure you use and refine your career skills more deliberately and with greater proficiency.

Thus, this is a book that focuses on the twenty generic life skills that come into play whenever an individual acts to seek a new career. Past volumes have paid scant attention to specific skills. Instead, they exhort the individual to "know thyself," "take the initiative," and "be persistent," without ever explaining the processes involved. Many career seekers find it difficult to make progress following this standard advice, but cannot determine why they are failing. A highly structured program may tell them what to do on Day 1, Day 2, and so forth, but they cannot put the advice to use. Why? Because people lack the skills to carry out well-meant advice. A person told to prepare for a job interview must guess what that means when he or she has no research skills. A person cautioned to speak more clearly needs help with communication skills. An individual told to look harder needs detective skills to translate the advice into action. Advice givers who criticize clients without teaching the necessary skills are only creating frustration.

While I encourage you to diagnose and treat your career search problem through use of several skills that seem appropriate, I caution you not to expect a cookbook solution to your difficulty. I cannot tell you what to do in ten easy steps. Precious few successful career searches are conducted in so mechanical a fashion. You must decide the best sequence of events for yourself.

A small but important proportion of readers will be systematic and patient enough to digest the book from beginning to end. Those who do will discover that the twenty career skills are presented in an orderly sequence, as outlined in Chart 1. Though many individuals will choose to study and practice these skills in a sequence different from the one I have presented, I believe this sequence best represents the order of events in a career search.

You must begin with an understanding of your uniqueness (self-assessment skills) in order to determine which employers are likely to be most interested in you. Specific methods of exploration (detective skills) then enable you to accumulate a list of prospective organizations. Once having identified such a target list, you must gather data (research skills) that help you become intimately acquainted with target employers at the top of your list. Finally, the skills of interpersonal exchange (communication skills) are vitally necessary for the many occasions when you talk with or write to an individual who has career possibilities for you. Transition skills, which help you to manage the entire career search process, are used during all four categories of the career search sequence.

None of these five skills categories is a stage you must complete before moving to the next category. You move back and forth among categories frequently. However, I offer these twenty skills in a sequence, rather than as a list, because I believe this parallels the course you would try to follow on your own.

| Self-Assessment Skills | Detective Skills | Research Skills | Communication Skills | Transition Skills |
|---|---|---|---|---|
| Values | Prospect List | Printed Materials | Listening | Support Group |
| Feelings | Personal Referral Network | Inquiring Reporter | Questioning | Self-Marketing |
| Skills | | Participant Observation | Assertiveness | Remote Control |
| Creativity | | | Self-Disclosure | Interim Job |
| Risking | | | Writing | |
| Goal setting | | | | |

Chart 1. The twenty skills of the career search

Perhaps more importantly, the chart allows you to see the entire career search process as an organic unity, reminding you that the several parts of career exploration are interconnected and that proficiency in one career skill undoubtedly aids progress with all the others.

# The Twenty Skills of the Career Search

The twenty skills discussed in this book fall into five categories: self-assessment, detective, research, communication, and transition skills. Each skill is briefly discussed below.

### • Self-Assessment Skills •

1) *Values* • Identifying and clarifying the highest priority rewards and satisfactions you hope to obtain in your career; discriminating sharply among competing opportunities.

**2)** *Feelings* • Heightening your sensitivity to your own emotions so that you recognize career-related feelings when they occur and describe them with greater precision than "like" or "dislike."

**3)** *Skills* • Identifying and labeling your most prominent strengths or abilities and choosing the ones you most enjoy using in work situations.

**4)** *Creativity* • Learning to envision new and previously unimagined career possibilities by using creative thought processes such as adapting, reversing, combining, and magnifying.

**5)** *Risking* • Recognizing that risk is an inevitable part of your career search and learning to distinguish among risk styles so that you choose one most appropriate for yourself.

**6)** *Goal Setting* • Translating your self-assessment into an action plan by framing short-term objectives that set the stage for first-hand exploration.

### • Detective Skills •

**7)** *Prospect List* • Building a comprehensive list of people, organizations, and situations that seem most likely to offer the kinds of work you desire.

**8)** *Personal Referral Network* • Learning how to create contacts for yourself by establishing relationships with people who can refer you to other people who are connected to your prospect list.

### • Research Skills •

**9)** *Printed Materials* • Using readily available published materials quickly to obtain data about a target employer, an industry, or a given individual you hope to meet.

**10)** *Inquiring Reporter* • Obtaining information and insight directly from people in careers you may desire to enter; learning what questions to ask and how to conduct the entire exchange.

**11)** *Participant Observation* • Gathering data about an occupational field or a specific employer through direct experience; participating in a career setting without having to make any commitment to it.

### • Communication Skills •

**12)** *Listening* • Attending fully to another person's words, feelings, hidden messages, and subtle meanings; learning how to detect when you are not listening effectively.

**13)** *Questioning* • Using questions in ways that encourage the other person to talk freely and offer more information that will aid your exploration; learning effective and noneffective methods of questioning.

**14)** *Assertiveness* • Taking initiatives in the career search process; learning nonaggressive methods to interest people in talking with you and providing you with assistance.

**15)** *Self-Disclosure* • Expressing yourself freely and comfortably when asked to talk about your accomplishments, aspirations, and past experiences; practicing self-disclosure.

**16)** *Writing* • Using written forms of communication in a personal way; writing letters to prospective employers that convey your inner motivations and spark a personal response.

### • Transition Skills •

**17)** *Support Group* • Reducing the aloneness of the career search by involving other people as your cohorts, assistants, and cheerleaders; assembling a team of helpers.

**18)** *Self-Marketing* • Sensitizing yourself to elements of your background that are most likely to be marketable; collecting evidence of your abilities so it can be presented to an employer.

**19)** *Remote Control* • Practicing your career skills when you are far away from your target geographical area; deciding what skills to use before the move and when to move to the target area.

**20)** *Interim Job* • Accepting stopgap employment that allows you to survive financially but also makes it possible for you to continue exploration toward your career goals.

## Diagnose Your Own Career Ailment

Perhaps you already understand many of the career skills and have used them successfully. Or perhaps you have precious little time and must be selective in deciding where to devote your energies. Or maybe many of the skills simply do not apply to your situation. Even if you can eliminate some career skills from your agenda, you may still be confused about where to start. You don't care to do everything, but would like some definite instructions to follow. To help you use your time most judiciously, I have distilled several typical career search problems and proposed that each problem can be attacked best by concentrating on a small number of skills. Your special predicament requires that you look at certain career skills before you look at others. In other words, I am giving specific directions for the shortcut that best applies to you.

Find yourself in the eight problem situations described below. You may be out of work and desperate for anything that pays money, or you may be solidly entrenched in a job but bored enough to contemplate a new career. Go directly to the problem that correlates best with yours, and put those skills listed into practice without delay. As your career search proceeds, you will use other skills, but I have advised you to use these skills first because they will produce results most quickly.

All these shortcut strategies are designed to reduce your task to a manageable size so that you do not feel overwhelmed. There is nothing sacred about the skills chosen for each problem. You may choose skills other than those I have proposed. You may see yourself in more than one problem area and thus have to concoct your own strategy. My main concern is that you use a strategy simple and brief enough so you don't wear yourself out, but specific enough so you are enthusiastic about getting started.

### • Problem One: I'm Panicked, • Desperate, at My Wits' End

I need to find work in a hurry. My income is fast shrinking toward zero. I have little time to spare, must get a job the fastest way possible.

**Interim Job (Skill 20)** • In your impoverished state, you must first get a job that provides enough income for survival. But make sure this is also a job that allows you sufficient freedom to keep looking for your real vocational goal.

**Prospect List (Skill 7)** • Most panic results from not knowing where the jobs are. This skill teaches you how to uncover potential employers with a minimum of effort, so you can conduct your search in an organized manner.

**Personal Referral Network (Skill 8)** • Once having developed a list of prospects, you need to establish personal contact with them. This skill tells you how to attract personal attention from people who offer career possibilities that interest you.

**Support Group (Skill 17)** • You probably have not made sufficient use of fellow job seekers, family, and others who have more than a casual interest. Surround yourself with a team of interested people who will gather information, share job search experiences, and refuel your enthusiasm.

**Remote Control (Skill 19)** • Your panic may result from being far away from your target geographical area. A special strategy is necesary for searching at a distance, knowing when to move and how to manage the transition between long-distance searching and in-person exploration.

## • Problem Two: I'll Want to Move • Eventually, but It's Not Yet Urgent

I have an orderly career timetable. I know my present job will expire x years from now, so I can plan systematically toward that end.

**Values (Skill 1)** • The most orderly transition is one that accounts for your changing needs, the subtle shifts in what you regard as satisfying in your work. What kinds of motivators elicit your best and most enthusiastic responses? What bores you today that excited you yesterday? If you are alert to these changes, you'll deal well with your future career transition.

**Creativity (Skill 4)** • Allow yourself to daydream about your future; propose several wild ideas for new careers. This skill will help you to break loose from thinking only of conventional or expected career alternatives.

**Writing (Skill 16)** • Chances are that creative thinking will jar loose a few employment possibilities that are not in your home area. Thus, you should make the acquaintance of target employers by letter.

**Goal Setting (Skill 6)** • Given the time, you can pay close attention to setting specific objectives that will lead you toward your ideal career. This skill tells you how to identify a goal and pursue it without dispersing your energy in several directions.

**Participant Observation (Skill 11)** • The more time you have available, the more you can devote to experiencing career possibilities firsthand rather than just talking about them. There are several ways to do this while keeping your present employment intact.

### • Problem Three: I'm Bored, • I Need a New Challenge

I am secure in my present job situation, but cannot stand this place anymore. I have fulfilled my usefulness here, solved the big problems, and now need a new challenge to get the juices flowing again.

**Risking (Skill 5)** • How much risk are you willing to take in exchange for eliminating your boredom? You are about to make a new departure in your life, so examine the several risk styles open to you.

**Inquiring Reporter (Skill 10)** • You probably have been in your present job a long while; hence, you must reactivate the skill of getting information from others. Information interviewing is the key link between you and a new career. This skill gives you specific guidelines for gathering data from other people.

**Questioning (Skill 13)** • The success of your information interviews will depend heavily on your ability to question tactfully and with clarity. Certain questioning methods have a high likelihood of yielding positive results; others are almost certain to discourage your respondent.

**Participant Observation (Skill 11)** • If you are determined to leap into a difficult field, you should participate in it directly before deciding you want to embrace it. This skill reveals how you can sample a work environment before committing yourself to an irreversible change.

**Self-Marketing (Skill 18)** • When changing occupational fields, you must be aware of the marketable talents you can transfer from one field to the other. This skill tells you how to assess your marketability and how to present yourself to a new employer.

## • Problem Four: I Have Been •
## in School and Have
## Little Work Experience

I don't know where to start. I have never been in the real world before. My only experience is in the classroom.

**Skills (Skill 3)** • Make a thorough review of your prominent strengths. Persuade yourself that you do have a lot to offer, even if you are young and inexperienced. By knowing your own assets, you can judge which jobs need you more than others.

**Values (Skill 1)** • Obstacles move aside for people who know what they want. Take a close look at the activities you find most satisfying and the reasons these activities stimulate you. You need not have work experience to discover career-related values. These values appear in your informal, out-of-classroom experiences.

**Self-Disclosure (Skill 15)** • As soon as you have a firm grip on what your strengths are, you should learn to talk about yourself and practice with others until it becomes second nature; this skill tells you how to describe yourself without appearing to be overly self-important.

**Goal Setting (Skill 6)** • You can begin putting your career search into action with short-term goals. This skill teaches you to make tentative goal statements that sharpen your search for long-range objectives.

**Prospect List (Skill 7)** • While you have access to a career resource library (in your school's guidance office or career planning center) and other libraries, this skill is easy to develop. You can put together a list of prospective places of employment by using these handy reference materials. Use these resources to convince yourself there are jobs out there when you're ready to find them.

**Printed Materials (Skill 9)** • Once again, your access to libraries gives you the advantage of gathering research data about employers long before they interview you. Let the research competencies you developed through your academic work prepare you for future career exploration.

### • Problem Five: I Don't Want •
### to Change My Job,
### Just My Assignment

I don't want to move from my present employer at all, but I do need a different kind of work, a different project, assignment.

**Values (Skill 1)** • Review the sources of your disenchantment by clarifying the values you feel are not satisfied in your present job responsibilities. Try to define or identify positions in the organization that would rekindle your enthusiasm.

**Self-Marketing (Skill 18)** • When leaving a comfortable position for a new assignment, you should review what is most marketable in your work background so you can readily interest another department in your services.

**Assertiveness (Skill 14)** • In order to change assignments or job titles, you'll probably have to initiate the request, follow it up, and perhaps persuade someone else to be uprooted. All this requires assertive skill, the ability to present ideas openly to those in power.

**Inquiring Reporter (Skill 10)** • Because you are already on site, you have abundant opportunity to interview people about their work in other departments. Even though you may believe you already know what they do, a few interviews will convince you otherwise.

**Support Group (Skill 17)** • You may have better success if you enlist the aid of several others in the organization who desire changes too. If you create an informal support group, the members can help one another pool information and perhaps even generate a few job trades in the process.

## • Problem Six: I'm a Late Entry, •
## Returning to the Work Force

I've been away from organized employment for many years. I've been a homemaker, odd jobber, traveler, or self-employed person.

**Skills (Skill 3)** • You will feel out of place and somewhat immobilized until you use skills-identification methods to generate some self-esteem. You'll discover that you have cultivated numerous job skills even though you weren't paid for them.

**Personal Referral Network (Skill 8)** • To acquaint yourself with job markets you've hitherto ignored, you should tap a pool of personal contacts who can lead you to sources of employment. This skill details how anyone can build a personal referral network, especially those who have not been employed by someone else recently.

**Assertiveness (Skill 14)** • Anyone has the right to initiate contact with a target employer, but many people don't know how to practice the skill. Assertiveness is always painless and usually pleasurable when done correctly; the skill can be practiced in many everyday settings.

**Prospect List (Skill 7)** • In addition to your personal referral network, you should use readily available employer directories to build a list of possible places of work. Using these directories gets you started quickly; with these and other prospecting materials, you can generate a list long enough to keep you occupied indefinitely.

**Creativity (Skill 4)** • As a person new to the career search, you will probably overlook many career fields that might interest you. You should stimulate your thinking by applying a few creative processes to your own background, and be willing to try the results.

## • Problem Seven: I Have •
## Tried Everything

My methods don't work. I have tried every job hunting technique under the sun. What am I doing wrong?

**Listening (Skill 12)** • If you are at your wits' end, you probably have had a hard time listening to other people fully. Your antennae are dulled by your desire to be heard. Recycle your listening skill by practicing it informally; then renew your search.

**Inquiring Reporter (Skill 10)** • The most frustrated career searchers are usually those who fail to take advantage of information interviewing. They are too busy seeking job interviews prematurely. This skill teaches you how to use inquiry techniques so that you are the chooser, rather than the one being chosen.

**Creativity (Skill 4)** • You are probably imposing unconscious restraints upon yourself. Let your imagination take you to some unlikely, even outrageous places. Try purposely to build a new career idea that does not even currently exist. In the process of looking for a new planet, you may discover an unexpected way of picturing your life on earth.

**Support Group (Skill 17)** • It is time you found some fellow sufferers and created a small network of help and reinforcement. Others will remind you that you have *not* tried everything. A team approach multiplies your pool of information and reduces feelings of despair and self-pity.

**Participant Observation (Skill 11)** • Chances are you need to back off from the active search for a little while. Participant observation gives you time to reality test your desired career by sampling it on an informal basis. This skill details several ways you can test your suitability for the career without being hired into it.

**Self-Marketing (Skill 18)** • Often people with the right qualifications are passed over because neither they nor their interviewers realize what they have to offer. Self-marketing is the ability to point out what is most salable about yourself and to support it with proper evidence. This skill teaches you how to judge what your marketable qualities are.

## • Problem Eight: I'm Trapped •

I know I must make a change, but family and financial priorities prevent me from considering it. I am sad to admit that this will probably be my position for many years to come.

**Remote Control (Skill 19)** • Just for your own mental health, take a fantasy trip to places and career settings where you'd like to be if you could free yourself. Draw as clearly as possible the pictures you imagine and then use long-distance skills to identify organizations and people who might satisfy your career wishes.

**Values (Skill 1)** • Isolate the factors that make your present work unhappy; this is the most demanding of career search skills, but worth the effort. What sources of reward would make a difference to you? Don't be vague; pin down the activities, resources, and specific tasks that would be most likely to change your attitude.

**Printed Materials (Skill 9)** • This skill allows you to explore your new interests with a minimum time investment. Use the nearest library for newspapers and journals that focus on your target interests, and write away to organizations for their free literature. Stimulate your imagination with these materials; perhaps these materials will prepare you for the day when you are no longer so "trapped."

**Writing (Skill 16)** • This skill encourages you to take an additional step toward creating a fantasy job while you are stuck in your present one. If you establish correspondence with just one or two people in a fantasy field, you have made contacts and probably the beginnings of friendships as well. Letters need not be scholarly or pushy, just personal, enthusiastic, and genuine.

**Goal Setting (Skill 6)** • You are not as trapped as you think. If you define one concrete goal that emerges from your musings, reading, and letter writing, you have taken the first step toward adjusting your present situation. Perhaps the adjustment can be a change of function in your paid employment or the start of a nonpaid employment. Having defined the first step in behavioral terms, you are making progress.

## Five Key Assumptions

Several assumptions pervade the recommendations given in this book; collectively they make up an attitude about the career search that is different from the view that job hunting is dreadfully hard work, highly competitive, and pressure-laden. I believe it is important to bring these central assumptions into the open so that you can understand a little better the attitudes and emotional tone of this volume.

**The Career Search Is Fun** • As long as you regard looking for work as drudgery or as punishment for leaving your last job, you will try to terminate it as quickly as possible and will accept the first thing that comes your way. I assume throughout this volume that the career search is an activity you can look forward to and become enthusiastic about. I believe it will become enjoyable for you about the moment you realize that you do have many options, that you can turn down an offer, safe in the assurance that you will find a better one. You can look forward to a job interview, instead of dreading it, because you will regard it as a chance to be curious and explore, rather than as an all-or-nothing situation.

**The Career Search Involves Exploring, Not Hunting** • Job seekers lose their patience and will because they are too single-minded about the task at hand. They easily become anxious and frustrated because they are trapped by the mentality that says: "If I don't get what I want the next time around, I will stop trying." Anything short of a job offer is interpreted as a failure.

People make the mistake of *hunting*, rather than *exploring*, for their work. Hunting implies the direct pursuit of quarry, zeroing in on a known adversary and moving in for the kill. Exploration, by contrast, is a process you conduct in a carefree, information-seeking manner designed to satisfy your curiosity. Hunting is deadly; exploration is for fun.

Job hunting is an all-or-nothing game that has many unpleasant conditions about it—long trips across town, detailed arrangements in advance, talking to strangers who ask you questions you may not understand, getting dressed up, acting sophisticated, and, worst of all, trying to convey your personal capabilities within a brief time.

I don't believe you will last long in the work search unless you treat it as an exploration process rather than a deadly hunt. Therefore, I recommend that your initial career search activity follow certain rules designed to maximize your positive experiences and minimize your negative ones.

**Multiple Skills Are More Important** • One of the complaints most frequently heard from job seekers is the no-talent refrain: "I don't do anything especially well, so why hire me?" Many people believe that a single prominent talent is necessary to attract employers; if you are not a financial wizard, an exceptional speaker, a skilled artist, or a persuasive writer, you may fear you are destined for mediocrity.

The power of a highly visible talent is somewhat overrated. Very few jobs exist that permit a person to depend solely upon one talent for success. It is far more commonly true that *multiple competencies* are necessary in any job for highest level performance. For example, an effective insurance salesperson must possess persuasiveness, competency with numbers, and long-range planning ability when discussing estate matters with clients.

In most cases, the combination of competencies is

more powerful than any single talent could be. I assume this is true because I want you to recognize that all your strengths can be put to use.

**The Career Search Is Largely Detective Work •** I assume throughout this volume that the most effective career search is fundamentally an exercise of detective skills, that the largest part of one's effort should be devoted to *finding* the right work situations. For every promising job you have found, another two remain undiscovered. The wise individual understands this and looks further. About 80 percent of your time should be devoted to detective work, because the seek-and-ye-shall-find motif incorporates all five of the skills categories; the detective attitude is at work in self-assessment, identifying job leads, research, communication skills, and transition skills.

Detective work is a state of mind. Once you adopt this attitude, you will regard your career as a complicated mystery story and become absorbed in following the clues and looking for new evidence; you will enjoy being the Perry Mason of your own career.

**You Need Time on Your Side, Not Against You •** Time works against you if you force yourself to make an instant career decision. Your strategy requires time, and you can buy time by either staying in your present situation or acquiring an interim job (see skill 20). Time allows you to maintain the search at a comfortable level and to let informal contacts begin working in your favor. The harder you look for work, the more it may elude you. It is an axiom among employers that the applicant who too clearly wants to be hired has a tough time convincing the employer that she or he is competent. Instead of mounting a campaign worthy of Sherman's army, let your search take a more leisurely course. The lower your desperation quotient, the easier it is for you to exchange views with a potential employer on a level of parity. Therefore, I assume in this volume that the career search is best conducted many months before you must actually make a change; if you practice these skills before your situation becomes urgent, they will work doubly well for you when you embark on an actual job search.

## The Career Search Is an Everyday Thing

Looking for better work is rather like learning to tie your shoes by yourself. You have to do it several times before you get it right, but once you have it, you wonder how you ever allowed anyone else to do it for you.

We have tried desperately to make a science of career decision making, and have succeeded in making a mystique of it. In fact, choosing a career is the most obvious of functions, relying on the natural rhythms of self-reflection and human interaction. An army of career-choice "experts" has mobilized because of people's inability to recognize their own opportunities for career exploration. The less an individual does for himself, the more he assumes that expert advice, outside consultation, and placement assistance are necessary. It is time to restore the natural order of things. Job seeking is as natural as any other kind of social interchange. By turning matters over to the pseudoscientists, we have assumed that (1) we know nothing or little about ourselves, (2) no one in our own circle of acquaintances can possibly be helpful, and (3) job getting requires a sophisticated set of techniques known only to the select few. The ultimate extension of this absurdity is to designate personnel officials as the soothsayers of the employment world, presumably capable of reading our palms, feeling our foreheads, or otherwise determining our capabilities from arcane criteria.

The more you believe that your ideal job is hidden away in a cave that can be discovered only by an experienced guide, the more helpless you will feel. Helplessness will lead you to desperation and a willingness to accept any employment as good fortune. By contrast, if you recognize that the skills of the work search are ordinary life skills and that they are available to anyone who cares to practice them, you can attend to the task yourself.

Looking for better work is fun. You can do it by yourself. It is relatively easy. Often it is about the least expensive thing to do with your time. Why is it necessary to state that the career search is pleasurable, self-propelling, and not complicated? Because of the way you've interpreted your previous job-seeking experiences. When you have obtained a job, you've assumed that your success was largely a matter of luck, fortuitous circumstances, or being in the right place at the right time. When you were not successful, you blamed bad luck, waited to see if your luck would change, and when it didn't, set about the chore of job hunting. And what a chore you made it! You laboriously typed application letters, sent out hundreds of résumés, spent hours scanning classified ads in the newspapers, and underwent interviews with potential employers to demonstrate your dedication to the Great American Work Ethic.

Let's take a closer look at the first part, the "I was lucky" statement, often used to interpret a previous job-seeking experience.

**EXAMPLE**

After Eileen's children completed their schooling, she decided to reenter the work force. Because she had not been in a paid job for twenty years, she didn't know where to begin looking. While at the beauty salon, she sought the advice of her hairdresser and asked if she knew of anyone looking for part-time help. "It just so happened" that the director of placement at a local college had confided to the hairdresser that she was "terribly busy—her assistant had just left." The hairdresser made a personal reference to the director. Eileen followed this up with a telephone call and her résumé and got the job. Later, the job was made into a full-time assistant director's position. Eileen feels she was lucky in getting the job.

Was it just "lucky" that Eileen stepped into her new career as a function of her visit to the hairdresser? Or was she smart enough to take advantage of a natural referral network that exists simply because people are curious about each other and enjoy passing information around? What would have happened to Eileen if she had followed formal channels only in her efforts to find work? Only her hairdresser knows for sure.

**EXAMPLE** _____

Bob wanted a job with a youth recreation group, so he hung around and helped out the local YMCA with its basketball games, its field trips, and anything else. He got to know Jane, one of the leaders, pretty well and showed her how the program could be expanded to include kids in his neighborhood. One day Jane invited him to a staff meeting; after the meeting there was a picnic. One thing led to another; a man was there from out of town who needed an assistant leader in his recreation center. Jane mentioned Bob's name, and he was hired a few weeks later. "All in all," Bob said, "I was pretty lucky."

Lucky, my foot. The young man in this example practiced naturally many of the skills outlined and detailed in this book. He found the target employer, asserted himself to become involved in its activities, used a personal referral to learn about a job opportunity, did information interviews with staff people, observed the activities of the center. No doubt he also used many self-assessment skills to decide that the YMCA was a good target employer and many communication skills in talking with the staff there.

People meet their lovers and employers in the strangest places. Exactly what implications does this have for you? It means simply that all your life activity can contribute to your work search. It means that your typical ways of getting together with people can be turned to your advantage. It means you can have your fun and profit by it too.

## Skills You Have Used All Your Life

The skills that will be most useful to you in the career search are hidden in much of the noncareer activity of your life. You have developed and nurtured personal strengths for other reasons, and perhaps unconsciously. No matter who you are or what your personal disposition, you have a personal style and corresponding set of strengths that can be used profitably in the work search. Find yourself in one or more of the prototypical personal styles described below.

**Charlie the Compulsive •** You are the person who lines up matchsticks in descending order of size, for no particular reason, or makes sure that your personal library is neatly catalogued, even though it has only one user and no need for checkout rules. You would probably arrange a Dewey decimal system for your own clothes closet if you could figure out a way to stamp the numbers.

Your hard-core compulsiveness will enable you to keep complete and accurate records of everyone you visit, their pertinent data, and the appointments you have arranged for future dates. You will also be a supreme cataloguer of research information and will probably do a painstakingly detailed self-assessment.

**Gertie the Gregarious •** You are the sort of person who would walk up to strangers at a bus stop, ask them about their marital happiness, and probably get away with it. You have a talent for beginning conversation, engaging people on a friendly, nonthreatening basis, and enjoying the exchange as though there were really nothing else in life but talking and passing the time of day.

Clearly, you will be able to swing the walk-in information interview with consummate aplomb. Your ability to engage people easily will allow you to play the personal referral game for all it is worth. You can make maximum use of personal contacts and will not require much encouragement to use all your social activity for career search purposes.

**Donna the Detective •** Nothing pleases you better than to unearth the solution to a mysterious problem or discover clues to hidden information. If someone told you that a bag of peanuts was squirreled away in a downtown office building, you would like nothing better than to try to find it. You regard detective problems as challenging in themselves, for no other reason than because they are there. You defy anyone to keep a piece of information from your inquisitive mind.

The hidden occupation, the mysterious referral person lurking in some far corner of the city's commercial district, or the reference source in the library that cannot be found by the ordinary mortal will titillate your seek-and-find antennae. Your talent in this area will enable you to track down the most remote of information sources, to look for clues to future employment possibilities lesser beings would miss, to piece together items of seemingly disconnected origin, to discover—*voilà!*—a career possibility no one else has noticed.

**Calvin the Con Man** • Your persuasive skill has shoehorned you into many a good situation and extricated you from many a scrape. You can talk old ladies into buying you lunch, bus drivers transfer you all over town, and even the tax collector gives you an extra few days to pay. Most of us poor working stiffs know at least one person who can finesse a situation with a few words in the right place, and you are that person. Perhaps your chief talent is to outwit those who *do* have the talents, by influencing someone to help you.

You should look more closely at what subskills allow you to operate so smoothly. As the Dr. Feelgood of interpersonal relations, you probably possess extraordinary timing, sensitivity to others' moods, and strong verbal facility. Your talent bodes well for getting secretaries and others to help you to walk-in career interviews. You will also get reams of help from reference librarians when researching an employer and will have little difficulty orchestrating your personal referral network.

**Freddie the Forecaster** • You have made a life style of predicting future events, trends, and personal preferences. You're not prescient or accurate beyond normal expectations, but you are occasionally able to foresee happenings when they are only in their formative stages. You enjoy peeking around the corner, looking for changing winds and signs of things to come. You have always believed that the advantage belongs to the person who can sense widespread movements, be at the leading edge of transition.

Your sensitivity to the prevailing winds will help you foresee new directions in hiring, both on a local scale (company expansions) and on a more universal level (products people are beginning to buy, new markets that result). Your skill at anticipating future movements will probably heighten your skill as an information interviewer and sharpen your antennae when you review the newspapers and popular magazines for items about target employers.

**Sam the Systematic•** You cannot undertake any project without planning it in the most elaborate detail, including time schedules, expected results, delegation of tasks, and record-keeping systems. Even when you arranged to lose twenty-five pounds, you organized yourself so that your menu included certain items on each day of the week, you were allowed "free" eating periods every Sunday morning and Thursday afternoon, and meals were measured meticulously in their preparation.

Obviously, your attention to detail will lead you to plan information gathering in explicit form. By having a thorough examination of your values and skills at hand, a systematically derived list of target employers, and a highly organized set of research tasks, you should proceed from one step of the career search process to another with strong preparation. Your questions to interviewer and interviewees will emerge from a strong foundation of knowledge and background data.

**Iris the Imaginative •** You don't pay much attention to detail or adhere to well-planned methods of doing things, but your creative powers are continually in operation. You are a "relational" rather than an "analytical" thinker. You perceive relationships between phenomena that others miss completely and can view matters in a holistic perspective that eludes the individual who tries to find the missing piece or errant part. You are a whiz at combining materials in playful ways, creating new uses for old objects, and adapting old solutions to new situations.

Your imaginative powers will add a dimension to self-assessment that allows you to combine diverse elements of your values and skills. The tapestry you weave from seemingly unrelated traits should give you an advantage in searching for unusual job descriptions that would not occur to a straight-line analytical thinker. Furthermore, you will probably have a superior ability to relate your strengths to needs that the employer has not envisioned himself; you will be trying to create your own job description.

**Lewis the Listener** • Your most prominent asset is the ability to tune in to other people—their sensitivities, feelings, moods, inner thoughts, and even their deeper concerns. You can empathize so well with the other person's viewpoint that you have a hard time maintaining a grip on your own attitudes and opinions. People like the fact that you attend to them so well. In addition, you retain information about people, yet are able to keep it to yourself.

Though it sounds as if I am describing the ideal counselor or psychologist, these traits will also serve you well in gathering information from people in your referral network. Listening is probably the most convincing way of persuading others that you really *want* to hear what they are telling you about their work and about themselves. Effective listening flows comfortably with the natural egotism in each of us. Your powers as a listener will encourage the information giver to keep his pipeline open.

**Oliver the Observant** • You're not strong on talking or constructing elaborate project plans, but you do an effective job of watching the behavior of others. You can observe and file away the tiniest of mannerisms, food preferences, arrangements of pictures on walls, speech patterns, and personality quirks. Very little escapes you because you seldom draw attention to yourself and can therefore gather observations without being noticed.

First of all, you will be helpful in watching others because you can help them with their self-assessments; others will give you similar feedback. Second, you are a natural for the on-site visit at employment settings. If you take it a step further and do volunteer work, you should be able to gather data galore. You also will be a competent information interviewer as you record signals during the interview that give you clues about what direction to take next.

**Vicki the Verbal** • You love to play with words. You'll speak at the drop of a hat, write letters to neighbors just for fun, compose poems to your dog or cat, write limericks in your spare time. The mellifluous sound of a well-turned phrase is your favorite kind of music.

No doubt your skills will find their mark in conversations and correspondence with prospective employers, if you are careful not to get carried away with yourself. Verbal skill will increase the probability that you can tell another person clearly about yourself, your experiences, and what your aspirations are. Keep practicing with that verbal paintbrush; you will have many opportunities to use it.

## Stop Resisting the Career Search

Like the child who can think of a thousand reasons for going outside, or ten thousand reasons for not doing his homework, many people have bottomless wells of excuses for their fear of getting involved in the business of searching for better work. It probably requires only one of the following to arrest any work-seeking behavior, and chances are you can lay claim to several.

**I'm Too Old** • A person my age doesn't do all that running around looking for a different job. It takes too much foolish energy that I must be careful to conserve.

Furthermore, I think it's a little undignified to admit I made a mistake in the past and go around confessing it to everyone.

Answer: Older folks look for new challenges because they have already licked several tough problems and want new ones. Changing work is not the confession of a sinner, but the spirit of a missionary who has something good to offer and wants to pass the wealth around.

**I Can't Do Anything Else** • I must admit, if you press me, that I am afraid there's nothing else I can do as well as what I am currently doing. I'm afraid of getting caught in the middle, losing my present work, and being unable to make the grade elsewhere. I was lucky to get my present work and am not so sure I'd be that lucky again.

Answer: The major currency in your work experience is transferable skills, which are abilities that can be marketed in numerous contexts. For example, if you have been an effective organizer in your present office, church, or community, chances are you can carry these abilities to a different work setting and put them to use without starting all over again.

**I'd Better Hang on to What I've Got** • There is no sense in building a record of good work and then throwing it away by looking for something new. Maybe my work isn't the greatest, but I should capitalize on the progress I have made, and not dismiss it for some uncertain future. I can't afford to surrender the experience I've accumulated.

Answer: No one is asking you to start over at the bottom. When you find a setting where your skills are transferable, you can reasonably request an appropriate level. If you are bored with your current situation, you cannot afford *not* to look for something more stimulating.

**My Job Takes All My Time** • My work doesn't give me time to think about doing anything else. I would have to take three weeks off just to explore this subject and would undermine my present responsibilities in the process. It's too large a price to pay for just shopping around in the dark.

Answer: Take a close look at the people you encounter routinely in your work and ask yourself how they might lead you to others. Who do they know in other fields of work? Do't be so busy painting yourself into a corner that you fail to look for a way out.

**I Don't Like Rejection** • I would rather not push myself in situations where I am probably going to be turned away. No one likes that kind of treatment, and I am no exception. Why walk into a buzz saw when you know it's there? That sort of experience will only tend to reduce my confidence.

Answer: When you set about the work search, it is *you* who are doing the choosing, not the other way around. There is no risk of failure when you are the customer rather than the salesperson. Perambulate through the work search as a data gatherer and let the job offers take care of themselves.

**Let Fate Take Over** • I would prefer to trust that the unseen hand, the mysterious flow of events that has been my life so far, will continue to shape the story of my career. I like surprises and have faith that good things will happen, that whatever comes my way, I can handle it and adjust to it. Going out to make my own changes is too much like tampering with a higher-order process. To my vocation I will be called. I believe opportunities will cross my path and I will be wise enough to know which ones are marked for me.

Answer: If you are so closely in touch with divine powers that you prefer not to develop an organizer strategy, then play it your way. However, allow me to suggest it is not fate that guides you, but your sensitivity to yourself and your willingness to trust your instincts.

**I Am Just a Complainer** • I am really a chronic malcontent. It's just a life style with me. I really don't want to change, but would simply rather complain, moan, attract sympathy, and just stay put where I am.

Answer: There are better ways to entertain yourself than crying wolf. I believe people who grouse about their work are in need of help, but don't know how to ask for it. If you are sinking in vocational quicksand, please call for a rope and pull yourself out.

**The Alternative Might Be Worse** • What I like about the miserable work I've got is that at least I know what sort of misery to expect each day. Whatever job I might get in exchange could be worse, even more debilitating. I am comfortable in a perverse sort of way with my present situation.

Answer: Risk is the tariff for leaving the Land of Predictable Misery. Secure a temporary visa—give yourself permission to roam the countryside and look at what other people are doing. If the alternatives demand too high a price in uncertainty, you can still come home again if you insist on it.

**It Doesn't Hurt Enough Yet** • I really cannot change because my present work is tolerable. I have nothing much to look forward to, but I can keep the pain to a minimum by dodging around, doing a little something different, and fantasizing that it will get better. I'm sure other people have it much worse, so why shouldn't I put up with my share of discomfort?

Answer: Is the pain really tolerable or is your head just numb from repeated encounters with the wall? When *will* it hurt enough? When your children talk about what a kind, calm, and likable person you *used* to be?

**I Don't Want to Shake Things Up** • Life is comfortable and predictable, even if it is not exciting and filled with challenges. If I look around for a change now, I will have to unsettle myself, my entire family, and everything that is orderly in my life. That's an awful price to pay in search of a rainbow that might not be there. I will not take chances with my family's security.

Answer: The emotional health of you and your family may be more important than a certain amount of financial sacrifice. Ask your family members first before you make assumptions about how they would regard a shakeup. Perhaps they have been waiting for you to give the word.

**Nothing May Turn Up •** Then what? Suppose I pour myself into a search for something better and then discover, after all that turmoil, that nothing is available, that I must stay where I am after all? Wouldn't that be a terrible waste of effort? Why even expose myself to that possibility? At least when I go to a store, I know I will usually find merchandise. Job hunting is shaky business. I don't like the odds.

Answer: Sure, and there may be no trout in the stream, no friends at the golf course, but you still go there hoping something lucky will occur. Charles Kettering's well-known saying about luck is especially apt here: "No one ever stumbled across anything sitting down."

**No One Encourages Me •** I am not being cheered on by those around me. My family and friends really don't know how I feel about my present work, so they see no great urgency for me to change. Besides, it is more comfortable for those close to me if I stay put. They won't have to adjust to my new ways or ideas.

Answer: You probably have not allowed them into your secret chambers. Any person with whom you share your struggle will cheer you on, because he or she wants the same attention when getting up the courage to move in a new direction. Don't suffer in silence; you will become your own worst critic.

## Conclusion

Of course, you have looked for work before. You probably did so, however, as an adolescent might seek to break into a strange social group. Job hunting has much the flavor of a ritual dance in which the initiate must perform in certain prescribed ways. The dance is a passionless affair because the individual does as told—send your forms here, sit there, talk now, go have this or that examined, cross your fingers, breathe deeply, wait ... and wait some more. Ritual dances, with employers calling the tunes and job seekers dancing to them, will remain the dominant rites until work seekers learn to orchestrate their own methods.

You cannot depend entirely on college degrees, reference letters, other people, good fortune, or paper qualifications to get the job that is best for you. You must exert more active control over the process and take initiatives as often as possible.

Your success will depend heavily on your ability to use many skills of the career search process. Without these skills, you are at the mercy of other people's arbitrary judgments and whims.

No doubt you already apply many of the career skills naturally in your normal life routine. Other skills probably represent areas of serious deficiency for you. The following chapters will show you how to acquire the skills you need most.

Career skills are lifetime skills. They can be used repeatedly in a person's life and work history. By possessing these skills you can reduce your fear of the career search because you can take better control of the search process.

You are most likely to regard the career search as enjoyable and effective if you put the skills to use many months before you have an urgent need to change your employment or your career direction.

part

# 1

**Self-
Assessment
Skills**

# · chapter one ·

 # Values

*He who has a why to live can bear with almost any how.* • Friedrich Nietzsche

*What we call "creative work" ought not to be called work at all, because it isn't. . . . I imagine that Thomas Edison never did a day's work in his last fifty years.* • Stephen Leacock

Values are the emotional salary of work, and some folks are drawing no wages at all. "I can't quite put my finger on it, but I feel empty all the time on my job." "I can't figure out why I am doing this; it all seems to add up to so much nothing." "It's just a job. Why should I expect anything more? So what if there are no fireworks; it's a living. . . . But I'm not living very much." And so we defend ourselves against criticism or regret about job choices we have made that defy the laws of emotional gravity, jobs we took because they were there, jobs devoid of purpose and redeeming virtue. The choice seemed reasonable at the time: "I had to do something, and this seemed as good as anything else."

Many people literally hate their work because they can find little or no value in it. As used in this chapter, the word *value* has a personal meaning: it reflects how you feel about the work itself and the contribution it makes to others. Value has other meanings (How much value will this product have in the marketplace? How valuable is this employee to our profit picture?) that are separate from the values that must dictate your individual choice.

Your selection of one particular kind of work from among the thousands available must reflect what you regard as important, worth doing, inherently valuable. If you do not value the work you do, then no other incentive can possibly compensate for your lost sense of being significant, important, part of something you value. On the other hand, if you value the work you have chosen, then neither small office, nor lack of recognition, nor poor working conditions can stay you from your appointed rounds or dissuade you from your objectives.

Most folks dance the Safety, Security, Seniority, Longevity Polka.

Security is the usual trade-off for work a person regards as dull, routine, and meaningless. "I would have quit long ago, but the paychecks keep coming in." "I just can't afford to surrender the terrific security this place gives you." "I put up with this place because they don't make you fight for your job every week." "I'll hold on to this job if it kills me." How many unhappy people do you know who buttress their positions with arguments of that kind? How much mediocrity, ennui, and routine acceptance of things as they are masquerades as job security?

# What Values Are

Raths, Harmin, and Simon, in their book *Values and Teaching*, define values as "those elements which show how a person has decided to use his/her life."[1] Work values are those enduring dimensions or aspects of our work that we regard as important sources of satisfaction.

Here is a representative list of work values:

*Help Society:* Do something to contribute to the betterment of the world I live in.

*Help Others:* Be involved in helping other people in a direct way, either individually or in small groups.

*Public Contact:* Have a lot of day-to-day contact with people.

*Work with Others:* Have close working relationships with a group; work as a team toward common goals.

*Affiliation:* Be recognized as a member of a particular organization.

*Friendships:* Develop close personal relationships with people as a result of my work activities.

*Competition:* Engage in activities which pit my abilities against others where there are clear win-and-lose outcomes.

*Make Decisions:* Have the power to decide courses of action, policies, etc.

*Work under Pressure:* Work in situations where time pressure is prevalent and/or the quality of my work is judged critically by supervisors, customers, or others.

*Power and Authority:* Control the work activities or (partially) the destinies of other people.

*Influence People:* Be in a position to change attitudes or opinions of other people.

*Work Alone:* Do projects by myself, without any significant amount of contact with others.

*Knowledge:* Engage myself in the pursuit of knowledge, truth, and understanding.

*Intellectual Status:* Be regarded as a person of high intellectual prowess or as one who is an acknowledged "expert" in a given field.

*Artistic Creativity:* Engage in creative work in any of several art forms.

*Creativity (general):* Create new ideas, programs, organizational structures, or anything else not following a format previously developed by others.

*Aesthetics:* Be involved in studying or appreciating the beauty of things, ideas, etc.

*Supervision:* Have a job in which I am directly responsible for the work done by others.

*Change and Variety:* Have work responsibilities which frequently change in their content and setting.

*Precision Work:* Work in situations where there is very little tolerance for error.

*Stability:* Have a work routine and job duties that are largely predictable and not likely to change over a long period of time.

*Security:* Be assured of keeping my job and receiving a reasonable financial reward.

*Fast Pace:* Work in circumstances where ... work must be done rapidly.

*Recognition:* Be recognized for the quality of my work in some visible or public way.

*Excitement:* Experience a high degree of (or frequent) excitement in the course of my work.

*Adventure:* Have work duties which involve frequent risk-taking.

*Profit, Gain:* Have a strong likelihood of accumulating large amounts of money or other material gain.

*Independence:* Be able to determine the nature of my work without significant direction from others; not have to do what others tell me to.

*Moral Fulfillment:* Feel that my work is contributing significantly to a set of moral standards which I feel are very important.

*Location:* Find a place to live (town, geographical area)

which is conducive to my life style and affords me the opportunity to do the things I enjoy most.

*Community:* Live in a town or city where I can get involved in community affairs.

*Physical Challenge:* Have a job that makes physical demands which I would find rewarding.

*Time Freedom:* Have work responsibilities which I can work at according to my own time schedule; no specific working hours required.[2]

Values are only labels, the words we attach to sources of reward that are inherent in a certain kind of activity. Values usually are associated with occasions when you expend great effort, both physical and emotional. The value is simply the descriptive marker you use to denote the reward you have experienced. For example, you may get your greatest kicks from, and expend the most energy in, overcoming obstacles and beating the odds, whereas I may not care much about obstacles, but would push myself to the limit to acquire power or authority.

We can discern our values in what we do *not* like as well as in those activities we consciously choose. If you avoid all work that involves selling products or ideas, you are making a strong statement about your preference for nonpersuasive activities. Positive values may lie on the opposite side of what you are avoiding. For example, if you hate all kinds of committee work, you probably are attracted to jobs in which you can make decisions by yourself. This may be obvious to some, but less apparent to others until they observe their own behavior.

Let me remind you that the term *values* refers to many different kinds of rewards. The previous list showed you much of this variety. These rewards can be further classified into three fundamentally distinct categories:

- *Enjoyment.* Work you choose because the activity itself is pleasurable, in terms of topic interest, creativity, achievement, adventure, or other kinds of stimulation inherent in the work itself
- *Conditions.* Work you select because of favorable circumstances that accompany it, such as physical setting, money earned, vacation time, people with whom you have contact, and other external features
- *Value to others.* Work you choose because you believe it

will benefit or please someone outside yourself (*others* can refer to clients, members of your community, or a much wider sphere of influence)

You make career choices in order to satisfy all three of these value categories. Each of the three exerts veto or approval power at one time or another. When you settle into a rocking chair fifty years from now and roll back the film of your life's work, you will want to know that your jobs possessed value. Work without value is mere labor, and work with value justifies any burden you may have to shoulder or effort you may have to put forth.

No particular values are any better than any others. You may choose on the basis of greed, spirituality, comfort, adventure, egotism, or any of a thousand other reasons. What matters most is that you understand what is important to you and act upon it forthrightly. If you are in touch with your values and pursue them vigorously, you need not fear the ancient viper of regret.

## How Your Values Are Exhibited

Identifying values is the single most fundamental process in a successful career search because every other skill depends on your ability to state your motives with clarity and some precision. In this section, I have outlined some specific methods you can use to crystallize your awareness of your values. Each method represents a different way of tapping into your values and is followed by an example of some results the method might produce. There are many more strategies for eliciting values than can be noted here. Simon, Kirschenbaum, and Howe, in their book *Values Clarification*,[3] have an excellent compendium of such strategies, many of which you can also apply to career concerns.

All methods for identifying values yield one or two essential kinds of information: (1) *past experience*—what you have already done in your life that you have valued, and (2) *future desires*—what you hope to do in the future that you would regard as highly rewarding.

Past experience is a rich source of your work values because your behavior is strong evidence of your preferences. Even if you are young, twenty years of personal choices can yield many clues about your prominent motivators.

Future choices are expressed in daydreams, fantasies, and

plans, which cannot be verified by actual behavior. Hence, the values they reflect may be more tentative. Dreams, however, are powerful forces when they are vivid enough to be imagined in great detail. Often they are harnessed to your understanding of your past experiences. When you shape past values in the light of your presently unfolding and changing needs, you can forge a powerful vision of a desirable future.

Mattson and Miller, in *The Truth About You*,[4] assert that your key values can be determined by a thorough review of your peak life experiences—occasions or periods when you have exerted yourself strenuously, have performed successfully, and have been pleased with what you accomplished. These occasions can be studied for the presence of values, and, Mattson and Miller claim, your one or two most prominent values appear consistently in these life experiences.

---

**EXAMPLE**

Won spelling bees at age twelve. Wrote essay on psychoneurosis at age sixteen. Wrote and presented a show for children at age eighteen. Edited a sports section and wrote column at age nineteen. Wrote songs for a camp show at age nineteen. Edited book manuscripts at age twenty-four. Read poetry at age twenty-six. (Values: personal recognition, precision with words.)

---

I subscribe to the view that values are extremely important in career behavior because our culture is intensely dominated by a work/achievement orientation. An individual typically expends far more effort than the minimum required to earn a paycheck when it is possible to satisfy prized values. The individual climbs a personal Mount Everest not only because it is there, but also to satisfy a compelling personal need.

Because people's needs change with age, you may have some career aspirations that are linked only marginally to your past experiences. These desires can also be examined for the presence of consistent themes.

---

**EXAMPLE**

I would like to: build bookcases, understand decisions made on the commodity exchanges, buy and sell antiques, study American folklore, collect historical anecdotes about the Civil War, raise farm animals for profit. (Key themes: interest in historical America, manual activities, and the farming business.)

Of course, these aspirations must be tested in the crucible of life experiences, but dreams should not be damped down by skepticism or taken too lightly. Your visions for the future are your assessment of your past, as you reject certain values and embrace others. Effective dreams grow from your being in close touch with past successes and especially with failures. The strongest drives often result from earlier disappointments or half-successes that were aborted by circumstances.

You may protest that dreams and values are fine, but few people get a chance to fufill career fantasies in their lifetimes. Most of us are stuck, you say, with marginally satisfying jobs. Changing your dull job for someone else's will not help matters.

The mistake in this reasoning is in viewing jobs as finished landscapes. Of course, values will not magically appear once you have discovered them. And employers will frustrate your dreams. However, knowing what the dream looks like will help you piece it into your current situation. Finding even one source of value in a sea of boredom is a powerful antidote to a deadly job:

- If you dream of architecture but are only a mechanical draftsman, try designing your best attempts at floor plans during your spare time and ask the professional staff to evaluate your work.

- If you can barely tolerate your job but see no way out, find a source of stimulation incidental to the job that will allow you to endure it, such as joining the company bridge team, starting a local investment club, or organizing theater trips.

- If the only enjoyable part of your present job is public speaking, but your boss lets you do precious little of it, look for another department that might want to borrow your services.

- If you want a job with complete independence, but the only available ones are too risky financially, decide how much security you are willing to surrender in exchange for some autonomy. Perhaps a part-time source of income where you have decision power will help you to tolerate submission in your regular job.

- If you love exercising control over budgets, but have little authority to do so, try seeking an outside source of funds for your organization (government grant, foundation money, or other) and then put yourself in charge if your proposal is successful.

In *Clarifying Values Through Subject Matter*, Harmin, Kirschenbaum, and Simon outline the seven subprocesses that help people make value choices that are both personally satisfying and socially responsible:

> *1. Choosing freely.* If we are to live by our own values system, we must learn how to make independent choices. . . .
>
> *2. Choosing from alternatives.* For choice-making to have meaning, there have to be alternatives from which to choose. If there are no alternatives, there are no choices. . . .
>
> *3. Choosing after thoughtful consideration of consequences.* We need to learn to examine alternatives in terms of their expected consequences. If we don't, our choice-making is likely to be whimsical, impulsive, or conforming. . . .
>
> *4. Prizing and cherishing.* Values inevitably include not only our rational choices, but our feelings as well. In developing values we become aware of what we prize and cherish. . . .
>
> *5. Publicly affirming.* When we share our choices with others—what we prize and what we do—we not only continue to clarify our own values, but we help others to clarify their values as well. . . .
>
> *6. Acting.* Often people have difficulty in acting on what they come to believe and prize. Yet, if they are to realize their values, it is vital that they learn how to connect choices and prizings to their own behavior.
>
> *7. Acting with consistency.* A single act does not make a value. We need to examine the patterns of our lives. What do we do with consistency and regularity?[5]

At the end of this chapter is an exercise that uses these seven subprocesses to help you determine your values.

## Values of Significant Others

Values are chosen by your own standards. You may choose to reflect the values or standards of others around you, as you see fit. You are not likely to reject everyone's values entirely, but neither are you expected to be a mirror image or composite of the people and ideas with whom you come in contact. To understand what is meant by *others*, imagine several circles of people moving from your immediate environment outward: (1) family members, (2) people in your immediate living community, (3) members of your religious or ethnic group, (4) people in the country or society at large.

You may want to reflect for a moment now upon the values of those closest to you and how you feel your own values correspond to theirs or show definite differences. It can be helpful to imagine some career choices that are not regarded by the general population as highly desirable, and then imagine how your family's or community's values would lead you to feel about such choices. For example, how would your mother react if you told her you were going to become a motorcycle racer? a chicken plucker? a sewage inspector? an alligator wrestler? a big-time gambler?

## Values-Clarification Exercises

The data for discovery of your values are all around you. Your values weave through the fabric of everything you do. The kinds of work to which you are attracted, the forms of play that exhilarate you are revealing. Those activities you regard as both work and play say even more about where your values lie. Building a tool-shed, watching horror movies, scaring old ladies, plotting the course of a caterpillar, digging with your hands for seashells, listening for little harmonies in sounds of the night—any of these activities carries values to the person who does it.

You can learn to interpret any of your experiences or imaginings if you nurture the simple habit of putting words, however imprecise they may be, to your feelings about events. If you enjoy having time to sit alone and ruminate, for example, you can say: "I value quiet." If you get excited about NBA playoff games, you can assume: "I enjoy the noise of physical competition." If you get a good feeling from seeing your words in print, you can put that into words: "I value recognition from others."

Here are a few exercises you can do to clarify your values further.

### • Exercise One •

You may find important clues to your occupation values in how you view the work of those closest to you. Unless you choose to, you need never feel obligated to perpetuate the occupation or profession chosen by a significant relative; however, you should notice which parts of that work appeal to you in a natural way and take this as evidence of your own preferences.

Try making a list of your family and friends, and put the occupation of each person beside his or her name. *Occupation* is here interpreted broadly to include the major way in which the person spends his or her time, including student and other nonpaid activities. Which single part (activity, task, subrole, duty) of that person's job do you find the most appealing? Try your best to find at least one part of the occupation that represents a value you appreciate. Identify the aspect of the job you would choose for yourself and the value it represents.

**EXAMPLE** _____

Friend, barber: meets many people (friendliness)
Friend, carpenter: builds houses (body use/seeing results)
Mother, schoolteacher: supervises class (decision making)
Father, accountant: has steady income (security)
Uncle, banker: handles money (responsibility)
Aunt, dress designer: makes new designs (creativity)
Minister: exhibits concern for others (compassion)
Neighbor, treasurer: controls finances (responsibility)
Neighbor, professor: keeps knowledgeable (learning/reading)
Brother, coach: physically active (health)

Once you have identified all these separate values derived from the occupations of family members and friends, try making a composite occupation from the values you have identified. Be creative. Don't worry about whether such a career actually exists or whether you could enter it. Just try to stitch the values together into a coherent whole.

**EXAMPLE** _____

Values: friendliness, body use, seeing results, decision making, security, responsibility, creativity, compassion, learning, reading, health

Possible composite careers: health director for a summer camp, physical fitness consultant for private industry, forester or range manager or other outdoor administration

### • Exercise Two •

Refer to the seven subprocesses of valuing on page 48 for this exercise. Use them as a framework to review your own activity of the past week:

**1)** Name one choice you made freely.

**EXAMPLE** _____

I read a book about the history of the town in which I live.

**2)** Name another choice, this time one you made from among two or more alternatives.

> **EXAMPLE** _____
> I went to the farm show rather than the stock car races or the picnic.

**3)** What consequences did you consider in making your latter choice?

> **EXAMPLE** _____
> I knew my friends would be unhappy that I didn't join them at the races and the picnic afterward.

**4)** Did you choose on the basis of your personal feelings, because you prized the activity you chose?

> **EXAMPLE** _____
> I chose the farm show because I think raising animals is important and more enjoyable than tinkering with car engines.

**5)** Did you publicly clarify this choice?

> **EXAMPLE** _____
> I told my friends why I could not join them, even though they did not fully understand.

**6)** Did you act on your value?

> **EXAMPLE** _____
> I acted on my value by attending the farm show.

**7)** Have you acted consistently on this choice in the past?

> **EXAMPLE** _____
> I regularly refuse to attend auto races because I do not admire what they are doing, and I attend farm shows at every opportunity, even if it means I have to travel fifty miles or do extra work around the house to compensate for my time away.

### • Exercise Three •

It is often even more revealing to witness an event with other people and then compare what each of you valued in it. By exploring the differences among you, you may see your own values in sharp relief, because others have seen the same event in different ways.

Choose another person with whom to do this exercise, a person who will help you focus on your values by participating in the exercise with you.

**1)** *Recall an experience that made you happy* • Recount to your partner an experience that gave you a good feeling, made you happy, or left you feeling better than when you started. Try to distinguish between something you *thought* was good and something that *felt* good inside. Your feelings are more important than your ideas in this case.

**EXAMPLE** _____

I felt good about the summer weekend I organized for my cousins.

**2)** *Provide detail* • Describe the experience in as much detail as you can. What exactly did you do to make it happen? Try to remember as much of the sequence of events as you can, including not only what you did but also how you felt about it each step of the way.

**EXAMPLE** _____

I arranged a preliminary meeting of the group at a restaurant during the winter to see if they were interested. We had a lot of laughs, recalled old times, and told stories. I told the most. Then I proposed a summer weekend and outlined how we would plan for it.

**3)** *Identify a value* • Of course there will be more than one value involved in the experience, but start by clarifying only one key value. What one aspect did you like about what you were doing? What seemed worthwhile about the experience? For what purpose did you expend this time and energy?

**EXAMPLE** _____

I suppose the biggest satisfaction was doing something to keep a family and its bonds together, arranging an event that would make it possible for the cousins who were once close to revalidate a family tie. They all wanted to keep close, but would not do anything unless it was made relatively easy for them.

**4)** *Reach deeper* • Once you have stated a value to your partner, the two of you can take an even closer look by asking: "What in particular was satisfying about this?" It will seem you are repeating the original question, but you are actually reaching deeper to another layer of meaning. In fact, the question "But what did you really like about that?" might be asked several times until the deepest layer of meaning is reached.

**EXAMPLE** _____

Well, I guess I like to be a catalyst, a person who brings other people together. I really enjoy recognizing a situation in which a group of people would like to fortify their bonds, but haven't been able to do so because of circumstances. I really enjoy being the person who makes it happen.

**5)** *Check with partner* • At one or more points in the process of describing your experience and identifying the values inherent in it, you should ask your partner to use his or her own words to help clarify what you were trying to say. Ask this person to restate in different words the value(s) you seemed to be expressing so that the two of you can arrive at the sharpest possible definition and label of your particular value.

**EXAMPLE** _____

PARTNER: You seem to get a kick out of arranging things, giving people a chance to reach each other on an informal basis. Yes, you seem to have a definite preference for informality in the things you set up. You seem to believe that informality is the best setting in which to give people the freedom to get closer, enjoy each other better.

It is important to be able to place your own labels on your values and to derive and label these values by reviewing your own experiences. This exercise gives you an opportunity to practice examining your experiences and discovering values in them. This most basic form of value clarification can be used with any sort of experience, big or small. More importantly, it *should* be used with all sorts of experiences, because values may be revealed in even the tiniest of events. Your more enduring values are especially likely to be hiding in the tiny, obscure life events because such events occur naturally, unconsciously without your thoughts, shoulds, or oughts intruding. These are the kinds of life experiences you can include:

- Teaching your little sister how to tell time
- Knocking over the bottles at the county fair
- Cleaning out your files till you know where every last item is located

- Losing the fourteen extra pounds you've been carrying for years
- Keeping a shell collection
- Walking barefoot in the rain
- Seeing how fast you can add up the restaurant check
- Reading every historical marker on your cross-country trip

# · chapter two ·

# Feelings

After dinner tonight, slip your mind across the events of the day and ask yourself: "How did I feel about each of the things that happened today?" Many things occurred that you and several others witnessed at the same time; however, you probably had an individual feeling, conscious or unconscious, about each thing you observed or participated in. No doubt your private emotional reactions were different from those of the others who were there with you. You listened to dogs barking on your street and enjoyed the feeling of protection they afforded you. Someone else felt annoyed that the dogs made so much noise. You traveled downtown to a steel-and-glass building and felt impressed with its importance and stature. Another may have felt that the building lacked artistic value and was inappropriate for the landscape surrounding it. You played cards at lunchtime and felt exhilaration at the sense of competition. You listened to a company speaker that afternoon and felt boredom because he was saying nothing you hadn't heard before. You rode the train home and felt relief that the boss had not asked you about the project you were working on. You sat with the family and felt anxiety that you hadn't been with them enough lately. You read a magazine article and felt nostalgia because it reminded you of a particularly happy period when you were eighteen years of age.

My purpose here is to make the clearest possible distinction between content and feeling. *Content* may be described for our purposes as an event that can be observed by anyone in the area; *feeling* refers to the emotional reaction of a given individual to that event.

We have been taught, perhaps by hard-nosed athletic coaches or task-oriented parents, that feelings are not quite legitimate, or at least not nearly so respectable as thoughts. Feelings are only for sob sisters, social workers, and grandmothers who wipe the tears from the eyes of four-year-olds. Feelings are presumed to be fuzzy, amorphous, and imprecise. No one will ever be accused of saying: "I feel, therefore I am."

People talk in nonfeeling words because they have been taught that facts count and everything else is opinion. Of course, feelings are personal, biased, private, and not necessarily rooted in factual data. Nevertheless, feelings are the mirrors of your soul and of the way you respond to events. A denial of the legitimacy of feelings is nothing less than a denial of individuality.

Whatever difficulty we experience in talking about feelings may derive in part from not knowing what words to use to express inner responses. In *Alive and Aware*, Miller, Nunnally, and Wackman suggest a starter list:

| | | | |
|---|---|---|---|
| Pleased | Confused | Eager | Uncomfortable |
| Comfortable | Excited | Weary | Discontented |
| Calm | Lonely | Angry | Anxious |
| Satisfied | Elated | Glad | Solemn |
| Bored | Uneasy | Grief | Apathetic |
| Jubilant | Silly | Contented | Hopeful |
| Fearful | Hesitant | Cautious | Sad |
| Daring | Surprised | Confident | Proud[6] |

Feelings are infinitely more subtle and complicated than mere like or dislike. Liking can range all the way from ecstatic joy and elation to a quiet sense of comfort or calm. Dislike can span the scale from intense anger and outrage to sadness or puzzlement or indifference.

More than occasionally, a positive or negative feeling on the surface is a cover for a more subtle feeling that is the reverse. For example, you may feel upset about a staff meeting at work because you feel the meeting would have gone better if you had been in charge. Almost any event deserves a more sensitive feeling response than mere like or dislike if you are to understand fully how you feel about what you have experienced.

A simple stop-or-go mentality cannot do justice to the richness of feeling. Emotions are an intricate web. We use words to try to unravel them. Metaphors are used to convey complexity of feeling where ordinary expressions will not do. Even these images are often not sufficient. Currents of feeling run more deeply than the words available. However, images give you a chance of capturing the spirit of your work in words:

- I feel like a trapped gopher when my boss gives me this computer job.
- I imagine myself a gypsy dancer in my role as waitress in the restaurant.
- I feel as dean of students that I am a maestro of young development, orchestrating the delicate growth of maturing psyches.
- I approach this sales job as though I were being thrown to the wolves.
- I live the life of a wealthy Arabian potentate when I travel for the company.

## How Feelings Affect the Career Search

A career decision is based on how you feel about a proposed area of work, rather than on an accurate portrayal of the way that work really is. Indeed, "the way the work really is" doesn't matter. What matters is only the way you respond emotionally to the work, the feelings you expect to derive from participating in it. Being in touch with your feelings enables you to exercise greater control over your happiness.

Feelings are also the barometers of your values. The feelings you experience when engaged in a particular kind of activity provide the first clues to whether you will value this activity in your work. The following self-statements, which anyone might make during a day's activity, mirror the work-related values they represent:

- I am bored doing copyreading now, even though I used to like it.
- I feel elated whenever I get a chance to interview a congressman.
- I get angry if the boss asks me to do something when my car pool leaves in five minutes.
- I am proud that I got all those numerical totals correct, even under a lot of pressure.
- I feel uneasy when the phone rings late at night.

You can monitor your feelings for the first clues about where your career search should go next. Ask yourself these questions:

- What tasks am I doing when my energy level is highest?
- Which parts of the day do I look forward to?
- Which tasks make me feel most satisfied?

As you begin your career search, look for these feelings you have just described. Use them as major clues for all your career detective work.

## Feelings-Identification Exercises

### • Exercise One •

**1)** Identify any recent event in your life, preferably one that seems innocuous and relatively unimportant, but that you had some feelings about.

**EXAMPLE** _____
I watched two friends have an informal two-mile race. About twenty other friends were there and cheered them on. We all went to the tavern after it was over.

**2)** Name at least three feeling words you associate with this event.

**EXAMPLE** _____
At the race, I felt excited, comfortable, and involved.

**3)** Which of these feelings do you believe applied most to you, compared with the others who were present?

**EXAMPLE** _____
I was probably more excited than the others because I have done a lot of running myself and could understand the strategy of the race, the pain they were feeling coming down the backstretch, and the exultation of hitting the last straightaway.

**4)** Which of your feelings derived from the behavior of others?

**EXAMPLE** _____
I felt comfortable because I was among my usual companions, people who kid around with each other, have a good time, but don't care much about tearing each other to pieces with competition. It didn't really matter who won, as long as we all enjoyed the experience.

**5)** Which of your feelings derived from your own behavior?

EXAMPLE _____

My experience as I watched them race was purely a private one, as I imagined I was circling the track myself, felt the pulsations of pushing my physical limits, and wished I could be involved in the next event of this kind.

## • Exercise Two •

**1)** Identify another recent event, this time one that occurred in your workday.

EXAMPLE _____

I went to a three-day workshop to learn about management by objectives and see how it could be applied to my supervisory responsibilities in the bank where I work.

**2)** Name at least three feeling words you associate with this event.

EXAMPLE _____

At the workshop, I felt curious, cautious, and hopeful.

**3)** Which of these feelings do you believe was unique for you, compared with the others who were present?

EXAMPLE _____

I was probably more cautious than the others, because I had read about MBO before and had heard from friends in management jobs at other companies that it created a lot of problems initially for a supervisor and staff.

**4)** Which of your feelings derived from the behavior of others?

EXAMPLE _____

I felt hopeful because some other staff employees in the bank told me we needed more systematic organization in our work load. They encouraged me to explore MBO in depth and give it a try.

**5)** Which of your feelings derived mostly from your own behavior?

EXAMPLE _____

My sense of caution derived not only from what I had heard about MBO from other managers, but from my experience with the bank and changes we had attempted to implement in the past. I was aware that new business methods often got a quick burst of enthusiasm from top management and then were discarded in favor of older, more comfortable techniques.

## chapter three

#  Skills

Dear Howard:

I will surely never amount to anything. Lots of things I do are okay, but I never really get good enough at anything so that anyone sits up and takes notice. My dog runs faster than I do, my brother gets more girls, and every new idea I get has been thought of by someone else first. It would be nice to charge ahead carrying my banner into the world if I had something outstanding to offer, but mediocrity haunts me everywhere I go. To the talent-rich go the spoils, and the rest of us take what mud is left over.

Signed,
*Destiny's Plaything*

Dear No Destiny:

Modesty is truly the curse that kills a thousand careers. You would rather be put in prison than claim you're really good at something, so you sit around mooning about the few who seem to have exceptional talents and count yourself as one of the rejects on the slag heap.

Your modesty is the back door of your existence. It is the hedge against anyone who might come along and say you're really not as good as you said you were. You figure that if you don't claim to be great shakes in the first place, you can always slip out the back door you've conveniently left open for yourself.

Enough of this self-deprecation, protecting yourself against mythical judges who might appear from nowhere to compare you unfavorably with others. Behave as if you are permitted to use your better talents, regardless of how they compare with the next guy's.

You really are better with your hands than most. And you can supervise people easily and calmly. And you take criticism well and have a lot of endurance. You're not so good with numbers, but you know enough to consult people who are. Go on, admit it. You've done certain things well before, and you'll do them again.

Modesty is all right in deference to the skills of your friends and respect for their right to have abilities too. However, modesty has no place when it disqualifies you from respecting yourself. Don't expect anyone else to notice your talents as well as you do.

Signed,
*Howard*

There is no putdown quite so devastating as the self-putdown. It sticks, because you make it stick. We prize modesty; the individual who is enraptured with his or her own accomplishments can be a pain. Yet strongly needing to present yourself as modest usually undermines your ability to acknowledge your own accomplishments. You become so worried that others may think you egocentric or pompous that you build a hedge factor into every victory or achievement so no one will accuse you of boasting. You use hedges. "I had a lot of help from my friends." "I couldn't have done it without old so-and-so." "It wasn't much; I certainly should have done better." "I was playing over my head, out of my tree."

You protect yourself from future criticism, but short-circuit your ability to derive praise from your achievements. Praise is the precious fuel that propels you to surpass yourself. You need not depend on the compliments of others or judge yourself by their opinions of you, but you must maintain (or regain) the capacity to congratulate yourself on a job well done. Remember—*there is no praise like self-praise.*

Recognition of your skills\* is nourished by your own self-statements, your own ability to recognize your accomplishments and interpret them in terms of abilities that can be added to your personal tool kit:

---

\* *Throughout the book, I use the word* skills *to denote those competencies that are important to successful completion of a career search. In this chapter,* skills *refers to all competencies that can be used by people in the widest possible variety of work settings and tasks. Thus, identifying one's marketable skills is a skill of the career search. I trust you will understand this double use of a most valuable word.*

- Once I acquire a skill, I will always have it to call upon.
- I will stockpile my skills for future use.
- I can detect one or more skills in everything I do.
- I won't be concerned about how long a task takes me.
- I will judge a skill by my own standards or satisfaction.

## Skills Inventory

What is a skill? I have in mind any of the widest possible variety of attributes that represent your strengths, your key abilities, the characteristics that give you your greatest potency, the ways in which you tend to be most successful when dealing with problems, tasks, and other life experiences. There can be little doubt that you do some things better than other things. You are more comfortable in certain situations than in others. You consistently prefer particular tasks over all others. Your strengths reveal much of what makes you unique, a person who is different from any other individual alive.

Here is a sample list of skills found in a cross section of careers:

administering
  programs
advising people
analyzing data
appraising services
arranging social
  functions
assembling apparatus
auditing financial
  records
budgeting expenses
calculating numerical
  data
checking for accuracy
classifying records
coaching individuals
collecting money
compiling statistics
confronting other
  people
constructing buildings

coordinating events
corresponding with
  others
counseling people
creating new ideas
deciding uses of
  money
delegating
  responsibility
designing data systems
dispensing information
displaying artistic ideas
distributing products
dramatizing ideas or
  problems
editing publications
enduring long hours
entertaining people
estimating physical
  space
evaluating programs

exhibiting plans
expressing feelings
finding information
handling complaints
handling detail work
imagining new
  solutions
initiating with strangers
inspecting physical
  objects
interpreting languages
interviewing people
inventing new ideas
investigating problems
listening to others
locating missing
  information
managing an
  organization
measuring boundaries
mediating between
  people
meeting the public
monitoring progress of
  others
motivating others
negotiating contracts
operating equipment
organizing people and
  tasks
persuading others
planning agendas
planning organizational
  needs
politicking with others
predicting futures
preparing materials
printing by hand

processing human
  interactions
programming
  computers
promoting events
protecting property
questioning others
raising funds
reading volumes of
  material
recording scientific data
recruiting people for
  hire
rehabilitating people
remembering
  information
repairing mechanical
  devices
repeating same
  procedure
researching in library
reviewing programs
running meetings
selling products
serving individuals
setting up
  demonstrations
sketching charts or
  diagrams
speaking in public
supervising others
teaching classes
tolerating interruptions
updating files
visualizing new formats
working with precision
writing clear reports
writing for publication

---

# What Good Are Skills?

---

Why should you examine your skills? Aren't people who have been around for a while aware of their strengths and weaknesses? If a person cannot assess himself accurately by now, isn't it a little late to wake him up? A resounding no in answer to these questions. The plain, unvarnished truth is that almost all of us are blithely unaware of many of our key personal strengths. The Johari Window[7] (Chart 2) proposes four areas of self-knowledge; only one area is available to both self and others.

|  | Known to self | Not known to self |
|---|---|---|
| Known to others | Open | Blind |
| Not known to others | Hidden | Unknown |

Chart 2.
The Johari
Window

I propose that a similar statement can be made about skills and, further, that the largest proportion of this Johari Window for skills is the "unknown" area, where skills exist, but are known neither to the person who possesses them nor to others acquainted with him. Why is this so?

**We Have No Vocabulary for Skills** • Most people have a severely limited set of words to use when they try to describe their strengths. Thus, vocabulary must be created in order to make the task of skill naming easier. The skills inventory in this chapter serves this purpose. It is not an exhaustive list, but simply suggests a sufficient number of skills labels to allow people to talk about their strengths with the beginnings of a common language.

**Skills Are Trivialized** • Have you ever done something well, but then immediately thought to yourself: "What good would that possibly do me? That talent is useless, surely not relevant to anything in a career." Everything is practical in some special context. You should learn not to trivialize your assets, but to imagine contexts in which they might be useful. If you are a whiz at sorting mail quickly, determining its contents, and filing it appropriately, imagine someplace (other than the post office) where that skill would be useful (purchasing office of an organization? complaint department of a store? assistant to Dear Abby?).

> **EXAMPLE**
>
> Ever since I can remember, I have liked writing slaphappy, funny letters to my friends and relatives. They seem to pour out of me naturally, the more ridiculous the better. Well, it turns out that I have adapted this skill to my work as a claims representative at the insurance company, where I maintain the "personal touch" with those who file claims by writing to them in my own fashion, which they get a kick out of.

**Skills Develop Late in Life** • In contrast to the few highly noticeable skills that emerge early in life (musical talent, artistic talent, or mathematical facility, for instance), most skills come along much more slowly and are infinitely more difficult to recognize when they appear. Many of them relate to ways of interacting with other people (a talent for organizing other people into smoothly functioning units, a talent for persuading others to do things for you, a talent for explaining difficult concepts to others in clear, everyday language). Such talents do not ordinarily merit the status of "genius" and do not prompt standing ovations when displayed to the population at large. Nonetheless, they are strengths worth applauding because they move people and even mountains at times. Such skills may not become apparent until the age of thirty, thirty-five, or even forty-five, but they can be seen as they grow gradually into potency.

**We Put Ourselves Down** • It is probably only a minor exaggeration to say that we live in a putdown culture, a social structure in which claiming that you possess an extraordinary talent (especially one people have difficulty labeling) is an open invitation to ridicule. It is far easier to say "Oh, I'm not really that exceptional" or "What good could that talent possibly be?" than to value a skill and talk about it easily, even among friends. However, the quieter you keep about your strengths, the more easily they tend to fade into the woodwork and become invisible to even yourself.

## Put Your Worst Foot Forward

I believe everyone feels that some skills are more reputable or desirable than others. If this is true, then many of us probably suppress our talents because we suppose that others would think less of us, or even laugh at us, if they knew we possessed these attributes. The happy message of skill identification is that any skill is worth crowing about, and the so-called status of a particular skill has little meaning when it comes to getting a job done well. For a moment, take a sneaky sideways glance at one or more of your own attributes that you believe are prominent, but somehow a little less than desirable in the eyes of others. Do any of these skills belong to you?

- *Compulsive.* I do everything in the same order, according to schedule.
- *Confronting.* I cannot help being very direct with people, saying exactly what I feel regardless of the consequences.
- *Talkative.* I have an overwhelming desire to talk, even though I know others would like me to shut up for a while.
- *Nosy.* I cannot restrain myself from nosing into everyone's affairs.
- *Persnickety about detail.* I leave no stone unturned, cannot rest unless the last crumb is picked up, the last note jotted, the last word said.
- *Antisocial.* I prefer to do most of my work on projects that let me be by myself for long periods of time.
- *Loud.* I can usually be heard by most of the people around me when I am talking and have a habit of speaking louder than normal conversational level, whether to an individual or in a group.
- *Dull, methodical.* My work has always been described as unexciting, proceeding at an even pace, so steady as to have no highs and lows at all; I purposely maintain an even pace so I will not have to deal with uncertainties.
- *Offbeat.* I prefer to do things the wrong way, or at least the crazy cockeyed way, so I don't fall prey to dullness, so I can build some adventure into what I do. No one knows what to expect of me and it bothers them, but I don't care.
- *Slow.* I am slow as molasses in January in every task I

undertake, but that is all right with me. I enjoy consuming a lot of time so I never need to feel pressured by a deadline.

Is there any doubt that every one of these personal styles has been denigrated, ridiculed, or sneered at by many of your friends? If you are a closet practitioner of one or more of these traits (or skills), remember that you will benefit far more by acknowledging your particular traits, valuing them, and searching for contexts in which they are marketable than you will by trying to alter these traits simply to elevate yourself on a mythical status scale.

Here are some examples of how "low-status" skills can be used successfully in job contexts:

- The *compulsive* person keeps perfect and orderly records of all calls, correspondence, visitors, and intrusions (birds flying in the window, etc.) in this department.

- The *confronting* one has an excellent record in approaching bank customers who have borrowed money and failed to make payments on their loans.

- The *talkative* individual is the best person we have in greeting new people in the community, making them feel wanted, engaging them in conversation when they feel shy.

- The *nosy* person hangs around enough bars, courthouses, barbershops, and shopping malls to hear about things before they even happen; that's why we couldn't be without her as a news reporter.

- Mr. *Persnickety* shines all the pots himself before leaving at night, makes sure no chair is out of place, and sees that all supplies are replenished; we need him as kitchen manager, even though he drives the staff buggy at times.

- Ms. *Antisocial* works over there in the corner, reading stacks of old manuscripts; someone has to do it, and I'm glad she prefers this to buzzing around the library making idle conversation.

- *Loudmouth* can be counted on to liven up a new group of people who are having difficulty talking to each other. That is why we use him as a greeter for tours of visiting firemen; whenever he wants to announce a departure or a change in plans, he has little difficulty getting the group under control.

- The *dull, methodical* one takes care of the tremendous flow of paperwork in this department by subjecting it to careful and systematic attention; we know that no important document will be missed, nor will any schedule be ignored.

- The *offbeat* person provides the unusual whenever we need it to promote a new idea to our membership; she is creative and knows how to catch people's attention, even if the other staff members think she's a little nutty.
- The *slowpoke* takes care of difficult mechanical tasks that carry risks of overload or mechanical error; he's patient enough to work a task to death just so it will be done correctly.

## Transferable Skills

Sidney Fine[8] has identified what is probably the single most important concept in viewing how personal skills are usable in career development. Skills that have potency in career contexts are not limited to being useful within a single kind of work, occupation, or vocational setting. On the contrary, most skills valued in work have the virtue of cutting a wide swath across many occupational boundaries. For example, the ability to write effectively and in clear language is valued highly in private industry, government agencies, educational institutions, and nonprofit organizations alike. In fact, most of the skills that are important in any responsible job have a similar virtue: they can be applied in a wide variety of work contexts to a wide variety of tasks. They are *transferable*.

Fine distinguishes among three broad categories of skills: functional, adaptive, and specific. The first two categories—functional and adaptive—contain all the transferable skills. Adaptive skills can be distinguished from functional skills because they usually refer to personality traits, characteristic ways of behaving. Adaptive skills tend to develop earlier than functional skills, yet they may not be valued or even noticed until the individual has done many years of career exploration. Adaptive skills, like functional skills, are eminently transferable.

> *Adaptive skills* refer to those competencies that enable an individual to accept and adjust to the physical, interpersonal and organizational arrangements and conditions in which a job exists. Included are punctuality, grooming, acceptance of supervision, care of property, getting along with others, and impulse control. . . .
>
> *Functional skills* refer to those competencies that enable an individual to relate to Things, Data, and People (orientation) in

some combination according to their personal preferences and to some degree of complexity appropriate to their abilities (levels). . . .

*Specific content skills* refer to those competencies that enable an individual to perform a specific job according to the specifications of an employer and according to the standards required to satisfy the market.[9]

Adaptive and functional skills are frequently coded in specific content language. That is, the word you use to denote a skill that seems highly specific to your job obscures the fact that the skill is eminently transferable. If you are an accountant, for instance, and regard yourself as "good at being an accountant" (content specific), you may fail to recognize that you are effective working with numerical data, handling detail, or adapting to peaks of the seasonal work load.

In addition, the work attributed to a specific job title can be accomplished well by two different people who possess different functional and adaptive skills. An effective administrator, for example, might possess these skills in abundance: handling financial data well, diplomacy with other staff members, flexibility in decision-making routine. A different person, also effective in the same position, might possess these skills: planning for new programs effectively, supervising other people's work effectively, training new employees well. Admittedly, a good administrator would possess some minimum level of all these skills; however, two different people might emphasize some of the skills much more than the others. Thus, as you evaluate your work, you must ask yourself "What did I *do*?" rather than "What was my title?"

Let's take a look at how skills are transferable. Say you aspire to be a bank officer. You list the skills you believe are most crucial to effectiveness in the role of bank officer:

Being careful with
  money
Analyzing numerical
  data
Dealing with the public
Anticipating
  community needs

Working patiently
Making financial
  decisions
Reading detailed
  reports
Supervising others

Of course, the above list might be different if you knew a bit more about what bank officers do. However, for the purpose of this example, ask yourself: "If I were to take away the title of bank officer from this list, would the skills listed indicate clearly that it is a bank officer we are describing?" The answer is a clear no. The skills noted are either functional or adaptive, and they are clearly transferable. They might be applied to any of numerous other occupations.

When a person asks you (or you ask yourself), "What can I do in my life that will improve my chances of advancing in the world of work?" don't concentrate entirely on the specific content skills available from formal programs of educational credentials. Talk about the transferable skills that can be acquired anywhere:

- *Communication skills.* Writing reports, essays, and correspondence in plain language; speaking effectively to individuals and to groups; listening carefully and empathically whenever necessary; portraying ideas clearly and imaginatively

- *Thinking skills.* Defining a problem cogently; evaluating alternative courses of action critically; creating divergent solutions to a problem when more than one answer is possible; shaping new ideas in the context of old circumstances

- *Human relations skills.* Interacting cooperatively with superiors, subordinates, and peers; communicating orders, instructions, and feelings with openness, genuineness, and understanding; delegating tasks in ways that show respect for the other person and receptivity to his or her ideas

- *Valuing skills.* Being able to view and assess an area of work activity in terms of the effects it will have upon human welfare; making and enforcing decisions in terms that will maximize such welfare

- *Research skills.* Discovering and identifying people who have information that is relevant to a task or a problem; identifying resource materials necessary to the solution of that problem

- *Interviewing skills.* Acquiring information from people when they are reluctant to divulge it or when information is difficult to reach; generating trust in such situations, necessary for future contacts

- *Planning skills.* Being able to sense an idea whose time has come, to move toward work modes that capitalize on this idea, and to sell the idea to appropriate people

# You Can Acquire New Skills

Even though we have focused skill identification on what you have done before, new experiences will occur that will add to your stockpile of skills. Furthermore, you can be deliberate about choosing future activities that will nurture *new* skills. It is a deadly mistake to assume that your skills are fixed, that you are unable to acquire new talents. Most skills people bring to the work market-place are ones they have nurtured and practiced in their informal, nonpaid lifetime of experience. Many of the most powerful skills are developed by accident, in the name of just plain fun, for purposes other than their current use or perhaps even for opposite purposes (as when former criminals bring marketable skills to their work as law enforcers).

Here are a few hypothetical and whimsical examples of people whose job-related skills were cultivated in contexts far removed from the marketplace:

**EXAMPLE**

Organized Orville is chief steward at the Roney Plaza Hotel, which serves a thousand people nightly. He stocks the entire place every week by keeping track of drinks served, glasses washed, dollars spent, table napkins needed, etc. Orville's talent for detail is compulsive. He used to inventory his father's toolshed, his mother's cupboard, his uncle's auto parts store, and anything else in sight, just to keep himself amused when he got home from school.

Oratorical Olive is chief spokesperson for the United Fund of Jivetown. She promotes social services everywhere, raises funds with in-person appearances, and speaks to community groups at the drop of a hat. Olive grew up making speeches at the dinner table, imitating the politicians while they droned away on TV. Olive was applauded by the family, encouraged to speak out no matter what people thought. She ran for school offices just to get the chance to make more speeches.

Dignified Dan is maître d' at the Sans Souci Restaurant. His cultivated speech, attention to formality, and sensitivity to the subtle needs of his guests make Dan a natural for this posi-tion. Where did he acquire this skill? Dan's years on the stage in comedies of manners were not wasted, nor were his trips to Buckingham Palace with an uncle of royal lineage.

Persuasive Paula is a lobbyist in state government. She twists tails of tigers, bends ears of elephants, and tweaks legislators' noses when necessary to get their attention. Paula learned on her block as a six-year-old that bargaining is done best by tone of voice, persistence, and attention to the individual ego. She learned long ago that peanut butter and jelly can be traded for roast beef if the proper words are applied to the bargain.

## Six Cardinal Rules of Skills Identification

As you become accustomed to identifying your skills in your daily routine, keep in mind these six rules.

**Compare Only with Yourself** • Avoid at all costs having to compare your level of talent with others'. Your only consideration is that your skill rates highly within your own private system. Which activities do you perform better than other things? The only relevant comparison is internal.

**Be Sure the Skill is Fun** • A skill is really not worth calling attention to if you hate doing it. Only those activities you both enjoy and do well matter for future reference to your work. Count only those skills that wear comfortably on you when you are using them, ones you smile about when you anticipate doing them.

**Look for Evidence** • Make sure you are talking about actual life experiences, not just something you wish had happened. The only credible validation of a skill lies in a real experience; something you did cannot be taken away from you. If you have evidence of a skill, you cannot be argued into denying it by superficial criteria such as test scores, interest inventories, or other externally generated data.

**The Function, Not the Title** • Make sure you are talking about what you actually did, rather than any title you may have carried. Titles and labels of positions often do not reveal functions especially well. Camp counselors do not always do a lot of "counseling," for example.

**Label It Yourself** • Even though you will get some help with the vocabulary of skills by referring to the skills inventory on preceding pages, you should ultimately call the skill by its rightful name. Your own descriptors are more accurate than any label I have suggested. Since you are in the best position to describe the function as it really was performed, don't hesitate to use the words you feel best reflect exactly what you did.

**Focus on Irrelevant Experiences** • This rule may startle you a bit; however, I suspect you will instinctively look for those life experiences that seem somehow more "important" to you and will ignore those that seem irrelevant. Hardly any life experience can be called irrelevant. I insist that some of your most special and powerful skills can be found in the life experiences you would dismiss out-of-hand.

## Five Ways of Identifying Skills

There are several different ways you can tap into your particular skills. You should try using all of them at one time or another, because each method may elicit strengths that had eluded you before. Moreover, you can use one method as a check against another, to discover whether the same skills are being identified by different approaches.

**From Personal Achievements** • This method is detailed in the exercise at the end of this chapter. It asks you to describe an experience that made you feel good about what you did and satisfied with your behavior by your own standards, not anyone else's. Is it difficult for you to imagine you have done anything well? Then try something really tiny, a skill you bet is no good to anyone.

> **EXAMPLE**
> I wrote a short verse for my daughter on her sixteenth birthday, making fun of her talents, yet extolling them, to the tune of "Wizard of Oz." (This skill with words and music and sensitivity to an individual's traits bodes well for your ability to express yourself creatively.)

**A Happy Role You've Occupied** • If you still have difficulty thinking of things you did that were successful, try remembering any position or role you held that made you feel reasonably satisfied with yourself. Boy Scout leader, organizer of the kitchen on camping trips, keeper of the keys, leader of the drinking games at parties, editor of the social section of your school paper, the one who restores order when things get out of hand—any role has its attendant skills that enable you to perform the role successfully.

> **EXAMPLE**
> I was always the one who kept the group calm when something went wrong, by telling stories, creating a little foolish-

ness, and generally getting people's minds off the trial of the moment. (Interpersonal skill, timing as a skill, perception of tension, and so forth.)

**A Peak Experience** • You cannot think of anything you would call a peak experience? You say just getting out of bed each morning is the peak for you, and everything else is anticlimax? A peak experience need not refer to a high-level accomplishment. When was the last time you laughed really hard? Which single moment of the past week would you most like to repeat? Whom did you meet recently who sticks in your memory?

> **EXAMPLE** _____
> I heard this fellow talking at the grocery store about his life at home in Maine. I'll never forget his regional accent and way of expressing himself. I guess I just have an ear for speech, a fascination with it, and some talent for imitating it.

**Skills Inventory** • Use a skills inventory (p. 11) to help you recall experiences from your memory bank. As you spot a skill you have used before, you should be able to remember when you used it. Run through the inventory, clicking off skills as you go, and let your memory make the connections.

**Ask Your Friends** • Your family, friends, acquaintances see attributes in you that you may overlook yourself. They may even be more likely to notice the shady ones, but skills that are nonetheless marketable. Others will probably tune in to many of your adaptive as well as functional skills, because they are receivers of your personal traits every day.

> **EXAMPLE** _____
> You are really good at getting out of doing things. You have a talent for making other people smile. You are a champ at nagging people to get things done.

# The Curse of the Single Outstanding Talent

People born with a great talent, and many of those who depend on a single prominent skill, often get themselves into deep trouble.

They depend heavily on the single great ability to surmount any crisis and gain approval from others, and in general they expect the talent to compensate for any other shortcomings they possess. In fact, highly talented people are so hugely rewarded for their abilities that it becomes all too easy to rely on the talent and neglect everything else.

The biggest basket cases in career planning are professional athletes whose talents have dwindled with the years, college professors who have been denied tenure, beautiful women whose physical charms have faded, artists who haven't found an immediate market, and others who have depended on a single talent for many years. Their problem can be stated simply: It is not necessary for them to build other skills as long as the one big talent is working for them, drawing acclaim and winning temporary rewards, so by the time the one big talent fades, a vocational rigor mortis, known as learned helplessness, has set in. The talented one has been fussed over, catered to, and provided for. The whole idea of struggling along like us working stiffs has been anathema. Bill Bradley writes in *Life on the Run* that the end of an athlete's playing career is a death in every sense but the physical. We no-talent folk look for a skill to perfect that will answer all our prayers, solve all our career worries, and be always in demand. If you get too good too quickly with a particular skill, beware of the same perversity that afflicts the one-talent person who suffers decline after a brief period in the sun.

- A supersalesman who ignores management skills suffers when the time comes to direct the efforts of others.
- A whiz accountant who handles the numbers like a Ouija board finds his numerical skill small comfort when he learns that interpersonal skill is necessary to deal warmly and effectively with clients.
- A dean of students who can establish friendships on a personal basis with everyone enrolled finds to his dismay that planning skills have eluded him because he was too busy prowling the dormitories and making friends.

To become very effective with a single skill is to become drunk with power. For a time, this skill seems to work in every circumstance, people reward you for it, and there seems little need to waste time with other matters. Read on, however.

# The Hidden Charms of Multipotentiality

Artur Rubinstein has been known as the King of the Wrong-Note Pianists. There are probably scores more technically competent than he, but he brings an extra dimension to the stage, a sensitivity of interpretation and a personality that sparkles and breathes life into his music. People prefer him to the pianistically perfect drone who lacks the twinkle and personal magnetism. Rubinstein can also talk with the best of them, charm folks away from the keyboard, swing at parties; people appreciate this dimension of his talent too.

It would be extremely difficult to find a career that depends entirely upon a single talent. One might think of artists first, but Rubinstein and others dispel this notion. The blessing of calling upon a cluster of abilities instead of just one is that almost every career imaginable demands a cluster of different skills. Being a social worker, for example, involves helping others personally, researching sources of community information, writing reports to public agencies, and recruiting unpaid volunteers. A carpenter must be able to handle materials, measure with precision, and visualize space requirements. A store manager has to relate effectively to customers, organize the ordering of merchandise, and create effective visual displays. A secretary prepares written materials neatly, deals with the public, and develops a careful filing system.

The curse of multiple demands is also its blessing because you are never required to be flawless in a single category of skill. It is the cluster that counts, not the single outstanding strength.

**EXAMPLE**

John was a young man whose transferable skills included the ability to supervise other people, the ability to mix social life with promoting ideas easily, the ability to manage money, and a good sense of what kinds of leisure activities people enjoy. He had studied biology in college and had cultivated an interest in scuba diving. It occurred to him that the scuba background should not go to waste and that he might train a group of people to provide weekend lessons to vacationers. "Rather than get a real job, I decided to fool around in the sun for a while and see if anyone would pay me and my friends to teach them scuba." So he flew to the Bahama Islands without delay, rented quarters, and started the first of weekend excursions for scuba devotees. John's Underwater Explorers group is prospering today.

The contest between multiple talents and a single outstanding talent is a modern-day version of the tortoise versus hare contest. The single-talent person gets off to a blazing start, then is outdone by the industrious but nonflamboyant person who parlays many marketable skills into a winning combination. You need not regret your lack of a single prominent skill; your future success hinges upon your unique cluster of modest abilities that, when combined, are highly marketable.

## Skills-Identification Exercise

Remember that a skill can refer to any particular way you have of doing things. If you like working by yourself for long periods of time, if you're a hard-core compulsive who gets a thrill from absorbing detail, if you operate by conning people rather than overpowering them with logic, if you like to read a lot, if you do things the wrong way but they turn out right—all these activities are legitimately called skills here. Stick to your ways as long as they work for you, and don't worry about skills other people seem to have.

Do this exercise with a partner, a person you see on a regular basis and with whom you feel comfortable talking about yourself.

**1)** Identify an experience. Recall a particular experience you had within the past two weeks, one from which you felt some source of satisfaction.

**EXAMPLE** _____
I cleaned out and organized the materials closet in my office.

**2)** Describe in detail. Tell in the simplest possible terms what you did from beginning to end of this experience. Try not to skip steps, ignore the obvious, or summarize detail that deserves a closer look.

**EXAMPLE** _____
I pulled everything out to the open floor, threw away 30 percent of it we no longer needed, rearranged each thing according to the time of year it is used, created labels easy to see, made room to walk in and out easily, and left two or three open shelves for future acquisitions.

**3)** Use checklists. Refer to the skills inventory (p. 11) as a starter method for identifying some possible skills that were involved in what you did. Don't be wedded to these labels; simply use them to jog your memory about abilities you had to employ in this activity and as a stimulus for further information.

**EXAMPLE** _____
Possible skills labels include organizing data, displaying, handling detail, or even physical activity.

**4)** Look under the surface. Your first description of skills will probably be somewhat superficial. You will probably use a label that is convenient for talking about the skill, but hides some of the meaning in what you did. Many of the labels in the skills inventory (p. 11) will be too superficial for your purposes. Looking under the surface label requires using your own words to describe what you did.

**EXAMPLE** _____
I looked through every item in the closet to assess whether we have used this very much in the past year (evaluating), then put it in a different place so it would be located with other items used in the same way (classifying).

**5)** Generalize to a broader skill. Just as a surface skill label can be examined more closely to discover a more detailed talent, so can a detailed skill label be scrutinized so it reveals a talent that is broader in its implications. The words you use to characterize a skill may distort its larger importance or realm of application.

**EXAMPLE** _____
My ability to winnow out the materials that are not helping us from those that have utility is really a talent for patient reexamination of a total operation, an ability to view all our necessary activities simultaneously and then anticipate what our future requirements will be. This ability is really one of planning or organizing for future action and being able to conceive of a long time span without needing a narrative of the past year's activity on paper. Abstraction of present and future needs seems directly involved in what I did.

**6)** Check for meaning. Lest you get carried away with generalizing your skill to too wide a perspective, use your trusted companion to help you assess the most accurate label for the skill(s) you have identified. Compare your own words describing the skill with your friend's, and do your best to reach agreement about how best to characterize this skill before you move on to another one. You are the final judge of how to label the skill, but be willing to rely on the independent view of your friend.

**EXAMPLE** _____

I guess we agree that the skill can be best described as reviewing large amounts of material quickly, being able to assess the utility of the materials in light of organizational objectives, and translating these needs into an effective display for future use.

## chapter four

#  Creativity

Dear Howard:

Now I know where that term *pigeonhole* came from. Every job I look at has one requirement after another, so you can't figure out where there's room for yourself. Nothing but pigeon droppings left over from the guy who was there before. Every job might as well be a cave or other dark hole in which rodents secrete themselves, because I sure can't find any light for myself. Is there any elbow room in a new career? Is there a place for the real me?

> Signed,
> *All Boxed In*

Dear Foxhole:

There was the man who asked, looking up at a ten-ton behemoth facing him in the jungle: "How do you eat an elephant?" Came the reply from the wise old witch doctor: "One bite at a time." You may feel a new job or career is as big as an elephant and twice as formidable, but it can be digested one bite at a time. The creative process begins when you recognize that you are different from the person who did the job before you. Within the limits of organizational needs, the person makes the job; the job doesn't make the person.

Creativity is the accountant who recognizes that a filing system has been frustrating the office staff and does something to reformulate it. Creativity is the social worker who figures out that home visits might better take place outside the home, if the outside location keeps the family members from wrangling as they habitually do on their own territory. Creativity is the bus driver who notices a change of traffic pattern in his daily circuit and recommends a new route to his supervisor.

Creativity is also realizing you have a talent that's not been used lately and figuring out a way this talent can help you do your job better. People are bigger than job descriptions. Creativity is remembering that you have more abilities than can possibly be used in a single job and slipping in a new one when the job description isn't looking.

Creativity is also piecing together your various talents and traits into a new and previously unimagined whole. I know a woman who has theater background, an interest in antiques, and is very handy with figures. She dreamed up the idea that such a diverse collection of skills and inclinations could be combined in developing financial data (figures) for an antiques business and using dramatic presentations to attract customers to the shop. Most other antiques dealers sit on their haunches, but Sadie brings her "dead" things to life and sells them between gigs.

Signed,
*Howard*

All your carefully collected values and skills are destined to be lost, scattered like the pieces in a jigsaw puzzle, if you cannot put them together in creative and imaginative ways. Isolated attributes make little sense if they float in space by themselves, not hinged to any coherent whole. The ability to be creative with yourself allows you to pervade any job with a style of your own, allows you to take a seemingly senseless, unrelated collection of traits and attributes (your own values and skills) and weave them into a coherent pattern.

## What Is Creativity?

Ellen wanted all her life to be involved with cycling in some way, but recreation jobs seemed few and far between. So she poked around looking for work in state or local government, hoping someone might sponsor bike trail legislation that would trigger some new employment. She canvassed every bicycle club, volunteered her time to map possible new trails, and started a part-time repair shop on her own. One day a state legislator brought his children's bikes for fixing; Ellen rattled on about her plans for the future, and the legislator told her she should bring her ideas to the Community Service Department. Ellen discovered that, lo and behold, this department wanted a combined researcher/promoter for bicycle resources and two weeks later found herself writing grant proposals to the federal government to acquire funds for her favorite community service.

Brian was a college minister who, weary of the campus routine, decided to pick up and leave on a long trip. He toured forty-two states, exploring every new life style he could discover. His travels led him to the Personal Growth Center in Arizona, where he took a job as a dishwasher. He used his mechanical skills to fix the dishwashing equipment when necessary and his ministerial skills to develop relationships with the people in permanent or temporary residence at the growth center. This center had not thought of assigning itself a ministerial role, but Brian created it, relating to life crises as they occurred, providing gentle counsel to all members of the group. And supervising the dishwashing after every meal.

Creativity is really several different animals called by the same name. It is, first of all, combining diverse elements. Your ability to be creative in your work can perhaps best be demonstrated in your efforts to pull together values, skills, and traits that seem unrelated. What do you do with mechanical ability, a love of the outdoors, a desire to work with numbers, and a passion for furniture? Perhaps you investigate forests for future timber crops, count the trees, set up an inventory system for manufacture of furniture.

Creativity also means changing horses in midstream. The metaphor is a caution against giving up one work style for another, but when you think about the process—getting off one horse and mounting another in the middle of the water—it sounds like a lot of fun. Creativity is a way of periodically wiping the slate clean and asking: "What if this job had never been done before?" Whoever invented the ball-point pen had watched too many fountain pens spill too many times on too many pairs of pants. Imaginative people never want to do the same job the same way twice and are willing to risk falling off a horse or two in the process of figuring out a better way to negotiate the stream.

Creativity also involves taking new skills off the old shelf. Since the person is always larger than the job, we can assume you are forgoing the use of certain skills because the job does not seem to call for them. But wherever there is a job that might be done better, there is an opportunity for a new skill to be introduced. Which of your favorite little talents have you not used for a while but would like to send into the game? Writing is fun for you? You like to build things? You really get a kick out of interviewing people? Assume that you have the power to rewrite your job description at least a little, because you do.

We have become accustomed to thinking that creativity refers exclusively to the fine or performing arts. In the context of the work search, however, I call *creativity* all forms of thought that focus on the production of ideas rather than on the solution of problems. In its fullest sense, creativity here means *divergent* rather than *convergent* thinking. I assume there is always more than one solution to any career problem and expend my energy toward developing new ideas before becoming concerned about the direction the individual will take.

## Stimulate Creativity Through Wrongheaded Thinking

The more we submit career decisions to logical, analytical thought processes, the more such decisions seem to elude us. Hence, our solutions may lie in thinking *illogically*, or at least not deductively, so that we do not expect answers to flow in an orderly way from the gathering of data about the self.

Wrongheaded thinking encourages a plentiful stream of ideas, images, possibilities, and random meanderings. If we can accept that career development is more a creative than a scientific process, we must be most concerned about teaching you to think freely and imaginatively, like an artist, rather than strictly and deductively, like a scientist seeking a natural law.

What I call imaginative or nonscientific thinking will be recognized by scientists as the hypothesis-generating stage of scientific discovery or problem solving. Fresh, original ideas always precede scientific rigor. It is these that are most lacking in career awareness. The individual who cannot decide what to do gropes for the nearest alternative, not yet having learned ways to generate many career hypotheses.

Wrongheaded thinking suspends judgment and thus frees you

from conducting a pseudoscientific analysis of your possibilities when your sheaf of ideas is embarrassingly thin. For example: "I have good mechanical ability, therefore I must study architecture or become an automotive designer."

Several key propositions are central to your having the power to roam freely in designing possible career futures. I urge you to accept and practice all these propositions in order to accumulate a rich collection of ideas that you can sort, compare, and validate when the time for making choices can no longer be delayed.

**The Rigidity of Words** • Recognize initially that the words we assign to career matters—occupational titles, names of skills, and so on—may do more to bind and hinder our thinking than to assist it. Words are symbols that denote classification, and any classification restricts thinking. If we call a person an accountant, does that mean all he or she does is "account"? Of course not. An accountant manages, counsels, analyzes, writes, and performs a hundred other functions. Does your title adequately represent what you do? Do other people who have the same title as you perform the same functions or carry out their responsibilities in the same style as you? I doubt it. You must begin with a healthy measure of caution about what words mean when you are selecting a career direction.

**Thinking Visually** • Richer and more descriptive insights will occur as you begin to use pictures and symbols instead of words to describe your career hypotheses. Is your career a cyclone? A treasure hunt? A comedy of manners? A Noah's ark? I have often thought of my own career of counseling psychologist as a pinball machine, in which I bounce crazily from one standard activity to another, never being absorbed into a particular place. The pinball describes the process of my career; a kitchen blender characterizes the content of my work, a bubbling mixture of psychology, education, marketing, and applied mathematics. Visual imagery allows you greater use of fantasy and far greater latitude in portraying your own set of objectives and the environment in which you desire yourself to be. If you can picture your career—where you are, what you are doing, by whom you are surrounded, and other odd details—you will have a fuller version of what you hope for yourself than you can attain simply by attaching your wishes to one or two sterile words that carry nothing more than abstract meaning.

**Irrelevant Data** • If it is true that the obvious things we know about ourselves may be misleading ("Should I be a politician because I have a gift for giving speeches?"), then perhaps the missing pieces of our career puzzle lie in the darker corners where we would not immediately look. The little irrelevant things we know about ourselves may provide the best clues. If, for example, you are a social worker by training and inclination, but spend your spare moments in political campaigns and reading about new legislation, perhaps you belong in politics more than the person who has oratorical skills. If you devour stock market data when you are supposed to be preparing lesson plans, this may be a clue for your future involvement. Any activity that commands your attention is relevant, no matter how separated it seems from your professional training or visible career history. Stamp collecting or an abiding interest in psychotic murderers—either may be a missing piece in your career puzzle.

**Lateral Thinking** • DeBono, in *Lateral Thinking*, characterizes vertical thinking as digging the same hole deeper and lateral thinking as digging the hole in a different place. "Lateral thinking . . . has to do with new ways of looking at things and new ideas of every sort."[10] Lateral thinking raises questions without immediate answers and freely permits the individual to be as *wrong* as he or she wants to be. Lateral thinking allows rich interpretation of one's work. You may insist that a waitress is a waitress by anyone's definition, but a waitress in Studs Terkel's *Working* likens herself to Carmen, who dances fluently and exotically while her audience throws coins. Vertical thinking encourages objectivity, an agreement among observers about what is being observed. (It is nearly impossible to have such objectivity in your perception of your career; hence, lateral thinking is more suited to your interpretation of the work you choose for yourself.)

**Reversals** • You will increase your creative insights about your career by often doing what is not expected, by perhaps doing the opposite of what seems most obvious to do. Reversal thinking encourages you to turn a situation around or inside out in order to gain a completely new perspective. For example, to reveal what is most salient about your work, take a close look at your play. To discover your areas of strength, examine your most extreme weaknesses. To isolate what you really like best, identify the things you dislike the most. A clever reversal uncovers a new reservoir of data. Reversals can also be used in different ways. Suppose you took an obvious function, such as counseling, and asked: "How might a counselor do the work by being the object of counseling rather than the provider of it?" The answer might be a counselor who devises a new therapeutic process enabling people to counsel each other. Reversals are necessary to counter habitual thinking, at the risk of proffering ideas that may seem ridiculous. Whether a reversal yields right or wrong answers is beside the point; what are needed are new viewpoints and ideas.

**The Arrogance of the Dreamer** • Perhaps the more outlandish a goal, the more power it has to propel you and help you endure the misgivings and misunderstandings of those around you. A ridiculous goal provides direction for you and establishes incentive; an ordinary goal probably bores you. If you are not daring and arrogant enough to suggest a goal that others will view with skepticism, then your goal is probably not imaginative enough. Unless your goal offends someone, you have probably not succeeded in departing enough from what is already known. Welcome criticism and defense of present standards as signs that you have begun to say something new and that your career hypothesis is worth further investigation.

In *Your Creative Power*, Osborn[11] tells us three characteristics to develop in divergent, or creative, thinking: (1) strive for quantity of ideas, (2) defer your judgment—when being creative, do not be concerned about quality, and (3) make sure your ideas are as wild as possible. You must allow no critical judgment about the value or quality of your ideas to interrupt the creative process. Any and every idea is okay in the brainstorming stage; judgments of quality and worth are postponed until a later time. In the words of Blake, the poet: "The road of excess leads to the palace of wisdom. . . . You never know what is enough unless you know what is more than enough." George Bernard Shaw used to look at the title of a book and then write a full outline for the book before opening it up to read. He didn't want the book to disturb his creative powers for imagining what might happen in the volume.

# Nine Creative Processes

It may help you to know there are ways of thinking creatively—not formulas designed to reduce the creative process to technocrat's delight, but nine excitingly different ways of shaking up your thinking, looking at an old situation in a new way.

Here is a summary of some of the questions to ask about a situation in order to stimulate ideas:

*Put to other uses?* New ways to use as is? Other uses if modified?

*Adapt?* What else is like this? What other ideas does this suggest? Does past offer parallel? What could I copy? Whom could I emulate?

*Modify?* New twist? Change meaning, color, motion, sound, odor, form, shape? Other changes?

*Magnify?* What to add? More time? Greater frequency? Stronger? Higher? Longer? Thicker? Extra value? Plus ingredient? Duplicate? Multiply? Exaggerate?

*Minify?* What to subtract? Smaller? Condensed? Miniature? Lower? Shorter? Lighter? Omit? Streamline? Split up? Understate?

*Substitute?* Who else instead? What else instead? Other ingredient? Other material? Other process? Other place? Other approach? Other tone of voice? Other power?

*Rearrange?* Interchange components? Other pattern? Other layout? Other sequence? Transpose cause and effect? Change pace? Change schedule?

*Reverse?* Transpose positive and negative? How about opposites? Turn it backward? Turn it upside down? Reverse roles? Change shoes? Turn tables? Turn other cheek?

*Combine?* How about a blend, an alloy, an assortment, an ensemble? Combine units? Combine purposes? Combine appeals? Combine ideas?[12]

Let's take an example and show how each of these creative processes would operate. Let's assume you have a job that doesn't seem creative at all. You're a claims examiner for an insurance firm. Here is an example of how each process could function in your situation.

- *Put to other uses.* Can I arrange the claims files for other purposes? By last name, by type of accident, by geographical location, by year of policy, and so on?
- *Adapt.* How can I adapt my work as a claims examiner to another position within the insurance company? My skills in dealing with the public, corresponding, handling detail, and organizing files are transferable to other contexts.
- *Modify.* How can I take an essential procedure and modify it to work better? I have to file the claims in order of their occurrence, but will change the system to record also the dates the claims were filed, so that we can correlate type of claim with length of delay in reporting.
- *Magnify.* How can I magnify my passion for working with statistical computation to make it a larger part of the job? I can figure out how many claims were handled for how many dollars in each of the categories, or tabulate the environmental conditions that precipitated each accident, or figure the number of miles between home and accident for the actuaries.
- *Minify.* What detail in my work might be reduced to the smallest possible importance? If I can reduce the exchanges of correspondence until I have thoroughly researched each claim, I will save both myself and the claimant a lot of needless communication.
- *Substitute.* If I wanted to substitute a special skill in my daily routine, how would I do this? I can substitute my conversational ability for the painstaking correspondence I labor through by talking with claimants before writing to them, so they can understand what we are doing without my having to write it in great detail.
- *Rearrange.* Is there some way I can rearrange the sequence of contacts between myself and the claimant so that there are fewer steps each of us has to complete?
- *Reverse.* Is there some aspect of my work that is so boring or distasteful that I would like to reverse it? I have always hated answering the phone, so I will try calling the claim filers before they interrupt me, so I can answer their questions and then get on to my other paperwork.
- *Combine.* Which of my responsibilities can I combine without sacrificing effectiveness? I have papers to process, reports to write, and people to notify. I will design a form that can be used both to notify the claimant and to serve as

entry into the monthly report, so that one need not necessarily duplicate the other.

## Creativity-Stimulating Exercises

Here are a few mental devices that will stimulate your creative,
lateral, or divergent thought processes and enable you to postpone
vertical thinking, or problem solving, until you have generated a
large number of possible alternatives.[13]

### • Exercise One •

**1)** *Challenge assumptions* • Identify a key assumption in
your present idea and test whether the assumption can
be violated, eliminated, or otherwise altered.

**EXAMPLE** _____

Must all accountants work with numerical data? Is it possible
they might work instead with pictures (of financial records) or
computer languages that would eliminate the need for numbers?

Must all counselors counsel? Is it possible that counseling
service can be provided *indirectly* through the management of
resources, training others to do direct service, creation of self-
help materials?

**2)** *Fractionate* • Break your work idea into parts, examine
each part and discover which you like best. Or fractionate
a nonwork experience to look for new data.

**EXAMPLE** _____

What parts of being in a fraternity/sorority did you like when
you were in college? The socializing, the philosophical bull
sessions, being forced to live together, the group tasks, the
identity, the adventures?

**3)** *Analogy* • The analogy or picture or metaphor can help
you envision what you are trying to accomplish. Use
words to create a picture of your situation.

**EXAMPLE** _____

I have often thought of an individual's career as "stable as a
hog on ice." I also like to picture self-assessment as "sorting
out the pieces in a jigsaw puzzle."

**4)** *Random stimulation* • In this variant of creative thinking,
one uses an artificial device to prod and jiggle the collec-

tive memory bank. DeBono suggests looking up words randomly in the dictionary or wandering around a room or open space to expose oneself to a variety of stimuli without looking for anything in particular.

**EXAMPLE**

I tried the random word approach, came up with *wench* and *lobby*. I related these to career planning by wondering whether there could be special methods for women and musing about the political dimensions of the work search process.

**5)** *Force relations* • Osborn suggests that you take highly dissimilar concepts and try to force them into some sensible connection or find a common ground between them.

**EXAMPLE**

What do an engineer and a seamstress have in common? (Work with precision.) What do an oil rigger and an antiques dealer have in common? (Patience.)

**6)** *Deliberate exaggerations* • Take a normal, common work situation and stretch it to an unusual degree. See what ideas occur.

**EXAMPLE**

Sell insurance to dogs, cats? (Pet insurance.)

Education as total deprivation? (Wilderness experiences such as Outward Bound.)

A camera as big as all outdoors? (Radar.)

**7)** *Alphabet system* • Use the alphabet to generate ideas by hooking your problem to each single letter in turn, and see what results.

**EXAMPLE**

What kinds of employers might want a person with numerical skill?

Actuary, accountant, bookkeeper, computer programmer, credit manager, and so on.

**8)** *Attribute listing* • Brainstorm as many attributes as possible about a given occupation (the same procedure can be used to describe a person) in order to generate data relevant to the decisions you might make about this occupation.

**EXAMPLE**

Attributes of the work of an insurance salesperson: social, financial, personal, abstract-intangible, future-oriented, risk-related, numerical.

## • Exercise Two •

Find a relationship between a past experience and a future aspiration by using one of the nine creative processes outlined on page 87.

**EXAMPLE** _____

1. Rita is a program director for the local YMCA. She would like to get involved in the retailing business.

*Creative process: adapt.* Rita can adapt her experience in promoting programs and services to the task of learning how to promote merchandise to customers.

2. David has done a newsletter for his Hebrew school synagogue group. He would like to do personnel work with college students.

*Creative process: magnify.* David can attempt to magnify his writing and data-gathering skills into a research and program development position with a large university student personnel staff.

3. Phil has done numerous bake sales in his neighborhood. He would like to become involved with a community arts program.

*Creative process: substitute.* Phil can substitute a different artistic skill—such as handicrafts—for that of baking and apply his manual and creative skills to developing new programs of this kind.

## chapter five

#  Risking

*The basic paradox of the stress-seeker lies in his apparent engagement rather than avoidance of the painful. This paradox may be resolved by the fact that pleasure and pain both draw upon the same reservoir of underlying excitement.* • Samuel Z. Klausner, Editor
*Why Man Takes Chances*

Dear Howard:

All this information about career possibilities has me buffaloed. I learn about twenty new occupations every week, that everyone's estimate of future demand is different from everyone else's, and no matter what experience you get, the next guy has something else to compete with you. Where are the careers that are sure bets? Which fields guarantee a clear path to prosperity? Where is the rainbow on my horizon?

> Signed,
> *Impatient about Where I Am Going*

Dear Impatient:

Riding around looking for the riskless career is something like being the Headless Horseman. You have no idea where you're going, less idea where you've been, but a driving desire to get there in a hurry. I submit that to go riskless is to go headless, because the only kinds of work that offer certainty and predictability are the most pedestrian of all—watching trains go by, taking tickets, counting inventory, and others that have little hope of changing.

You might as well get used to the idea that risk rides with you wherever you go. Sure, there are some careers that seem to offer guaranteed annual incomes to their practitioners—medicine and accounting, for example—but they carry hidden risks such as malpractice suits from your patients or financial irregularities from your clients.

The harder you look for predictability and security, the more they may elude you. Every ten years or so, hordes of young people sweep their way into engineering curricula in search of the risk-free career, only to discover some years later that the demand for engineers is subject to wild fluctuations as a function of government contracts. Even the individual who finds the occupation that seems impervious to change, having a regular and respectable fountain of demand—optometry comes to mind—may discover that regularity carries the hidden risk that boredom will set in. Optometrists probably dream of big-game hunting and robbing banks, where the element of risk can be recaptured and savored.

Signed,
*Howard*

The very word *risk* conjures up images of people jumping off bridges, amateur gamblers laying down next month's mortgage payment, or wild-eyed youngsters climbing mountains without the proper lifesaving equipment. None of us likes to admit to entering a risky situation purposely. To do so is tantamount to saying that you didn't investigate the situation well enough to know things would work in your favor. All sorts of conventional wisdom persuades us that intelligent people avoid risks: "Look before you leap." "An ounce of prevention . . ." Risk tables in the insurance world deal in the probabilities of death or dismemberment. Even a derivative, the word *risqué*, suggests off-base behavior, not prudent, out of line.

Most of us, except the daredevils and purposeful chance takers, would rather convince ourselves that we have squeezed every last ounce of risk from our career plans, that every contingency has been anticipated, and that one stage of career advancement will lead logically to the next.

The notion that a career can be planned, risk-free, orderly, and predictable, is, of course, the most self-delusionary form of nonsense. You cannot foresee the thousand turns in the road, changes in yourself, and constant shifts of circumstance that will alter your plans, reshape them, and leave you wondering why you didn't foresee it all. Risking is the normal state of affairs in career development; it simply means you are open to opportunities, to changes in yourself, and to new ways of putting your talents to use.

Risking is the element of work search everyone wishes would go away, the stranger in the back of the room whom no one wants to acknowledge. You would prefer to think there is no risk because you have planned carefully and honed your talents sharply in the hope of minimizing the possibility that something will go wrong.

Guess again. Not college degrees, experience, personal referrals, union memberships, or all your piety and wit will keep the stranger from your door. Credentials, recommendations, apprenticeships, and so on are acquired for the specific purpose of reducing the probability of mishap, but the beast refuses to go away.

## The High Risk of Risk Avoidance

Risk avoidance leads only to the bomb shelter. The harder you try to wall yourself off from unreadable futures, the more you remove yourself from the sounds of everyday life. Hermits avoid risk successfully, but only at the risk of sensory deprivation and feeling their coping powers atrophy. Prisons, mental institutions, and other highly controlled environments manage to winnow risk behavior down to its barest minimum, but in doing so they excite the risk sensors of the inhabitants through deprivation. The inmates will do almost anything to escape the routine.

The risks of leaping to a new job are matched in kind and magnitude by the risks of sitting still: boredom and atrophy. "I will die of boredom if I have to open this ledger five thousand more times, make the entries, and call clients who have the same questions they asked me last year." "It is said that a limb which is not used for a long period of time will atrophy and die. If I continue to do as I am told, I may lose the ability to think for myself." "After years of performing the same tasks, however competent I may be, I will lose the fine edge of motivation, will perhaps get burnt out." "I will become the victim of my own fringe benefits, stifled by Blue Cross, smothered by the retirement plan, and strangled by reduced air fare on charter trips to Bermuda."

## Four Risk Styles

People differ widely in the attitudes they have about risk taking. While you may regard risk as enjoyable, exciting, the added element you need to keep your blood circulating, others may hope to minimize it and tame it.

**Minimum Failure** • You act to reduce the probability of failure to as close to zero as possible. You are less concerned with predicting success levels or watching the fascinating interplay of variables than you are with avoiding catastrophe. Anything that allows you to put to rest fears of failure will do, thank you very much.

**Maximum Possible Gain** • This sky is the limit. This strategy demands that the highest possible level of attainment be sought at all costs, no matter what the risk of failure or consequences that must be suffered along the way. You folks are the gamblers among us, the daredevils who would board the next mule in search of a gold strike or invest heavily in a venture only a few visionaries feel has a ghost of a chance.

**Probable Gain** • The prudent risk taker assumes it is necessary to take a flier now and then, but only if there is a reasonable chance of success. Possible gain and probable success are balanced against each other here, with neither allowed to get out of control. You will take a moderate risk if the value of success is high enough, but you prefer to have a better than 50 percent chance of success in most careers you consider.

**Maximum Probability of Success** • If most of us were forced to admit it, we would opt for stability and certainty first, and a little prudent risk taking later. Few of us like to take wild chances before a foundation of earning power has been established. Adventure is nice and risks are even stimulating, as long as you know where your next Thanksgiving turkey is coming from. Adventure and flying leaps are luxuries when the survival level has not been assured.

## When Risking Becomes a Necessity

A lifetime strategy of probable gain and maximum probability of success may seem prudent and the road most often taken by reasonable people, but when Frost wrote of a "road less traveled by" he had in mind that predictability and safety often beget their own downfall. When does the need to increase your risk-taking become so important you can no longer ignore it?

**When the Thrill Is Gone •** When your pulse no longer quickens at the thought of the work week, nothing pushes you to your limits anymore, demands a new response, or kindles the spirit of exploration.

**When You Know It All •** The person who must say "tell me something I don't know" feels the ennui of having been there a thousand times before, having learned everything there is to learn, and being able to anticipate any turn in the road that might occur.

**When They All Look the Same •** When all the clients begin to look, sound, or feel the same, it's time to ask yourself what you are doing in this place. If your work week makes you feel you're at a Shriner's parade, watching a hundred bands pass by, interchangeably, predictably, then this parade has run out of oompah for you.

**When You Become a Compulsive Worker •** When it's time to resort to your faithful work habits, your dedication to the cause, or your unwillingness to be regarded as a quitter, it may be just the time to quit. If all you have left to stimulate you is your reputation for punctuality and reliability, then you may win the good conduct award, but your spirit will wither in the process.

**When There Are No More Surprises •** When nothing in the job could possibly startle or surprise you anymore, there is no such thing as anticipating what will happen next, and every future project is as predictable as the office Christmas party, you've stayed longer than anyone has a right to expect of you.

## Risk Exercise

Following is a hypothetical situation designed to illustrate the four risk styles. After reading through it, make up another situation—or use your own case or that of a friend—and ask yourself how each risk style would respond. Notice that it is possible to choose consciously a risk style to suit yourself and a particular situation best.

Pam would like to be a legislative assistant in her state government. She has a comfortable job as a youth service director for the city parks department, but would much prefer to work on key legislative issues for a representative from the local district. If Pam leaves her current job, however, the department will hire someone else and Pam's changes of resuming her director's position would be small. The legislative job offers not only more money, but also the possibility of building a base for future entry into political campaigns. There is a middle road for Pam. She could stay with her present job and volunteer to work as local campaign representative for the representative. If she goes to the state capital now, she has no guarantee that the job of legislative assistant is hers, but if she *is* hired the chances of advancing are better because the representative is newly elected. If she waits, building her base on a volunteer level, the chances of getting hired are better in the future, but others will have joined the staff by that time, and they will be competitors.

What would Pam's decision be, using each of the following risk strategies?

- *Minimum failure.* Stay in her present job.
- *Maximum possible gain.* Quit the present job and apply right now.
- *Probable gain.* Stay in her present job, but do volunteer work and watch for an early opportunity to make the change.
- *Maximum probability of success.* Accumulate volunteer experience for a long period of time.

# · chapter six ·

 # Goal Setting

Goal setting is vaguely threatening. It brings to mind every coach's locker-room admonition ("Get four turnovers by halftime") and every stern mother's advice to her children ("You'll never get anywhere without a goal in life"). We answer meekly that life is a journey and not a destination, but the mystique of the proud goal setter lives on.

Goals give order and direction to our energies. Though they may be reshaped along the way, goals are energizing because they tell us what we can expect to accomplish. Goals are simply the landmarks and road signs of where we have been and where we expect to land next. Without them, we have no measures with which to heighten our anticipation. The observation of progress—intermediate goals attained—is the fuel that keeps us going.

## Getting Perspective

You want better work, but what is *better*? Do you want more of this and less of that? A review of your work-related values is helpful at this juncture. But more importantly, it is time to step back and get some perspective. Satchel Paige once said, "Don't look back, somethin' may be gainin' on ya," as a way of expressing his unwillingness to surrender. The older you get, the more acutely you will feel the need for perspective, the need to ask yourself: "What am I trying to accomplish in the years that are left to me?" Your finite timetable will make you want to set goals and watch your progress toward them. Goals put the harness on your energies, but paradoxically, this harness frees you from feeling worthless or scattering your efforts to the winds.

Any sequence of goal-seeking behavior must begin with a goal statement. The goal statement is developed by (1) identifying your highest-priority skills and values, (2) naming the organizations where you would most like to apply these skills and values, and (3) deciding what you would like to accomplish there.

**EXAMPLE** _____

My skills are supervising, negotiating, analyzing numerical data. My values are creativity, variety/change, choice of geography.

I would like to apply these skills and values in the Health, Education, and Welfare Department at any level of government.

I would like to accomplish the following: supervise contract negotiations and awards, research dollar allocations.

Goal statement: To supervise and negotiate research contract negotiations at HEW offices somewhere in New England.

A goal statement can often be simpler than the example above. Other goal statements might include:

Building houses for the Department of Housing and Urban Development

Doing estate planning as a financial consultant for a bank

Speaking and writing about agriculture for the county government

Training and raising horses for shows

Promoting and staffing services for the older population

## Goals Need Visible Deadlines

How many times have you said or heard a friend say: "I do my best work when I have a deadline to face." I suspect we all feel the same love-hate relationship with a deadline. It stares at us until we sweat and feel pain, but it squeezes the best efforts from us because we are compelled to act. A time goal provides you with an imaginary rival against whom you can pit your energies.

In 1832, the night before a brilliant 20-year-old French mathematician named Evariste Galois was killed in a duel, he feverishly filled sixty pages with notes and proofs that solved a long-standing mathematical problem. His calculations laid the groundwork for what has become the Theory of Groups, now considered the supreme example of mathematical abstraction.[14]

It may surprise you to know that many great writers fashioned their best and most creative work when faced with severe time deadlines and the unquestionable need to make money:

> No professional writes except for the promise or expectation of money. Dostoyevsky, forever under financial pressure because of his gambling, wrote most of his novels under contract to newspapers that serialized them. He wrote the last chapters of *The Idiot* in a tremendous burst of speed, writing around the clock for several days, because he was going to forfeit a substantial amount of money from future works unless he met his deadline. Balzac wrote throughout the night, every night, because he wanted money.[15]

We may dream of the day when no deadlines exist and we have time to think in a leisurely way, coalesce our thoughts, and reflect broadly and deeply. For most of us, however, this is idle daydreaming, because it takes a teeth-bared deadline to force creative action, as though the inner energies were waiting for a signal to respond to the call of alarm.

Most of us have the attention span of a gnat. We need to set short-range deadlines for our goals. We can pay close attention only to an activity that has a completion point in the very near future. Of course, we have long-range goals too, but our success in pursuing the long-range objectives is related to our ability to connect several short-term goals to the more distant objective.

Every goal should have a time frame with results that occur soon enough to let you experience some sense of progress. You may decide that you will finish reading a novel by Friday so you can move on to other works by the same author. Or you may promise yourself that your dancing muscles will improve by two months from now, in terms of your ability to do certain exercises.

## The Importance of Intermediate Goals

Ultimate goals are not always in your control. You must establish intermediate goals that allow you to move closer to an ultimate goal, facilitate your progress, and increase your preparedness. If your ultimate goal is to become a store manager, for example, you'd establish such intermediate goals as: acquire accounting skills, learn merchandise in the field, get experience as a customer.

For lack of a target, the entire kingdom can be lost. The work search often suffers from lack of something to do. If you don't have a real live job interview scheduled for the coming week, you may feel there is nothing to do. In fact, there is everything to do. Don't be in such a hurry to see your work search bear fruit. Think instead of the intermediate goals that stand between you and the ultimate job contacts. Ignoring intermediate goals is like trying to find apples on trees without first planting the seeds.

Each of the skills described in this book can be understood as an agenda for an intermediate goal.

**EXAMPLE**

To clarify my values, I will identify my high-priority values in some recent life experiences.

To develop a prospect list, I will make a list of at least twenty employers in this area who might be of interest to me.

To become the inquiring reporter, first I will gather data from at least three in-person interviews this week with target employers.

## The Sequence for Goal-Directed Behavior

You will find it helpful to recognize that all goal setting can proceed through a fairly predictable sequence, one that allows you to review whether you are dealing with your goals in the most effective way:

**1)** *Goal statement* • State the skills you would most like to use, the values you would most like to satisfy, what you would like to accomplish, and the employer with whom you can imagine this all would be possible.

**EXAMPLE**

I would like to use my interviewing, researching, and writing skills to work with a small-town daily newspaper as a reporter covering political issues.

**2)** *Strategy* • Translate your broad goal into a strategy that explains the things you must do or learn en route to your goal.

**EXAMPLE** _____

I must become a good enough writer, find out whether I can handle the hectic pace of newspaper reporting, get some experience, and see whether there are any job possibilities in this area that appeal to me.

3) *Intermediate behavior* • Translate your strategy into observable behaviors so you will be able to monitor your own progress.

**EXAMPLE** _____

I will have an idea of my writing talent after I take this journalism course and get some feedback from the professor. I will volunteer for six months of part-time experience with a local paper to test my reactions to the pace and acquire necessary experience in the process. Some intermediate behaviors I could measure are my willingness to volunteer on a regular basis, completion of my assignments in journalism class, written comments from the professor that are encouraging.

4) *Resources* • Identify the materials, funds, and other resources you will need to move toward your goal.

**EXAMPLE** _____

I will need several beginner's books on journalism, enough funds in the bank to afford six months of volunteer work, and a car to cover assignments.

5) *Timetable* • Can I spell out specific times in which the steps of my goal can expect to be accomplished?

**EXAMPLE** _____

I will complete the journalism course in September, will have done six months of volunteer work by December, and will have saved enough money by January to quit my current job and look for paid work as a reporter.

6) *Measure results* • What observable data will I have that tell me the progress I have made toward my goal as originally stated? How will I know when I have made it?

**EXAMPLE** _____

Grades and feedback received in my journalism course. The willingness of my sponsor (person with whom I volunteer and apprentice) to help me actively with the job search. My ability to write stories the local paper is willing to publish. I will consider my progress successful when: I receive a grade of B or better in my journalism course; my sponsor agrees to read my stories and provide criticism to me; I submit three stories to the paper that the editor is willing to publish, one each in the categories of feature, sports, and news; I can research a story, conduct the necessary interviews, and write it acceptably without significant revisions from the paper and with no more than one rewrite by me.

# Goal-Setting Exercise

The simple sequence of goal attainment outlined above can be applied to any goal you have in mind. Practice this skill and get comfortable with it before testing it on more serious goals. Then use it on some of your career goals.

**EXAMPLE**

Goal statement: To learn how to cook.

*Strategy:* Ask mother for guidance and try a meal each week in our house.

*Intermediate behaviors:* Complete each meal and serve it to the family.

*Resources:* Cookbooks; advice from mother, sister, Uncle Harry.

*Obstacles:* Adverse response from family when they eat my cooking; to be overcome by requesting their patience and having Mom make a backup quick meal.

*Goal sacrified:* Cannot read my novels during predinner hours; must contribute part of my earnings for the food.

*Timetable:* I intend to make a satisfactory meal from start to finish, without assistance, within a two-month period of once-a-week trial meals.

*Measure results:* I will know I have succeeded when I do the meal on my own and someone in the family believes my mother did it herself.

part

2

Detective
Skills

## chapter seven

#  Introduction

The image of the sleuth or detective is my favorite for characterizing the career search because it merges the elements of excitement and anticipation with judiciousness, the awareness that your quest for information will always bend to intellect and persistence. Just as a good detective knows the puzzle can be solved, the necessary information is at hand, and what may be invisible to the eye is deducible by the inquiring mind, so the work detective can say with assurance: "The work you want is out there; all you must do is find it."

The best work is awarded to those who are most diligent at finding it, at putting themselves in the *right place at the right time*. Since most job contacts have an element of luck in them, it follows that a good detective takes advantage of every ounce of luck available. Most employers are grateful to find a capable person at the time they need him. Once you have made yourself available, the employer will have no particular compulsion to conduct a cross-country search for the best candidate. He will assume you are the best that could be found, because the others simply have not appeared.

## The Work Detective Has It Easier

When you consider that the crime detective and the work detective function according to similar principles, you realize that the work detective enjoys the advantages of the trade without the disadvantages of having criminals, paranoids, and competing sleuths attempting to hide information from him. Everything you are looking for as a work detective is open to public view. Furthermore, it is offered by people who want to help you, if you will only ask them. If I want to learn more about what a carpenter does, I don't have to sneak around corners and bribe people to give me hot information. I can approach my target directly and ask for the assistance he is willing to give.

A friend of mine wondered where in the world she would learn about the banking field and get the contacts she so desperately needed. Meanwhile, she sat beside a bank teller on the bus to work, tripped over a bank vice-president on her way into the building, had lunch with a friend who lived next door to a big money man in the financial district, and went bowling that night with a city manager who was about to close a deal with his local bank for downtown redevelopment. The best sources are walking past you, if you have the presence of mind to tap them on the shoulder.

Don't look for the proverbial needle in the haystack by yourself. It does not make sense to conduct all your detective work alone. You are not paid to be a full-time sleuth. You certainly don't have the time or patience to track down every detail on your own. What then? Let others do most of your work for you. Find the people who know the most about what you want to know and give them the privilege of showing you their storehouse of information. It has been said that the smart manager proves it by surrounding him- or herself with people who are even smarter.

When doing your detective work, don't get hung up on precision or on being overly careful. An old friend was afraid to change career fields until she knew everything there was to know about city planning, the field she proposed to enter. She verified every fact, interviewed every person on the professional roster, examined every statement for possible bias; in other words, she subjected her detective work to the scrutiny one would expect from a professional scholar. That sort of precision and care will drive you to an early grave because you will be sacrificed on the altar of veracity. Don't try to weed out bias and inaccuracy in your searching—expect them. There is nothing impartial about the opinions of people about their fields of work. Their biases are their passions, and their opinions about what is right are their daily challenges.

# How to Get Started with Detective Work

As you set forth in search of people or information about your intended career, the questions to ask yourself routinely are: Who would know? Who would know anyone else who knows? Where would they meet? Do they have any formal association or affiliation group?

Any good detective looks in the places that have the greatest promise. Don't wait on park benches for the clues to sit in your lap. Let's say you want to make contacts in the field of recreation.

- *Who would know?* Town recreation boards, youth groups, anyone engaged in athletics, and people who teach recreation at the state university.

- *Who would know anyone else who knows?* People who participate in recreation a lot, such as children, older people, church leaders; and people whose business it is to know what is happening in recreation—retailers of recreational equipment, keepers of parks, and so forth.

- *Where would these people meet?* Try the obvious first, places where people engage in the recreation itself; then try the less obvious, places where people meet to plan recreation activities—church groups, youth groups, town councils.

- *Would they have an association?* Of course. Don't any groups that share common interests, problems, and needs for enrichment find a way to get together? Ask any active recreational specialist where colleagues meet when they want to share new ideas or have a good time together.

You can make useful connections through seemingly unlikely sources. Butchers know bankers, and street cleaners have made the acquaintance of government officials. I know a college professor who knows mideastern high potentates. It is within your grasp to start a chain from potentates to that special camel dealer you've been wanting to meet all these years.

**EXAMPLE**

Steve always wanted to meet an alligator wrestler. He really half-suspected there were no such people. He tried the local zoo and they laughed at him. Undaunted, he slipped into the town's luggage shop on a lark and asked where the alligator suitcases came from. "I just get them from my wholesaler, Mac," replied the store owner. Thus began a trail from the owner to the wholesaler to the manufacturer to the alligator trappers in the bayous of Louisiana. A few letters and a phone call later, Steve was invited to an open market for trappers and traders. He declined the offer of a summer job, but made contact with a Louisiana guide for the day he plans to make a firsthand visit.

# Seeing It from the Employer's Perspective

Consider who is really the helpless one in this job search process. It is the poor employer, even more than you. The employer must discover you from among thousands of potential applicants. The employer has precious few resources to find you easily and literally no systematic method for even detecting your existence. You at least have the advantage of knowing what you want and being able to find the employer, who is listed in the telephone book or some other convenient directory. By contrast, you are nearly invisible to the employer who seeks you.

**The Employer Doesn't Even Know You Exist •** Directories are little more than organized frustration for the employer who wonders: "Who would want this job? What is this person doing now that is relevant to our situation? How do I find this person without having to interview everyone at the national convention?" It is far easier for you to know that the employer exists. Numerous reference books, stock market reports, annual reports, newspaper stories, and other research materials tell you whether an employer should be included on your target list.

**The Employer Must Talk to Whatever Walks in the Door •** Typically he has to deal with hundreds of the wrong people in the effort to find you. Misfits of all shapes and sizes must be reviewed, notified, tested, coddled, and rejected, as the employer hopes against hope that you will show up. By contrast, you can reject any employer at all, with a wave of your hand. Every employer you interview adds to your storehouse of worthwhile information, and you can pass an employer by without any elaborate personnel procedures. After all, you're just doing research—for yourself.

**The Employer Is Usually Under Great Time Pressure** • When an employer has a job vacancy, it must be filled in a specified period of time. How many hires are made because the employer simply got tired of the hiring procedures and took whoever was handy at the time? You will never get a good answer to that question, but most employers will admit there is a ring of truth to the old adage: "If you want to keep a business meeting short, schedule it close to dinnertime." As the job seeker, you can take whatever amount of time suits you because you are answerable only to yourself, not to a corporate hierarchy or personnel department. The concept of an interim job is an important one. It is a job you take to buy time for exploring the work you really want the most.

**The Employer Must Depend on the Least Reliable Data** • Anyone who has ever stared at a pile of a hundred résumés, trying to decide which of them reveals the right person to hire, will understand that a stack of résumés can be characterized as a parade of wooden soldiers. Any relationship between résumé data and what the person is capable of doing is often purely coincidental. Following the résumé screening process is the thirty-minute canned interview, in which the interviewer asks questions hoping to elicit the essential qualities an individual has cultivated during twenty-one or more years of living. Small wonder that a blind interview, based on a résumé that has been carefully manufactured to present a selective truth, often results in a process resembling a Martian talking to a person from the moon.

**The Employer Doesn't Know What Is Needed for the Job** • The employer has either just lost a good worker and doesn't quite know how Jim/Jane got the job done, or had to let a bad worker go and thus knows only that the job can be done poorly. Employers seldom know what it takes to do the job better because they have been hypnotized by watching the previous occupant do the job in a particular way for years and have a hard time conceiving of someone who might do it differently. You, however, know what you can do, and if you have done your research on the employer properly you have some glimmer of what the employer needs to get the job done more effectively.

**Where Are You When the Employer Needs You?** • While the employer can at least be given credit for knowing when there's a job to fill, you (the individual who is needed most) may very well be unconscious that you need to make a change from the work you are currently doing. If you have failed to absorb anything about career risk taking from this book, and are thus oblivious of your other possibilities, it is impossible for the employer to find you because you do not want to be found. This, of course, is the ultimate dilemma of all employers: "How do I awaken the person for whom I have a job that will better make use of his or her talents?"

There will be many moments in your life when you will say to yourself: "How could so-and-so have ever hired that cluck?" At such moments, you should take pity on the employer, who must cope with the miasma of difficulties I have outlined here.

The moral of this story is: *if you don't find the employer, the employer will not find you.* Hence, the employer will be forced to hire the cluck instead of you, and you will become some other employer's cluck because you too have managed to find the wrong job for your particular talents.

It is much easier for you to find the right employer among thousands than for the employer to discover you among millions.

## chapter eight

# 😕 Prospect List 😕

The first step in any active work search is to identify a list of prospective employers. Such a prospect list can be created in two ways: (1) through use of direct contacts with other people, and (2) by gathering information from printed materials and telephone calls.

Remember, there is no central clearinghouse that can tell you where the job opportunities are in this country, or even in your little town, at any given moment. The government keeps track of many things that stand still, but when it tries to follow individual employment changes, it discovers the task is no easier than getting wild horses to align themselves in an orderly row or counting raindrops for the next census.

You must begin your search with the assumption that *any employer at all may have a job for you.*

Pay no attention to what you have heard or read about where the jobs are. Include any organization on your prospect list that appeals to you. And always keep in mind these four things:

- *There is a large hidden job market.* Three-fourths of available jobs are hidden from public view. There are reasons for this, including, among others, the employer's unwillingness to advertise to the public at large, and the time lag between the start of the job vacancy and the moment it is announced.

- *Jobs are created.* A job may be created as a result of your initiative. Stranger things have happened. Your presence, your ability to describe your skills and experiences, and the employer's needs could come together in a chemical reaction that results in a new job.

- *Jobs open up later.* Though a job may not exist at the moment you see the employer, one may occur in the weeks following, and you will be among the first to be notified.
- *Jobs come through referral.* When you talk with a target employer, you have the extra benefit of being able to ask where the employer believes the jobs exist. Because data about job vacancies are never centralized, you must depend on individual sources for your information.

## Obvious and Less Obvious Prospects in Your Work Search

There is more than meets the eye to looking for work situations that will satisfy your needs. One of the most frequently fatal errors in making a prospect list is assuming that all people who work in an organization carry job titles that reflect the purpose of that organization. Are all the people who work at an accounting firm, for example, necessarily accountants? Are all the members of a community guidance staff really counselors?

The purpose of the organization and the functions performed by its staff may differ widely. There are financial experts who work in educational institutions, plumbers who work in embassies, and human relations specialists who work in engineering firms.

You can avoid the mistake of overlooking hidden prospects if you remember that the relationship between the purpose of the organization and the function performed by an individual employee can be classified as obvious, less obvious, and least obvious.

**Obvious Relationships** • The purpose of the organization and the function of the employee sometimes correlate very highly or perfectly. In these situations you can apply directly for the work designated by the avowed purpose of the organization.

**EXAMPLE** _____
Psychologists who work in a center for psychological services.

**Less Obvious Relationships** • In the organization of your choice, there may be functions performed that do not correlate with the major purpose of the organization.

**EXAMPLE** _____

You apply to a theatrical agency but discover they also have accountants there; you can use your business background to apply for that job.

**Least Obvious Relationships** • The skills you most want to use are often performed in organizations where you would not expect to find them and in jobs with titles that do not designate these skills.

**EXAMPLE** _____

Counseling employees in your role as manager
Teaching in your role as training specialist
Accounting work in your role as administrator
Writing articles in your role as sales manager

How do you take advantage of the less obvious prospects? When you have decided the type of work you are seeking (selling computers, counseling youth, whatever), make three lists of your target places of employment: (1) places where almost everyone is doing the type of work you are seeking, (2) places where only one person or very few people are doing that kind of work, and (3) places where no one is doing the work you want, but someone with your talents and inclinations is needed. Do not assume your targets are only where you expect them to be. Always ask the people you meet: "Where can I find the people who do this kind of work and to whom would you suggest I talk?"

## Strategy for a Prospect List

Every prospect list you develop should proceed through four stages.

**1. Making a Goal Statement** • Every search for prospects must begin with a goal statement, an operational definition of the kinds of organizations you are seeking and the work functions you hope to perform there.

**EXAMPLE** _____

I want to use my organizational and writing skills in working with any organization that involves international finance and economics.

**2. Focusing the Geographical Area** • You want to get your work search started without having to launch a thousand ships or invest a thousand dollars, so focus yourself on a tight geographical area. Decide on a town, city, or small region of a state that captures your fancy.

**3. Identifying the Kinds of Organizations** • What categories of employers might satisfy your needs? How would you find out? You have Ma Bell and other phone companies to thank for the handiest employer-search reference known to humanity—the good old familiar White Pages and Yellow Pages. A phone directory can be counted on to provide the names of employers by functional category (banks, manufacturers, recreational organizations, and so on), standardized across all towns and cities. The local phone company usually makes out-of-town directories available free or at modest cost. The Yellow Pages organize every functional category; the White Pages provide a handy classification of federal, state, and local government offices.

**4. Narrowing Down to Specific Organizations** • Once you have identified the categories of employers you seek, it is time to create the target list itself, the names of actual organizations and their key offices if possible. Of course, the phone books and other publications noted above will tell you many of these names. However, there are even better resources available for this purpose.

## How to Find Information About Specific Organizations

Anyone who works in a profession or occupation knows that there is probably a book somewhere that lists all organizations similar to his own. Often these directories sit unused in libraries, and even the librarians hardly know they are there. I have coined the generic term *employer directories* for our special purposes to denote such books. Use these to build your prospect lists, to obtain names of actual people you can phone or write, and to get a measure of the volume of employment in your target area. If you were interested in becoming a literary representative for writers, for instance, you would find in *Literary Market Place* a list of scores of literary agencies, their addresses and telephone numbers, and even the names of agents working in each organization. You would also find that there are no literary agents in Casper, Wyoming, and that 80 percent of them are in New York City.

If you are unsure who heads the particular department in your target organization that interests you most, pick up the phone and ask someone in the firm's public relations department, especially if you are preparing to write a letter or make a personal visit. Telephone contacts can also help you learn quickly about branch offices, personnel changes (any employer directory is at least a little out of date), and the functions of a given department. You will be surprised to discover how many of these questions a secretary can answer for you, if you explain your purpose and ask politely with patience.

Another good source is a directory. If the employer directories elude you or you cannot find one that covers your particular target organizations, try the *Directory of Trade and Professional Associations*. It lists thousands of trade and professional associations (each of which has a list of its member organizations). If you do not find names of employers through a reference in the directory, contact a person in your town who you believe might be a member of the profession and ask to see his or her personal copy of a membership directory. It may be national or local in scope, but it will always organize people by geographical location and specialty of their work.

Finally, alumni directories can be helpful. Call or write your college's alumni office and ask if it has a listing of the graduates of your school who work in a particular field or whose job titles come close to that category.

## The Importance of Sampling Widely

Every time you interview individuals about their work, you run the risk that what they tell you will be biased, colored by the particular lenses through which they see the situation. Therefore, you must sample as widely as possible among people who work in your field of interest. Take special care to include some of each of the following:

Happy workers—
people who are
pleased with what
they are doing
Unhappy workers—
people who are
dissatisfied with the
nature of the work
itself

People who have
different frames of
reference toward their
work, perhaps
because of their
previous work history

The "career bureaucrat" in government work, for instance, has a different perspective and set of attitudes about the job than does an academic person who works in government for a year or two on a temporary assignment.

## Prospect-List-Identification Exercise

Here is a step-by-step breakdown of the four stages involved in a good strategy for making a prospect list. Go through each as it applies to your own situation.

**1)** Write a goal statement that defines the skills you want to use and the broad categories of employers where you would like to use them.

**EXAMPLE** _____
Use managerial skills with financial organization

**2)** Choose a geographical area that you prefer—a town, city, or small region.

**EXAMPLE** _____
Boston, Massachusetts

**3)** Choose one of the four major employment sectors—private industry, government, education, or nonprofit—in which you'd like to work.

**EXAMPLE** _____
Private industry

**4)** Select one employer type in the sector you'd most like to work for.

**EXAMPLE** _____
Stockbrokerage house

**5)** Choose three skills you would most like to use in your work.

**EXAMPLE** _____
Writing, organizing people, speaking to groups

**6)** Name three other types of employers (organizations) that could offer you work in the field of your choice.

**EXAMPLE** _____
Insurance companies, banks, mutual funds

**7)** Choose a size of organization you would prefer, in terms of number of employees in a single location.

**EXAMPLE** _____
No more than five hundred employees

**8)** If you have gotten this far, you have done much to identify the kinds of target employers for whom you are searching and can use the employer directories in your target geographical area to make a prospect list of manageable size. Choose the names of three employer directories that seem most likely to contain organizations for your prospect list.

**EXAMPLE** _____
Look through the *Financial Market Place, Thomas' Register of Manufacturers*, and *Moody's Industrials* for information on stockbrokerage houses, insurance companies, banks, and mutual funds in Boston.

## chapter nine

# Personal Referral Network

Dear Howard:

How will I ever get out of the miserable job I'm in? I've been hidden in this rathole for years and don't get any chance to meet people who have the good connections. I'm a forgotten soul, sinking into the swamp of mediocrity and nonrecognition. How does a rinky-dink like me get to meet the big guys? I think I might have a shot at something a little better if only I could plug in to the right sockets.

> Signed,
> *Faulty Wiring*

Dear Wired for Sound:

Do you walk with both feet on the ground? Do you live somewhere on the planet Earth? Can you fall over a stranger at the bus stop? Are there at least three people in the world who love you or at least tolerate you enough to refer you to their friends?

If you can squeak a hesitant yes to these questions, there is hope for you yet. "Contacts" do not hide in smoke-filled rooms; nor do they travel, as a rule, in bullet-proof cars or walk around shielded by entourages of henchmen or hangers-on. Contacts ride buses like the rest of us, eat in cafeterias, go to ball parks, and sidle up to pizza stands. They don't wear red carnations. Contacts are you and me, Uncle Harry, and the guy who fouls you when you reach for the basketball at the local YMCA.

Your best connections are the ones you trip over every day, the people who cross your path on a natural, routine basis. They may not have the keys to the executive washroom, but they inevitably know people who do and can introduce you in casual contexts—the next company softball game, the tavern after a day's work, or the motorcycle trail where everyone is the same dirt digger with gravel in the ears and sand in the windpipe.

If you have lived with people, you have contacts. Don't bury yourself with the false assumption that your friends could not possibly know anyone worth knowing. Uncle Harry may look like a toad, but he plays handball with the bank president and cuts cards twice a week with members of the city council.

Signed,
*Howard*

---

# The "I'm a Nobody, I Don't Know Anyone Important" Blues

---

"You need to know people in high places to get ahead." "Only people with connections get anywhere." How many varieties of this tale of woe have you heard or said to yourself lately? I do not claim that all people have equal footing as they begin the work search; some folks *do* have contacts that are more influential than others. However, this complaint is still a weak excuse for not doing anything about your situation, for not mobilizing yourself and taking advantage of the contacts you do possess.

No matter how lowly you believe your station in life to be, or how private a person you think yourself, you still have valuable contacts. This chapter discusses the wealth of possible contacts within your comfortable grasp. No, contacts will not necessarily obtain a job for you; nonetheless, they provide a vital link between you and the people you are trying to meet.

"I just fell into it." "Every job I got was the result of a lucky break." "I was just in the right place at the right time."

How often have you said one or more of these things to yourself as you looked back on your job history and breathed a huge sigh of relief, wondering what on earth you would have done if a handy friend, an unforeseen break, a fortunate connection hadn't happened to bless you with a job?

People more often find their work through direct referral by other people—usually friends or acquaintances—than in any other way.

Crystal and Bolles, in *Where Do I Go from Here with My Life?*, call this *organizing your luck:*

> There is always an element of "luck," "the fortuitous crossing of paths," or "serendipity" that is beyond your control. But the question is: "How can you best organize your luck, so the factors that *are* within your control are working for you?" The answer is by choosing a target area and running it to death.[16]

Like the guy who hangs around the firehouse or the emergency room of the local hospital just on the chance something might happen, you *can* develop special antennae for work opportunities and the people who know about them. Many people who call themselves lucky are ones who have unconsciously refined their ability to learn about things as quickly as they happen and have developed the habit of putting themselves in touch with the right ears. If questioned, these talented people may not be aware of how they do it.

**EXAMPLE** _____
Jane asked the local automobile dealer to tell her about antique cars, where they are located, how they are acquired, and all that. She was just curious, you understand. The dealer invited Jane and her grandmother to an automobile show where antique cars were on display, and there Jane met another dealer who was looking for a young person to get into the business. Thus did Jane have the "lucky" break of meeting her future business partner in the trade that is her heart's desire.

Every planned contact can lead to unexpected ones. Expect the unexpected breaks and ask for them if they are not immediately proffered. Every time you make contact with a person who is in direct line with your career interest, you set up the possibility that he or she will lead you to more people of similar persuasion.

## Intermediate Contacts

"But I don't know anyone in that field at all," you protest. "That's like trying to meet the Prince of Wales." The intermediate contact, the person who knows both you and the Prince of Wales, is the person for whom you are looking.

The skill of expanding a personal referral network is the skill of connecting people, the skill of stringing together enough intermediate contacts so that you can reach anyone. Anyone. Acquiring employment is a *social* process. People are connected to one another by a nearly infinite number of pathways. Many of these pathways are available to you, but you must activate the circuits to make them work to your advantage.

An illuminating research study known as the "Small-World Problem"[17] reveals the extraordinary power of having and using your own personal contacts. Milgram estimated that any person of adult age has accumulated between 500 and 1,000 personal contacts, and he reasoned that each link between two individuals generates a total pool of contacts numbering between 25,000 (500 × 500) and 1,000,000 (1,000 × 1,000). Three links in a referral chain permit an astronomical number of contact possibilities. Therefore, he reasoned, anyone ought to be able to reach anyone else in a populated country simply by putting a few links of the referral chain into operation. He tested this empirically by asking a sample of people in Massachusetts to use their personal contacts to reach a randomly selected group in Nebraska whom they did not know at all. Results showed that the Massachusetts people reached the town in Nebraska typically within two links ("I know a plumber here who has a brother in Nebraska who has a friend in the target town"). The implications of this research for job seekers are little short of staggering. It means that you have the power to reach almost anyone if you simply use your existing contacts.

There is no such thing as a person who cannot be contacted, reached, tapped, exploited, or otherwise made a friend. Everyone has a friend who also has a friend. Somewhere in that chain of friends you are standing with your arms at your sides and your eyes closed. Now if you carefully open your eyes, reach out to the two friends waiting on either side, and grasp their hands firmly, you will feel the electricity of a personal contact network begin to course through your body. It will be stimulating, but not shocking. You will feel alive with the circuit of energy that comes from plugging in to people networks. However, be aware that any time you drop your hands and close your eyes again, you have broken the connection. The life of the circuit depends on your ability to keep the switches open. I don't know how to help people who are asleep at the switch.

People like to make their contacts known to you. It takes a lot of restraint *not* to tell another person about your contacts. Try it sometime. Most people's natural egotism takes over. "Why, of course, I know Dradnatz. Been a good friend of mine for years." Once you subtract a constant for puffery, you have a good measure of a person's contact potential. By telling you the people I know, I accomplish two things: (1) I reaffirm my membership in the human race and show that I have some history of having kept my relationships over a period of time—no small matter; and (2) I can be helpful to you in a way that requires little effort, yet does you some definite good.

To take the fullest advantage of natural contact networks:

- Never underestimate the value of any person you know. The milkman, the druggist, the country butcher, or the sandwich-board man (now there's a person who meets and greets a lot of people) can all be helpful to you. You-never-know-who-you're-talking-with incidents happen every day. The street-sign painter on your block this summer may be the son of the local bank president.

- Keep your mouth open at all times. Get in the habit of asking anyone and everyone what they do, whom they know, where they have been lately. Curiosity opens the most unexpected doors. I once asked a woman at the dry cleaner's where she got the Maine sticker on her car and discovered she had taught at a camp in that state where I had been trying to establish a contact for several months.

- Keep your ears open at all times. Listen more closely than you usually do to what people say about themselves, where they have been, who they have met along the way. Be curious about everyone's travels and meanderings.

## You Don't Need to Know Important People in High Places

There is a prevailing myth among work searchers that one must be wired directly to the seats of power in order to have a chance of being recognized. The mysterious business of personal contacts may seem the privilege of the moneyed class or the private territory of a so-called power elite, but contacts are available to you or anyone who chooses to pursue them.

Granovetter has found: "The more different social and work settings one moves through, the larger the reservoir of personal contacts he has who may mediate further mobility."[18] Every personal contact you make leads to a multiple of potential future contacts. The math is simple: If you have three friends, and each of them has three friends, and you contact each one, and each one of the nine has three friends . . . The huge potential here is apparent.

Granovetter found that in one out of every four cases a person acquires a job through a contact he didn't even initiate, from a person who had no idea he was looking.[19] If this much job contact can take place on a purely accidental basis, consider how much greater your activity can be if you choose your social activity wisely so that you are likely to run into people whose work interests you. Don't go to the woodchoppers' ball if you'd really rather work for the Sierra Club.

## How to Acquire a Personal Referral Network

There are three basic rules for acquiring contacts.

**The Best Time to Look for Contacts Is When You Are Not Looking for Contacts** • When you are in a desperate hurry to find the right contact, you will probably turn this person off with your impatience. You will also probably fail to relax enough to ask the best questions, wait patiently for the answers, and allow the person the freedom to reflect. You will be focused less on the person and more on your own private anxieties, and this will transform him into a functionary for you, which he will not like at all.

The less pressure you feel to ask the person for direct job information, the more likely you are to develop a comfortable rapport, talk easily about your mutual enthusiasms, and give the other the space in which to offer personal referrals without feeling compelled to do so. I can only conclude that you should be looking for personal referrals *at all times*, especially when you are under no pressure to change your work, when you are satisfied with what you are doing.

**You Never Really Know Who You Are Talking to** • Take, for instance, the man who went to a magazine office one day to get some back issues, fell into conversation with the receptionist, asked her a few questions about her work, got interested a little in her as a person and, lo and behold, discovered she was the niece of the magazine publisher, just working there for the summer. She introduced him to her uncle, who led him to the newspaper editor he had been wanting to meet. There is nothing at all mysterious about the skill of generating personal referrals. To some extent, you may have been doing it naturally all your life. Now make it more conscius and systematic, and you will have your hand gripped tightly around the throttle.

**Always, Always Ask for the Names of Other Contacts•** You can then say: "So-and-so suggested I call you." These linkages between colleagues, friends, or associates in the same line of work are your magical door openers. If you fail to take advantage of these connections, your work search will bog down.

## The Best Places to Hang Around

If you are in the early stages of seeking personal referrals and don't know where to get started, there are a few standard places that offer you a better-than-potluck chance of meeting someone who has good contacts. These places, listed below, are ones where your conversational behavior will not be regarded as odd because they are characterized by natural social intercourse. They offer you nonthreatening ways of introducing yourself.

- *Stockbrokerage office.* Sit where everyone watches the ticker tape and trades items of information, opinion, ecstatic glee, or curses as the market rises and falls.
- *Race tracks, taverns, and bars.* These are the old standbys for meeting people easily, as reliable as ever, provided you aren't overly obvious about your conversation and allow enough time for things to develop naturally.
- *Courthouse and courtrooms.* These are places where things are happening; there are a lot of curious-citizen questions you can ask, and the sorts of people who frequent the area like to share stories and opinions, anyway. Don't tamper with the jury or the judges. You can spot the ones who like to talk.
- *Travel agency.* A bit more difficult for natural conversations, but there is a lot of traffic, topics of mutual interest ("How did you like New Orleans?"); and people who take trips are often contemplating employment changes.

- *Real-estate office.* Just curious about these summer list-ings, you understand. Ask people who frequent the place about their property or the deals they are thinking about, and you may discover some referrals in the bargain.
- *Ball parks.* Especially during long double-headers, when fans have a lot of time on their hands and will talk about anything to get through the scoreless pitchers' duel.
- *Church committees.* Many of the town's knowledgeable and influential people show up on such committees. They are socially conscious and know their community well, includ-ing people in a wide variety of occupations.
- *Investment clubs.* People who devote time and energy to their investments usually make it their business to be ac-quainted with numerous corporation executives. If you can find a club to join, their acquaintances can become yours as well.

## Don't Get Ahead of Yourself

When you set about meeting people who have the power to hire you, it is important that you keep the brakes on and resist the temptation to rush headlong into asking someone to hire you on the spot. Proceed slowly. Give the person reasons to be interested in you. Give the personal referral and information-seeking process a chance to work in your favor. Don't pervert it by asking for too much too quickly.

Don't play the hidden agenda game. Don't ask to see people on the pretense of wanting information and advice, when you are sneakily trying to edge close and ask for a job. This tactic insults the other person and may haunt you for the remainder of your job search. Let the interview be a pleasant and nonthreatening one. If the person volunteers information about job leads, that is so much gravy for you, but not something you asked for.

## People Who Should Become Your Close Friends

Regardless of where you are searching for better work or what kind of work you desire, when you arrive in your chosen location, there are certain categories of people who are always in a favored position to be helpful to you. They are special people because they have more knowledge of the citizenry than almost anyone else in town. They are also people you would be likely to ignore if you had not read this book because they are part of the human landscape of any town, but not officially designated as job information experts. They would not think of themselves as such, but they are, nevertheless.

**Policemen •** Probably no individual sees more of what occurs in a town or makes it his business to know more occupations and what they are doing than the policeman. He knows where the bank presidents are, where the dope pushers hang out, and where the politicians can be found when the legislature is not in session. He has to know these things because he depends on these people for information when he needs it. People make it their business to know him, so he has continuing flow of information.

**Bartenders and Beauticians •** These folks may well see a steadier stream of people on an individual basis than anyone else. For this reason, they know not only who does what kinds of work, but how they feel about it, the organizations they work for, and probably who's going where, how it all happens, and when the openings will occur. No one ever accused a bartender, beautician, or barber of being 100 percent accurate about his or her information, but you are less concerned with total accuracy than with getting leads and gathering data.

**Cab and Bus Drivers •** These people are the traveling bartenders and beauticians. They too have the gift of gab; they get a rider's ear because they are anonymous and catch him breathless between engagements, ready to spill the latest crisis. Unlike the bartenders, they may not know the names or even the faces, but they know a lot about who's doing what to whom and where you should go to learn more.

**Other People Supplying Personal Services •** This category includes manicurists, masseurs, masseuses, house cleaners, and a variety of others with whom you come in personal contact. Many of these people acquire a great deal of information from the people they routinely see, their regular customers or occasional contacts. They usually enjoy sharing this information. It is part of the reward of *their* work. Make them happy; encourage them to talk at will.

**Retailers** • Anyone who operates a retail establishment of any kind—grocery, clothing shop, toy store, sporting goods store—sees a lot of customers and tries to know them as well as possible. He also does his best to find out which customers occupy positions of prominence because it may affect his sales.

**Secretaries/Receptionists** • These people are gatekeepers; they have the keys to the executive chambers and the knowledge of everyone's comings and goings. They have to know the people they serve in order to survive the daily blizzard of inquiries. They are your experts in discovering where the target people can be found, who is grumpy to talk with at what time of day, and how the information you need can be obtained without violating anyone's privacy, sanity, or company regulations. They can lead you to your destination or frustrate you at every turn, depending on how well or how poorly you have persuaded them that you are worth helping.

**Librarians** • These almost forgotten people would probably escape your attention in any work search where you are walking streets, taking buses, and focusing on office buildings. However, librarians know more than most of us about almost everything because they are surrounded by so many resources. Even if they don't have the exact sources directly at hand, librarians are some of the few people who see it (usually) as their professional *obligation* to help you find what you want. Librarians are detectives by another name.

## Exercises for Developing a Personal Referral Network

### • Exercise One •

**1)** Stop the first five people you encounter today in your usual routine. Don't be concerned about who they are or whether they are relevant to your intended work.

**2)** Ask each person: "Do you know anyone who does the kind of work I am looking for and would this person be willing to meet with me informally to answer a few of my questions?"

**3)** How many of these people were able to give you a referral to another person of some relevance to you, without having to think very hard or refer to any written lists?

## • Exercise Two •

Choose the name of an employing organization at random from the Yellow Pages. How many people in your neighborhood must you query before you discover someone who knows a person who works there? It may be as few as one, two, or three in a small town. Even in a large city, if you cheat by crossing town to the right neighborhood, you will be pleasantly surprised at the results.

## • Exercise Three •

Review any checklist of one hundred or more occupations and ask yourself: "In how many of these categories do I know at least one person who does it?" If you have lived and worked in your own city for a while, chances are you can tick off at least half of the list. I tried it for myself and managed 89 of a list of 125 occupations.

## • Exercise Four •

Choose any two occupational titles at random and imagine how many different other occupations would have connections between these two.

**EXAMPLE** _____

Plumber—insurance broker. Connecting occupations: home assessor, contractor, city manager, and others.

## • Exercise Five •

Identify the occupation of your next-door neighbor and imagine how you could use his working acquaintances to help you link up with a particular kind of employer.

**EXAMPLE** _____

If your neighbor is an oil company representative and you desire to meet a publisher, use the neighbor to contact the city manager, who will help you contact the Board of Education, which can lead you to textbook sales people, who then lead easily to the publishers themselves.

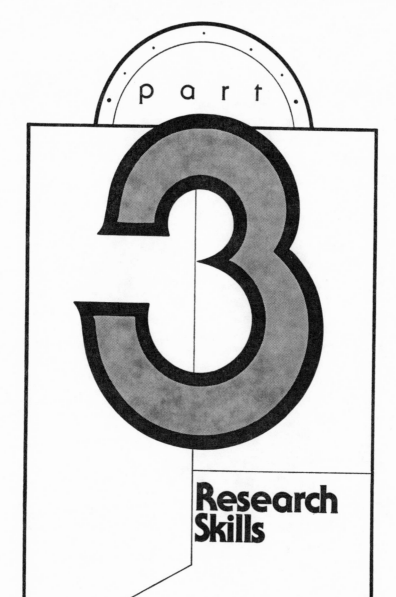

part

3

Research
Skills

## chapter ten

#  Introduction

Few job seekers care to gather information about their prospective employers. They prefer instead to assume that what they have heard or guessed is true and that "you don't really know what it's like until you work there, so why try to find out anyway?"

What stops the individual from gathering research information? What makes the task so unpleasant, more than most people can bear to endure? Why would most folks prefer to trust luck or conventional wisdom rather than gather information in their own hands? I can suggest several hypotheses, and I propose that each reason for avoiding the research process is largely unfounded and can be countered by a clearer understanding of how such research can be done with a minimum of effort and resources.

First of all, people too often think: "This information is not available to me." Not true. As detectives will tell you, most of the information vital to their livelihood is easily available in public records or other accessible locations; undercover work is kept to a minimum and skullduggery is reduced to low priority. Similarly, almost any job information you desire is readily available. Consider the following sources of information.

- *People.* You can make contact with *employees* of an organization, *customers* (or clients) of a business or other service organization, and *competitors* of a company in your efforts to discover what the target employer is doing. Each has his or her own perspective and can offer special insights. For fullest enlightenment about a target employer, all three categories—employees, customers, and competitors—should be tapped.

- *Written materials.* Most employers try their best to represent themselves in print. Corporations and public and private agencies produce annual reports and newsletters about their operations. They are only too happy to provide you with these materials because they regard such distributions as good relations with the public. Even small organizations like you to have their brochures or other reports so you can carry away their "image." Ask for these materials, and you will get them, in profusion. It has been said that the surest way to achieve immortality is to have your name on several mailing lists for public relations materials.

- *Public opinion.* Even the most superficial inquiring reporter survey you conduct about an employer in your local area will yield some information about the firm's general reputation. People who have never been employees, customers, clients, or competitors of your target employer will still venture opinions about the organization's reputation, purposes, future plans, and about all the mistakes it has made in the past several years.

A second reason people don't like to gather information, I believe, is that they simply don't know how to begin. The way to begin is by obtaining some easy-to-get reading material. Write the public relations office of your target employer and ask for annual reports, brochures, statements of purpose, and anything else that would help you understand better what the organization is doing.

Another way to conduct this kind of low-risk research activity involves being a customer of the organization with whom you are considering future employment. If, for example, you would like to work for a publisher of children's books, start investigating the books they sell; read the books and try to analyze the overall impact this publisher is trying to make on its market. If it's a service organization you're researching—say, an employment agency—try its services. If it's a government agency you're interested in, visit the place as a citizen seeking information for a local constituency. In all situations where you seek to gather data as a customer, constituent, or other user of an organization's product, you'd be wise to enter this customer role far in advance of your actual job-seeking activity, so that you can minimize the chances that such research activity will conflict with job interviews or other formal job-seeking behaviors.

Third, people think all this inside information is kept secret.

Despite my best efforts to persuade you that job information is public and accessible to the ordinary citizen who does not have connections in high places, you will insist that much of what you need to know is beyond your power to obtain.

Let me ask you this: What methods would you use to arrange meeting men or women for social or sexual reasons? I suggest that the following are typical methods. First, you would ask your close friends for advice on how to meet a particular person: "Where does he hang around?" "Do you know her? Where am I likely to meet her casually?" Second, you would watch the person's behavior to learn personal interests, places frequented, other aspects of life style that provide clues for conversation when you meet. Third, you would arrange, if you wanted to be really industrious, to be in places where you think the target person is likely to show up and be available for conversation. You might even join a club or other group the person belongs to, if you wanted to be downright manipulative. Finally, you would assert yourself at the appropriate moment and speak to the person on the basis of your common interests.

This seek-and-ye-shall-find behavior for improving one's social life is similar to seeking contacts with potential employers in the job search process. Thus, you have probably been cultivating many job search skills in your pursuit of daily relationships. The analogy can be developed as follows.

You can begin your search with anyone you know in the world of employment. Since each person who is employed has an estimated 500 to 1,000 personal contacts, you should be able to gain referrals to desired employers more easily than you would think. There is much to be gained from naturalistic observation of the setting where you hope to work. The physical arrangement of the workers, the emotional tone of the people at the work site, the requests of customers or clients, the kinds of equipment in view, the smoothness of the operation, the pace of activity, and many other factors contribute to your impression of the employer. A good detective always cases the joint, and you should do likewise. Carrying the on-site visit to its logical extension, there are many ways in which you can arrange to spend time in the same place as the people whose work interests you. Professional conventions are ideal settings for contacting target people. Conventions occur only a few times a year at most; hence, you should supplement this activity with volunteer time, if you have an especially strong desire to learn more about a particular employer. In many respects, a continuous volunteer experience is the equivalent of paid work experience and certainly its equivalent in terms of learning more about the person you may one day work for. Conventions or volunteer experiences are perfect places to use your assertive skill in meeting people who have information and insight that can help you. Of course, you should choose those people whose priorities correspond most closely to your own.

The research skills described in the following chapters can be used by anyone because knowledge of prospective employers is easy to obtain. You can do effective career research simply by using written materials that are readily available, by interviewing target people, or by visiting accessible work sites. Furthermore, such research will always give you a competitive advantage over people who choose to remain ignorant about target employers.

# · chapter eleven ·

# Printed Materials

A great deal of the information about your intended employers is in readily available printed form—annual reports, newsletters, company magazines, articles in the commercial press, and brochures describing products and services available.

Job seeking can be a war of paper airplanes. Your paper credentials—résumés and the like—are pitted against the employer's paper job requirements. Read what the organizations have to say about themselves and turn their words to your advantage. You can demonstrate your devotion and good intentions with substantive knowledge instead of repeating a tired litany: "I wanna work here; I wanna work here."

You have probably been cultivating research and library skills for several years of your life and could produce information and references at will for a topic to be discussed in a formal classroom situation. It would be a sad quirk of human development if you should suddenly abandon these research skills when perhaps you need them most.

Once you have identified an organization or place where you would like to work (prospect list) and have identified people who can tell you more about that organization (personal referral network), you are ready to gather as much information as possible about the people and institution where you hope to be employed. You are ready for in-depth research of a few target employers. While I have stressed that personal research is usually the most powerful, you should concentrate on getting data in two other ways in addition to approaching people directly. The first of these ways is through the use of printed materials. The second, discussed in Chapter 13, is participant observation.

In its simplest terms, making use of printed materials involves locating any form of published material that can expand your pool of career information. Such information can be as broad as that which describes an entire occupational field that interests you (for instance, architecture), or it can concentrate on the particular company, organization, or department you seek. Published information can also help you illuminate the background of a given individual with whom you would like to work.

The knowledge you get from printed materials enables you to do a crucial thing: to act like a professional. When you are seeking entry to a profession, it helps to adopt the attitude that you already *are* in that profession; to regard yourself not as an outsider, but as a person who has decided this is the field for him. Your research is the first step in establishing your right to be regarded as a respected member of the group. Though you may not yet have the credentials, degrees, or other imprimatur for that profession, you can behave as though you *will* be so accredited one day; it's just a matter of time. Your attitude will influence others' behavior toward you and the seriousness with which they respond to your requests. Therefore, the research skill is important because it is an opportunity to demonstrate that you are so serious about your future work that you will devote time to becoming better informed.

This skill is important also because it saves you time. If you are armed with data about the company, you can leap directly to the more personal and penetrating questions when you talk with someone personally. You can focus the information interview on those questions that cannot be answered easily in print ("Why did your company decide to get out of the war materials business?").

## Make Good Use of Libraries

Libraries are invaluable resources. The bigger ones have vast collections of materials helpful to job hunting, including industrial reference books, employment directories, annual reports, pamphlets, and catalogues of every kind. In addition, libraries contain another wonderfully useful source of limitless information: librarians.

When asking a reference librarian for information about your topic or prospective employer, be careful to be neither too specific nor too general in your request.

> If you were to go to a grocery store, and ask specifically for oranges, you might get the answer, "Sorry, we don't have any." And you would leave emptyhanded. But if you were to ask for breakfast fruit, the same clerk might suggest grapes, prunes or apricots, either of which would serve your purpose. . . . At the same time, if you were to make your request so general as to ask for "food," the storekeeper would hardly know where to start looking unless you carefully explained what you wanted it for and why.[20]

If you ask the reference librarian, "What kinds of information do you have on scientific research?" your question is so general as to make an answer difficult. On the other hand, "What information do you have about research laboratories for organic tree sprays?" is too specific. A manageable question lies between the two extremes: "Can you give me information about chemistry laboratories involved in scientific research and development?"

The research librarian will tell you that one of the best resources you can use is *Subject Collections: A Guide to Special Book Collections in Libraries.*[21] *Subject Collections* tells you whether your local library, or the metropolitan or university library in the neighboring town, has special information that relates to your work search. If, for example, you are seeking employment with a food-processing company, and the library has a collection of books on cooking, you might profit from a visit to that collection.

Library research affords you an opportunity to acquire a historical perspective on your subject, because you can review what the organization has done for a long time, perhaps see trends, and possibly sense what it will do in the future.

## How to Research an Occupational Field

Any one or more of these sources is handy for researching an occupational field.

**Professional Organizations** • See the *Directory of Professional and Trade Organizations* for whichever group pertains to your interest. Write to this group and ask for printed literature. It will be pleased to honor your request because it exists for the purpose of promoting its profession to you and others.

**Local Societies** • Many areas of work have their local societies as well as their national groups. Ask anyone in town who does this kind of work where the local group keeps its library materials.

There may be many small or large professional societies in your area, all of which are communications agencies for the membership they represent. You can visit many of them and learn how to reach their members by simply making a polite request.[22]

**Books in Print** • This is a reference book available in any library or bookstore. It lists all the books written lately, organized by subject, author, and title. You can find in it a listing of books on the occupational topic you seek to research.

**Periodicals References** • The *Reader's Guide to Periodical Literature*, the *New York Times Index*, and the *Wall Street Journal Index* are three standard reference works available in any library. They allow you to research magazine and newspaper articles pertaining to your subject area. If you are focusing on pharmaceutical companies, for example, use *Reader's Guide* or the *New York Times Index* to tell you all the articles that have been written lately about drugs, drug abuse, pharmacology, and so on.

**Join the Professional Group** • Perhaps the best way to act like a professional is to join the professional society itself, so that you can attend conferences, correspond with members, receive journals, and be eligible for in-service training workshops.

If you seek employment in private industry, cultivate the habit of reading one or more of these publications: the *Wall Street Journal*, *U.S. News and World Report*, *Fortune* magazine, *Business Week*, and *Money* magazine. All these journals and others are directly involved in telling you about *change*, the shifts of human behavior and attitude that have implications for the marketplace. If you come across an article entitled "Population Shifts to the Sunbelt Region," for instance, you can conclude that more jobs will be available in the southeastern and southwestern states. "Physical Fitness Activity Upsurge" may indicate that leisure industries that market fitness equipment can expect to prosper. "Water Problems in the Nation's Rivers" implies that scientists will be needed to improve water testing and control indiscriminate use.

# How to Research a Specific Organization

To research a specific employer, these sources of published information are most readily available.

**Annual Reports •** The first source you should seek is the annual report of the company or organization because it offers a summary of all the operations for the year, products involved, highlight events, and names of key personnel, plus budgetary data you may want to see.

**Organization Chart •** This chart shows all the departments and how they report and relate to each other. If it does not appear in the annual report or any of the other company publications, call the public relations office of the company and ask if one is available. If not, ask one of your personal referrals to see whether he or she can get you a copy.

**Stock Reports •** This is a more unbiased source of information and is available at any stockbroker's office for an organization that is sold by shares to the public. Several research services provide the brokers with data that can help you analyze the company's potential for growth, stability, and other relevant factors.

**Library References •** The *Reader's Guide*, the *New York Times Index*, and the *Wall Street Journal Index* can help you locate quickly and easily stories that have been written about an individual company, government agency, or other employer, provided the employer is prominent enough to rate news space.

**House Organs •** While you are asking for annual reports and the like, request a copy of the organization's in-house newspaper or magazine, which gives inside stories about company operations that are more up to date than what appears in an annual report.

**Public Relations Office •** Ask this office for any other printed materials that can help you. The staff will know about company reports you cannot identify by name, company magazines they would like to send you, and so on.

**Local Newspapers •** Get in the habit of reading the local paper each day to see whether your prospective employer is mentioned.

Perhaps an exposé of company graft, maybe a citation by the mayor will appear.

**Historical Society** • If you are dying to know more about how this organization got started and the library fails you, try whatever historical group there is in town. Such groups sometimes keep documents no one else cares about.

# How to Find Out about Specific People

To obtain vital background data on individuals who are employed at your target organizations, especially those who will eventually make the hiring decisions, research these people in any of the following publications: *Who's Who in America*; *Who's Who in the East*, *Who's Who in the West*, and so on; *American Men and Women of Science*; *Directory of American Scholars*; and the professional directories of national professional organizations. The directory of the American Psychological Association, for instance, provides a one-paragraph work history and statement of special interest pertaining to every member of the APA.

# Research Is Easy

Why is this skill easy to acquire? Every source mentioned in the previous section—the local library, the stockbroker's office, the public relations office of the company—is easy to find and is staffed by people who usually have a high degree of interest in fulfilling your request. All can be reached by telephone or in person, without complicated series of maneuvers. In most cases, the data for which you are asking are absolutely free. Most of these places are happy to give their information away because they often feel it promotes their selfish interests to the public, which is none other than you. And you will find that this is an infectious method because the more you know about a target employer, the more your appetite will be whetted for additional data.

# · chapter twelve ·

# Inquiring
# Reporter

The formal job interview is alien territory to the person who has not yet done research. Without any prior contact between you and the interviewer, you might as well be a Martian talking to a visitor from Saturn. Neither knows exactly what language the other speaks or how best to make a connection. Both you and the employer should avoid subjecting yourself to such an ordeal without having some prior knowledge of each other.

The artificiality and untrustworthiness of the formal job interview, without prior contact between the two protagonists, is the best reason why the Old Boy network has survived as an effective hiring tool. As you may know, the Old Boy network, from the employer's perspective, depends on having friends in other organizations who provide backroom information about likely job candidates, information from sources who can be trusted. Such channels allow the employer to reduce the huge volume of work entailed in interviewing people off the street and to reduce his dependence on the undependable formal interview as a selection device.

The passive voice of the phrase *being interviewed* suggests that you are on the receiving end of things, waiting for something to happen. Being interviewed immobilizes you and entrusts your fate to chance that the interviewer will ask the right questions, the questions you want him to ask. It is a performance not orchestrated by you and, therefore, out of your control.

When you, the job applicant, are passive, the employer has little choice but to depend on Old Boy methods. However, you need not wait for permission from an employer to become involved in the selection process. Enter the inquiring reporter, which is the single most powerful and versatile method for shifting your involvement in the work search process from the passive to the active voice. It involves your becoming the interviewer rather than the interviewee, the seeker rather than the sought, the hunter rather than the hunted. The two major potential disadvantages of the formal job interview—that it puts you in a passive role and that you and the interviewer know little about each other—are overcome through the main tool of the inquiring reporter: the information interview.

## The Information Interview

The information interview is the centerpiece of your research, the method you will use most frequently to gather data and collect the insights you are seeking. This special type of interview, much less formal than a job interview, is one in which you are the interviewer, the person asking the questions, controlling the agenda.

Your previous detective work included discovering target individuals or organizations and putting yourself in touch with target people in ways that make them likely to tell you what you need to know. Information interviews follow logically upon the heels of detective work.

All information interviews are not alike. They vary according to how much interviewing you have done in this field, organization, or department before, and how close you are to making formal application. A sequence of information interview categories is suggested below, ranging from the easiest and least threatening to a formal job interview in which there is the most pressure to perform. While the sequence is loose enough so that you can treat it as a rough approximation, you should take care to practice the earlier stages and acquire the data they can elicit before moving to the more compressed and difficult versions of the information interview.

1) *Surveying a hobby.* You talk to someone who has general information about your favorite form of leisure activity—canoeing, collecting stamps, playing chess. You would probably go to someone who does this for a living or as a profession, but you can also talk to a person who treats the activity as an avocation, as you do.

2) *Researching the organization.* You have a special interest in this company, agency, or institution and are doing a research project for yourself so you can become better informed about its operations. Be careful to specify your purpose here so that the respondent does not suspect

you of being an undercover agent or some other type he would want to avoid.

3) *Researching the people who work there.* This level of the information interview is different from the previous one in that you are concerned less with the organization and its objectives than with the individuals who have come there, get their satisfactions there, and are members of this working community. Of course, this level and the previous one often merge in a single information interview, and you should make the merger happen if you can.

4) *Finding target people.* At this level, you ask specifically for the person who would hire you if you were to apply for employment. Ordinarily, you should have had one or more information interviews earlier in the sequence before you tackle this one. You want to be as well armed as possible with information and as practiced as possible in your conversational skills before making your initial impression on the boss.

5) *Formal job interview.* You should recognize that the formal job interview always offers the opportunity for information seeking on your part, even though the overt format is one in which you are the respondent, not the questioner. Your questions may help you decide whether to accept, if you are given an offer.

The information interview is used at various stages of your work search, ranging from the earliest gathering of data about a career you know virtually nothing about, to the last stages of a search in which you have identified ideal target employers and are both presenting your views on why you believe you would be a good candidate and gathering detailed information about the nature of the work possibilities. To differentiate among the ways in which you would conduct various information interviews, depending on the stage of your work search, I will describe the conditions that should prevail in the two extremes: doing background research and meeting target employers.

## Using the Information Interview for Background Research

The purpose of this interview is to acquire information about work responsibilities, life styles, work conditions, and so on; to learn as much as possible while accumulating acquaintances from people in that field. Interviews for this purpose should be started many months before you intend actively to pursue a change of employment. You will have many of these interviews across a long period of time.

Certain behaviors are permissible in this type of interview that are ordinarily not desirable in a formal job interview. You may make an appointment on the spot, without the benefit of a previous phone call or contact, if you desire this approach and if the respondent is willing to see you. You may also bring a notepad with you and take notes occasionally, being careful not to let note taking detract from the attention you give the other person.

Typically, you should ask for about fifteen minutes of the person's time. You may well end up with more time than this, if you ask interesting questions and succeed in getting the other person to talk about him- or herself (not hard to accomplish), but you should not make a point of asking for a long meeting.

In most cases, you should not feel it necessary to write in advance of your meeting, unless you are at a distance from the person.

When you make your initial approach, smile warmly at the receptionist, secretary, or target person. People like friendliness, especially from strangers; it make the day a little brighter. A good initial approach to the secretary is to say something like, "I need to know more about the organization and its purposes," because this establishes the seriousness of your inquiry and makes it clear that you will have to see a person in a decision-making capacity to get your information. Act as though you know why you are there, because you do. Do not be timid about your request. If you are confident you know what you want, others will feel comfortable with you; if you are unsure of yourself, they will not be sure why they should want to see you (see Chapter 17: Assertiveness). Let the other person talk as much as possible. Don't try to control the conversation any more than you must in order to ask the questions you desire. Be genuinely interested in the other person. Remember that you are talking to a human being who has strong feelings about that work; you must begin by keeping in mind that you *really want* to hear those feelings. If you are just going through the motions in order to get to someone higher up, the person you are interviewing will sense your insincerity.

When you complete a meeting, always ask the interviewee to refer you to someone else in the field of work, *if* you continue to be interested in it.

## Using the Information Interview to Meet Target Employers

You hope your series of background research interviews will lead to a situation in which you can discover an employer who needs your services and to whom you can present a justification for your suitability. You should not leap to this stage of the information interview process until (1) you have done enough interviewing to determine that you are really interested in being hired and would choose this organization and department if asked; (2) you have sampled widely among people in this type of work and in similar kinds of work—both happy and unhappy workers; (3) you have reviewed enough printed material about this employer so that you are prepared for a formal job interview if it should occur; (4) you know at least one problem this employer is trying to solve; and (5) you can state why you believe you can respond to that problem, why you feel you are qualified to help the employer meet some of his needs.

As you make the transition from background interviews to this more serious type of interview, do not be concerned about the protocol of the formal application process. In other words, do not feel obligated to visit the personnel department and undergo the usual series of employment screening procedures. If you know the person you wish to speak with and what you want to say, be as direct as possible.

And you needn't be concerned that there seems to be no job opening. Your entire work search is based on the premise that 75 percent or more of the job market is hidden from public view. Any employer *may* have a job available, even though one has not necessarily been advertised and even though the employer may have disclaimed on a previous occasion that there is a vacancy. You are there on the assumption that a vacancy may occur in the future, which it most certainly will. Your purposes are more specific and focused than they were when you arranged interviews for background research. You are talking to a target employer in order to ask the questions that will help you decide whether you would like to make a formal application to this employer in the future. In the process, you will allow the employer's representative to learn about your interests and experiences so that if and when you make application, you will be a known quantity, not just another name on a piece of paper. Although your purpose is to do the evaluating, not to be evaluated, you should be alert for an opportunity to talk about your suitability as a job candidate if the employer introduces this idea. Don't expect this to happen, but keep in the back of your mind that it sometimes will as a natural result of the conversation.

What are the logistics of the information interview with the target employer? This sort of interview should almost always be arranged in advance, unless it occurs spontaneously. You should know the name and title of the person to whom you wish to speak, and you should know from your previous search efforts that this person has the power to hire for the work you seek. In all likelihood, the two of you have met before as a result of your background interviews, and you have sent written correspondence to this person between your background interviews and the proposed interview, to give some advance notice of your thinking. It is necessary to explain in detail on the phone why you want the meeting; for example, "I have thought about what we talked about before and would like to continue our discussion."

Ask for at least thirty minutes. You will need sufficient time to be able to ask detailed questions. Thirty minutes is usually enough and is not so much that you will present the other person with a burden. This time, do *not* bring notes with you; be able to talk from memory, for if you cannot, the ideas are not clear enough in your own mind yet.

Begin the interview by explaining your purposes right away. Don't beat around the bush, leaving your listener to try to guess why you made the appointment. State your purpose as soon as the pleasantries are over: "I came to talk with you because I am considering this profession as a career."

Be careful not to come on too strong. In any interview with a person you believe you may one day work with, it is a regrettable mistake to allow your style to overpower your substance. If you feel you are being interviewed instead of doing the interviewing, or evaluated instead of doing the evaluating, don't launch into a sales pitch. The anxiety you project as you seek to convince your listener can quickly dispel the gains you have made. It is hardly ever necessary to be a hard-sell persuader when you are talking about yourself and your qualifications. Most people can infer, from your simple assertive statements about your experiences, skills, and aspirations, what you are capable of doing. Furthermore, if you already believe the individual is interested in you as a possible employee, you can and should be even more low-key about proclaiming your capabilities. Tell what you can do and what you would like to do as parsimoniously as possible; then be quiet and let the other person respond.

## General Guidelines for Any Information Interview

On all occasions when you are interviewing people who can aid in your career search, you must follow certain guidelines that are fundamental to any effective exchange of information and feelings. Wherever the interview lies on the scale of formality, these are the guidelines to follow.

**Plan a Manageable Agenda** • Don't plan an agenda any longer than you believe your respondent can comfortably handle. You will cancel any gains you make in information gathering if you overstay your welcome by asking a few extra questions after the time allotted you has run out. Plan to ask no more than four or five key-open-ended questions and have a few questions in reserve, if time allows.

**Let the Interview Roam Freely** • You will seldom get to follow your anticipated agenda to the letter; do not mistake yourself for a tough investigative reporter who sticks to the questions no matter what. You are there to learn what the respondent has to tell you, and in all likelihood, any ramblings will answer most of the questions you had planned anyway.

**Ask Answerable Questions** • Be sure no question you ask stumps the other person. Be certain your question actually has an answer. Don't ask: "What kinds of products do you expect your competitors will be introducing five years from now?" Answerable questions allow others to feel helpful; unanswerable ones make them feel put on the spot and awkward.

**Ask Open-Ended Questions •** The way you ask a question controls much of the person's comfort in responding. An open-ended question ("How do you do that?" "In what ways is that different from . . . ?") permits complete freedom to the person who answers; closed questions ("Did you do that because . . . ?") sometimes imply their own answers, are often loaded questions, and always restrict the respondent to an abridged answer, usually yes or no.

**Ask Impromptu Questions •** Your best questions will be ones that you had not thought about prior to the conversation. They will be triggered in your head as you hear the person make initial statements.

**Focus on the Person •** Remember at all times that you are talking to a human being, not an organization. The best and deepest information you will get comes from that person's biases, private experiences, emotional responses to the work. Behind the view of the organization that is programmed for public consumption lies a set of personal attitudes that will tell you more about what it's like to work there. Moreover, most people prefer telling you their personal views to spinning the company palaver for you.

## How to Obtain Information Interviews

There are two ways to obtain an information interview: through walking in and through personal referral. In the walk-in interview, you identify your target employer without the aid of referrals from other people. Either you know this person yourself as a result of previous exposure or you approach directly without previous contact. In the personal referral interview, you are referred to the target employer through an intermediate contact person or sequence of such persons. The meeting with the target employer is thus arranged in advance, unless you decide to approach and use the name of your intermediary at the same time you request a meeting.

Each style has it own advantages. The main advantages of the personal referral are:

- You have easier access to the person because you have been referred by someone known and trusted; this increases your chances of getting a warm reception.
- You can build more slowly and patiently to your ultimate targets, using intermediate targets to practice your interviewing methods and sharpen your self-disclosure skills.
- Personal referrals usually give you a larger number of people to interview because each contact person has a circle of friends within his or her line of work.
- This method is less risky in that you do not blunder into situations where you do not belong, and you depend on the referrers to use their wisdom and experience to lead you to the best ultimate targets.

The main advantages of the walk-in interview are:

- You have shortened the chain length between yourself and the target employer; because you do not depend on intermediaries, you reach the ultimate target sooner, before others do, thus reducing the competition and enhancing the possibility that you will arrive in the right place at the right time.
- You can make more rapid strides in developing your assertiveness skill by approaching employers directly and obtaining meetings with them, without the buffer of referral sources.
- By eliminating a series of intermediate contacts designed to lead you to your ultimate target, you reduce the possibility that you will make a pest of yourself and oversaturate the target organization by seeing too many people in too brief a period of time.

There is no reason to pursue either the personal referral approach or the walk-in approach to the exclusion of the other. You will find they can be used together. For example, if you do a walk-in interview, and you believe you have dicovered an ultimate target, quickly seek a personal referral who knows this person; then use that intermediary to gain a second meeting. Or if your personal referral leads you to a brief encounter with a person who impressed you as an ultimate target, seek the second meeting on your own. The sequence in which you use walk-in and personal referral methods depends a great deal on chance and circumstance; do not expect these events to proceed in an orderly, predictable fashion.

## Other People of Interest to Interview

Any person, not just a target employer, can be of interest to the inquiring reporter. Don't make the fatal mistake of assuming that target employers are the only people who have good information for you. There are many other hidden sources of insight, some of whom can give you data that would not be available from the target employer himself.

Let us say for the sake of discussion that you have a target employer, and a department where you would like to work, in mind. Other than the people you believe will make the hiring decisions, whom should you seek for an information interview?

Talk with people who work there in other capacities. If you want to be in administrative work in a hospital, ask people in the other departments about the reputation of the administrative offices. Often you can get straighter information about what a department is doing by asking those who have no reason to color or otherwise protect their answers.

If you really want to know how the department is functioning, ask its customers, its clients, its students, or other people who use its services or buy its products. Even more than people from other departments in the same organization, the customers have nothing to hide, no reason to guard their answers or modify their replies.

If you can get access to the sources of funding, boards of trustees, or other governing groups, you may learn some things not even the employer is aware of. You might just live next door to a trustee of the college where you would like to work.

Finally, others who do the same work at similar organizations are in a good position to advise and inform you about your intended career. It is a good idea to practice your information-gathering skills on people you don't expect to approach for employment.

## Do Your Number Any Time

The inquiring reporter is always on the prowl. He recognizes that information interviews, unlike the formally scheduled job interview, can occur at any time under the most unlikely of circumstances.

The following rule applies: *any setting is okay, the more casual the better.* The less structured and formalized a meeting is, the more likely you are to reach a person under conditions of maximum comfort. Lawn picnics, swimming-pool gatherings, bus rides, and beach parties are great occasions for asking questions and getting inside information people cannot resist sharing with you.

Another rule applies: *any time is okay, not only when you are job hunting.* In fact, the moment you are under pressure to get a job fast is probably the worst time to be an inquiring reporter. The best times are when you are safely entrenched in your current situation but are getting curious about what may happen to you several years in the future.

## chapter thirteen

# Participant Observation

*One thorn of experience is worth a whole wilderness of
warning.* • David Campbell
*If You Don't Know Where You're Going,
You'll Wind up Someplace Else*

I have emphasized up to this point that research can be done by
collecting written materials and by talking directly with people who
have information and insights about your intended work. Though
these methods are powerful and can generate a lot of vital data for
you fairly rapidly, there can be a vast ocean of mystery and uncertainty surrounding what people tell you in printed materials or in-
person observations. Information interviewing and researching the
literature are vessels equipped to travel this ocean of uncertainty,
but they can leave you foundering on the rocks of misinformation
and bias if you trust them completely.

Most people accept new employment as though they were walking the plank—blindfolded, hands bound, last rites on their lips,
hoping everything will work out okay. You are leaping into the dark
unknown if you choose to enter and make a commitment to a field
of work you have never even sampled. I admit that there are
numerous such adventurers among us, but their existence does
not validate the ways in which they arrived at their chosen professions: "Oh, I just fell into it, gave it a try, and it worked out okay"; "I
heard what my neighbor said about it, and it sounded good, so I
signed up"; "Nothing better came along, so I figured what else
could I do."

Participant observation is any method of personal research in
which you can gather data and be involved in the actual work
activities at the same time. By both doing and observing, you have
the unique opportunity to look upon the work as insider and
outsider at the same time, to sample the wine before opening the
bottle.

# Levels of Participant Observation

A wide range of intensity and exposure is possible for the individual who wishes to engage in participant observation. I have described several levels of this kind of activity below, beginning with the least intense and demanding types of exposure, through the ones requiring more endurance and commitment. Choose whichever of these methods seems most comfortable to you, not necessarily in the sequence they are given.

**Academic Coursework** • It is stretching things a bit to say that school courses allow you to participate and observe the work you seek; however, many courses have field study and even on-site internships as well as intense scrutiny of the content from an academic perspective. This is the simplest level on which to begin participant observation because it allows you to gain entry as a learner, an academic voyeur, with the blessing of the parent institution.

**On-Site Observation** • The on-site visit is the most direct method of obtaining data and impressions you could not gather otherwise. The curious onlooker who combines his visual observations with casual conversations reaps the benefits of correlating what he is told with what he sees firsthand. Tours of the plant or the campus fall into this category, but you should try your best to conduct your own tour, one that is not colored by what the prospective employer *wants* you to see. A panorama of data is available from an on-site visit—facial expressions of the workers, orderliness of the equipment, energy level displayed by the workers, signs of close time regulation (bells, clocks), displays of the product, physical atmosphere of the workplace, and so on.

**Personal Projects** • You can conceive of a sequence of on-site observations that form a continuing project. You might, for example, make it your plan to track the harvest process at a local apple orchard and ask permission from the grower to be there at periodic intervals to record your impressions. Most employers, unless they are threatened by the thought that you are passing on this information to competitors (you must discover ways of dispelling these fears), will be flattered by your attention and welcome you as a person who validates what they are doing by your presence.

**Reality Testing** • A reality test is an activity in which you can simulate the type of work you desire by taking on a similar responsibility in your current life routine. A reality test, such as joining a stream exploration project when you intend to become a hydrologist, affords you the following benefits:

- You expose yourself to the uncertainties of the work itself, risking failure or disappointment, and, through your successes, increasing your confidence that you can prosper in this career on a full-time basis. You have an opportunity to try your abilities in order to determine how capable you are, without suffering severe consequences.
- You can discover whether the rewards you expected from the work are as valuable as you had imagined.
- You experience the gestalt, the whole of a work experience, the rhythms of the workday, the ways the job affects you when you return home at night.

Say your desired career is journalist. How do you go about reality testing? You can write articles for the college newspaper, set up a church newsletter, and send your material to the local newspaper. If you want to be a social services administrator, you can coordinate a fund-raising campaign for the local YMCA/YWCA or other nonprofit organization. If corrections officer is your ambition, become a member of the volunteer-in-probation program and spend time on a regular basis with probationers in the local area. The aspiring financial wizard can do what most graduate schools in business administration have students do: invest fictional money in stocks, bonds, and other securities and chart their progress.

**Volunteer Work** • Perhaps the best all-purpose method for gathering participant observation data is the volunteer experience, in which you offer your services for a regular period of time for the purpose of being as close as possible to the work setting you desire. Volunteer jobs can vary widely in the degree to which they give you exposure to the entire workplace; you must choose the situation carefully and attempt to define the kind of volunteer work and setting you most prefer.

**Part-Time Jobs** • If all else fails, or the other methods of participant observation do not satisfy you, the availability of part-time work is one you must consider. Many careers can be sampled on a part-time basis without your having to make a commitment, invest large amounts of time, or undergo a lengthy selection process.

## How Participant Observation Helps the Career Search

Business people use the phrase *caveat emptor* ("let the buyer beware"). In "buying" new work, there is even more to worry about than the quality of the merchandise—the personalities of the co-workers, their life styles, the demands of superiors, numerous other factors. Shoes, refrigerators, and automobiles can be tested in a relatively simple manner before they are bought. *Consumer Reports* has no laboratories for work environments.

As much as information you obtain from printed materials is useful, you must remember that printed literature distributed by the employer may distort the picture for the purpose of persuading you and others that the work environment is ideal. Furthermore, even newspapers and other commercial print media distort the picture because they are most concerned about portraying dramatic highlights in order to sell their product to the reader. The highlights do not necessarily offer an accurate picture. Does every policeman's day culminate in the capture of a million-dollar opium shipment?

While the respondents in your information interviews give you valuable insights if you win their trust and successfully entice them to talk, they still introduce bias in the form of the topics that interest *them* the most. You have no certainty that they will answer *your* questions or that you will even know what questions to ask. Participant observation raises questions and issues you would never have thought about because you didn't know they mattered.

Participant observation often paves the way for actual job offers because it gives people a chance to see what you can do. In such situations, your exposure to the employer accumulates and you develop close relationships with the people who may one day employ you. Two examples illustrate this point.

**EXAMPLE**

Mo was a young man who had a lot of sensitivity to the drug- and alcohol-abuse problems of college-age and other people who are captives of adolescent life styles. He spent most of his time during college and summers between terms getting to know drug users and the ways they think, the attitudes they hold toward their lives. During college, he spearheaded the creation of a study group and informal counseling service that would reach out to his friends and provide information, counsel, crisis support, and a place to ventilate feelings. He obtained a federal grant for the purpose and grew closely acquainted with community leaders in his efforts to build town support. When Mo graduated, he wanted to continue this work. Complete with major fields of study in philosophy and English, he sought the environs of a large metropolitan area and discovered that a suburb heavily populated by adolescents wanted to begin a community-based counseling and referral service for drug and alcohol abusers. Many trained scholars of pharmacology, psychology, mental health, and other disciplines applied, but Mo was hired to direct the center because he had experienced the problems of drug abuse and the difficulties of extending this service to adolescents. The selection committee felt that the youth population would trust Mo more easily and would respond to his experience.

**EXAMPLE** _____

Sara worked in an office of local government but longed to play a role in encouraging the growth of performing arts in her city. She attended theater, concerts, dance programs, music recitals, and every artistic event that appeared within a hundred miles. One day she heard from a neighbor that a few people in town were trying to create a summer arts program for high school students. She decided this was her opportunity to learn about arts administration firsthand, so she volunteered to help in every phase of the project. She raised funds, wrote publicity brochures, interviewed prospective students, surveyed the schools, talked with potential faculty, and helped develop budgets. The summer program eventually came into being, and two months later Sara was hired by the executive director to return with her to a nearby town and become assistant arts administrator for the county.

Participant observation becomes most important for you when you practice the more intense levels, such as volunteer work, reality testing, and part-time work. The employer who may one day seek a new assistant or other staff member, and wonder how to decipher from résumés and other standardized credentials the quality of candidates' abilities, will likely be glad to short-circuit the selection process and hire the familiar volunteer or part-timer—you.

## How to Obtain This Skill

How do you become a skillful participant observer? First, be curious. Cultivate a higher level of curiosity than you have ever had before. Snoop around as though you were a detective. It's great fun to pay attention to details ordinary mortals would not notice, pick up a few pieces of information that are hidden from public view, and push your limits of visual observation.

Second, practice taking the person-on-the-street role. This you can do in many ways: you might want to buy a new suit, seek information from a government agency, or inquire about child-abuse services from your local courthouse. Much of the on-site visit and personal project data mentioned earlier can be gathered using this method.

Third, play dumb. Except when you are asking someone to hire you, it ordinarily helps to approach a work site as though you know nothing. Take little for granted; ask questions about even the things you think you understand. People will be more willing to explain what you see if you approach them as though you are the novice and they are the advice givers, which is the truth. Let every informant tell you his or her own version of why things look that way, so you can collect and merge these data and opinions into a consensus view.

Finally, be willing to risk. Every instance of participant observation means doing or seeing something new to you. If your tolerance for change and variety hovers over the zero line, take some small risks first. Be prepared to try a new environment, knowing you can return to the old fireplace any time you choose.

part

4

Communi-
cation
Skills

# · chapter fourteen ·

# Introduction

Dear Howard:

Most interviewers are so professional at what they do that I am simply overpowered by their command of the process. Because of this, I feel my answers are ones they have heard a thousand times before. Furthermore, they seem so in control that I am happier to let them take over and ask me what they want to ask me. Far be it from me to disturb their professional style with my amateurish inquiries.

Signed,
Awed by Power

Dear Awed Man Out:

Pity the poor interviewers: (1) they know little about you and are hoping to discover what you are like in thirty minutes or less, including your chief strengths, personal qualities, what you'd be like to work with; (2) they know that many interviewees enter the room determined to be passive, and they're thus gloomily preparing themselves for saying the same things they've said a hundred times before; (3) they try to raise their level of excitement and anticipation to what *you* are feeling as you enter the room, but know they cannot simulate it; (4) they can remember only snatches of what's on your résumé; (5) they want *desperately* to hear you say something the others have not said; (6) they struggle to think what they will say next when you look at them blankly and sit very still.

And you are in awe of this? Under the professional veneer of interviewers are individuals who really wish you would accept some

163

responsibility for the two-way exchange so they will not have to use Ouija boards or divining rods to figure out what is inside you.

Interviewers are nervous too, in their own smooth ways. Take them off the hook. Give them a chance to depart from their prepared agendas. Live a little.

Signed,
Howard

## The Interview

The formal job interview is usually handled with great care. It is treated as though it were a sacred event, with high ritual. Many believe it has mystical qualities, that the interviewee must tune in to the special wavelengths of interviewers, adopt certain magical techniques, or adopt a new personality.

In truth, this view of the employment interview as a formal presentation is heavily distorted and surely oversold by those of us who teach others how to conduct the work search. The more you are led to believe that an interview demands acting talent, intense rehearsals, and decoding the interviewer's remarks to trigger the "right" responses, the more deeply in trouble you will find yourself when you engage in conversation with a prospective employer.

We must demystify this thing we call the interview process. Your success in an interview is a direct result of conversational habits you practice in your routine daily interactions with friends and others in your immediate life space. An interview is nothing more than a conversation between two people who desire information from each other. It has a special focus, but there are certain habits of conversational interchange common to *any* successful interview. I will assume that you know enough about the work by the time you reach the interview to affirm that you have something to offer the employer. Your problem is to *make this known* during the course of your meeting.

## You Conduct Interviews Every Day

Every time you speak or listen to what someone else is saying, you are most likely engaged in an interview. A job interview is simply a special, artificially contrived example of an ordinary two-way exchange. It is little more than two people trying to know each other better and consider a set of activities they might do jointly. You can bring your interviewing skills into play almost any time because these skills generalize to meetings with prospective employers. Practice interviewing in everyday situations like these: asking the gas station attendant how to get to the theater across town; trying to discover why your children strewed toilet paper all through the house one hour before the in-laws were due to arrive from the West; questioning your tax accountant about how to plan your next year's expenditures; resolving a quarrel with your companion, lover, or friend; explaining to your professor why you've chosen such an arcane topic; or negotiating with your family about a summer vacation trip.

## Interview Styles That Don't Work

There is no particular interview style that works best. In fact, any attempt you make to change your personality for the sake of impressing an interviewer is sure to fail because you will have made the fatal error of trying to be someone else. Here are a few examples of the personalities some people believe to be effective, and the reasons why they ultimately self-destruct.

**The Chatterer** • Never a moment of silence with you. Any lull in the conversation is cheerfully rescued by your witty, inquisitive, anecdotal, charming talk. You believe an interview should race along at top speed, so that the interviewer is overwhelmed by your ability to converse with facility. This approach will fail because the interviewer will feel overpowered, perhaps even insulted, by your need to display conversational talents.

**The Counterpuncher** • You don't commit or expose yourself or otherwise blunder into conversational error by leading with your jaw. You wait for the interviewer to let you know what is wanted, then give a short, careful response. You show only as much of yourself as you have to because you are terrified you will make a mistake. This careful bobbing and weaving will offend the interviewer because you are so difficult to engage in two-way interchange. Your efforts to be cautious will turn sour because the interviewer wants, above all, to know you in some genuine way.

**The Data Blabbermouth** • You provide as much evidence as possible that you are knowledgeable, bludgeon the interviewer with facts and figures you have gathered about the organization, drop names, and try to impress with the breadth and depth of your knowledge, even if it's not asked for. While I have emphasized elsewhere in this book that gathering research data is vital preparation for the interview, you will discover that a small display of your knowledge can quickly become overkill that offends because it distracts the interviewer from the more general purposes of your meeting. Information is good to have, but the interview is also a personal exchange.

**The Inoffensive Diplomat** • You were well-mannered as a child and carry into adulthood the belief that diplomacy succeeds where insensitive blundering fails. You take care to do whatever the interviewer wishes you to do and let the interviewer control the process. Your task is never to offend and to show that you have the talent for treating people with maximum gentility. This motif distorts the entire purpose of the interview and ultimately makes you appear an obsequious fool because you avoid any answer to a question that has the faintest trace of risk, and you are unwilling to take enough control to ask questions or say things you feel must be said.

**The Tiger** • You take charge at every turn and show your willingness to assume responsibility and be a self-starter by asking leading questions, proposing your own agenda for the inteview, and volunteering information you believe the interviewer wants. You reason that the interviewer really likes these qualities and is waiting for you to demonstrate them. This attack posture will ultimately bury you in your own ammunition because you will have taken away the interviewer's power to assume control and obtain certain information regarded as vital. Assertiveness is prized as a quality in job applicants but, taken to an extreme, becomes a display for its own sake rather than a skill that facilitates further discussion.

## Personal Chemistry

Jobs are awarded as often to people the interviewer *likes* as to people who are the best qualified. Let's assume you are reasonably well qualified for the work for which you are interviewing. How are you going to get the edge on people who are similarly qualified?

Employers seldom admit it, but the depth of the interchange between two people (the extent to which they reach each other, like each other, understand each other) has as much to do with the eventual hiring decision as the paper credentials the person offers.

## Questions Most Typically Asked in Job Interviews

The content of any job interview has certain commonalities, universal questions every interviewer seeks to have answered, regardless of the type of work being considered. Interviewers typically ask a wide variety of questions. A list of the most common questions follows:

- What career goals have you established for yourself in the next ten years?
- What do you really want to do in life?
- Why should I hire you?
- What qualifications do you have that make you think you'll succeed here?
- What two or three accomplishments have given you the most satisfaction?
- If you were hiring a person for this position, what qualities would you seek?
- Why did you decide to seek a position with this company?
- What two or three things are most important to you in your job?
- Why do you think you'd like to live in this community?
- What have you learned from your mistakes?
- How do you plan to achieve your goals?
- What kind of person are you?
- In what ways will you make a contribution to our organization?
- How do you feel a friend of yours would describe you?
- What are your prominent work habits?
- Why did you choose to enter this careeer?
- What questions do you have for me?
- In what ways would you change this organization?
- Where else would you like to work, if you couldn't be employed here?

- What motivates you the most?
- Do you work well under pressure?
- What kinds of work situations irritate you?
- What is one significant problem you have overcome and how did you do it?
- What is your chief ambition?
- How much responsibility do you like?

## Hidden Questions

The questions above are usually stated openly in an interview and must be answered directly. However, you should be aware that hidden among these openly stated inquiries are some other universal concerns that are more difficult to state in the form of questions. Nonetheless, they are equally important in the interviewer's mind. Consider how you might anticipate these hidden questions.

**How Much Enthusiasm Does the Candidate Have About Us?** • If you feel this employer's work has high priority for you, be sure you say so without hesitancy. Gushing your excitement is too much of a good thing. Instead, support your enthusiasm by telling of books you've read, experiences you've had that relate to the work, and people with whom you've initiated contact. An employer will judge your enthusiasm more by what you have done than by your bare expression of feeling ("Oh, I just love this kind of work").

**Will This Person Stay With Us?** • Employers are finally learning that the best candidate for a job may be the worst because he will stay only long enough to get a taste of what is going on and then move to other pastures. Assuming you are capable of doing the work required, the employer will attempt to determine how many years you are likely to remain committed to this kind of work and to this particular department or organization. In most cases, you should apply for a job as though you expect to make at least a two- to three-year commitment to it. Be sure to tell the interviewer the extent of your commitment, even if the question does not arise.

**Will We Like Each Other If We Work Together?** • This may be the most deeply hidden question of all, but when you are talking with the person for whom you may ultimately work directly on a day-to-day basis, this question is clearly an unspoken part of the interview. Personal compatibility is a two-way street. The best way to discover whether you two will enjoy each other's presence is to carry the interview to a personal level. Ask the interviewer questions ("Why did you choose to work here?" "What are you hoping to accomplish?"). Then ask yourself whether you like the answers. Conversely, give the interviewer a chance to like you by being open about your own aspirations and personal interests.

**Can We Get the Candidate Away from the Competition?** • In the cat-and-mouse game known as recruiting and selection, once the employer thinks enough of you to consider making you an offer, he begins to worry about whether you will accept if asked. Being excessively coy or secretive on this point can hurt your chances of being asked in the first place. Potential suitors do not want to be rejected when they ask for your hand, and employers are nearly as touchy.

**How Poised Is the Candidate?** • Many, many questions in the interview that appear to be content questions are really process questions in disguise. Often the interviewer doesn't expect you to have fully detailed answers to the questions; rather, the questions give opportunities to judge the manner in which you handle the response. Does she think well on her feet? Does he get rattled by an impossible-to-answer question? Does she speak confidently? Does he speak carefully, without rushing his responses? Does she try to say too much?

Interviews are fearful events for many people, but they need not be for you. If you can apply the fundamentals of clear and effective conversation as explained in the following chapters, you will represent yourself well in both formal and informal interview situations. I urge you to practice these communication skills on any occasion when you talk with another person so that you can recognize the relationship between everyday conversation and those conversations called job interviews.

## · chapter fifteen ·

# ✌ Listening ✌

Then there was the story about the host at a party who greeted his guest at the door. The guest wished to discern how closely the host would listen to her, so she said: "I'm sorry to be so late, but I just murdered my husband, and it took me a while to stuff him into the trunk of the car." The host, ever conscious of his role as gracious innkeeper, replied: "Well, it's great to see you; I just hope your husband can make it next time."

Total listening is the fine art of holding your own self in suspended animation while you tune in to all the signals you are receiving from the other person. Listening, in its purest state, is the ability to restrain all your inner thoughts, to keep from rehearsing what you are going to say next, to stifle all connections you may feel between what the other person is saying and your own experience, and finally, to reject the notion that "I've heard that before."

A good listener would wait in stunned silence after the other person had finished talking in order to collect his or her thoughts for a response, not having done this while absorbed in listening. An effective listener would not only absorb all that is being said, but would also be able to report to the other person such a clear understanding of the content and feeling of the speaker's message that the speaker could recognize his or her own messages, stated perhaps even more clearly than they were originally given.

A good listener would make the speaker feel that everything said or about to be said is of great interest, that the next part will be even more worth hearing than what's already been said, and that nothing less than the whole story will be acceptable.

Does this sound like any conversation you have ever had? Has anyone ever listened to your words in a state so enraptured? Of course not. We settle for a lot less than perfection from the people who listen to us because we are happy that anyone listens at all.

All of which explains why an effective listener has a great advantage in a work search. Effective listening is the key to trust in a talking relationship.

*Other people are more interested in themselves than in you.* This is a cardinal rule, and you must remember it. People who feel you have to come to deliver a soliloquy, give a prepared talk, or otherwise monopolize a conversation quickly lose interest in you. What you have to say has little power unless others are interested in hearing it. Their willingness to listen is a direct function of your willingness to show interest in them.

Given half a chance, many interviewers would prefer to talk about themselves, their own problems, anxieties, and ambitions, rather than listen to you. Of course, they are probably expected to listen to you as well, but your ability to allow for their needs in your conversation will influence their attitude toward you.

Furthermore, your ability to hear what they are saying gives you important clues about which of your skills or attributes is most likely to attract their attention. You will not have time to talk about everything you have ever done or are capable of doing; hence, it pays to be selective. Without knowing what the employer wants, you can only guess which parts of your experience or which items on your skill list are most relevant.

**EXAMPLE**

Dan hung around Mr. Karlson's camera shop every Saturday asking questions about the shop, what the customers buy, how Mr. K deals with the clients. In return for his curiosity he heard numerous stories about irascible customers, arguments that had ensued, return of photographic materials, and so forth. Dan even had a chance to witness an occasional spat firsthand. One fine day it occurred to Dan that he could probably handle the irate customers better than Mr. K, if he was given the chance. He proposed a part-time job in which he would field customer complaints. By this time, Mr. K knew that Dan knew all about the situation and had no choice but to agree with the young man's proposal. Today they are happily engaged as partners in the operation of the store.

## Fake Listening

I think you will agree that it is hard to talk about the art of listening because listening—like walking, eating, sleeping—is a thing we do all the time and believe we must be pretty good at by virtue of all the practice we have had. We resist with great passion the very idea that we might have to be taught such a thing. Any fool ought to know how to listen!

The problem is that we have learned pretty well how to *appear* to be listening, how to convince (we think) other people that we are in touch with them and taking it all in. We use certain cues to let others believe we are in touch—looking them in the eye, offering head nods of understanding, uttering uh-huh at appropriate intervals, delivering a knowing smile at just the right time, all this punctuated by "I know just how you feel."

But how many people really see you when they look at you? How often does a series of head nods occur *before* you have completed your thought or even before the sentence has begun? How many yeses, smiles, and other surface gestures are delivered with little connection to what you are saying outside and feeling inside? Is the person *with* you or just creating that appearance by catching enough snatches of conversation to keep the spark of interaction alive long enough to get a chance to talk next?

We have learned the skill of facilitating a conversation smoothly, at the expense of hearing a person fully. We become so preoccupied with keeping the train moving ("What will I do if the other person stops talking and I have nothing to say at that moment?") that we have trouble giving significant attention to what there is to see and hear during the ride. We figure that a conversation ends successfully if both parties were allowed to say something, there was a lot of smiling all around, and neither person made any grave errors or insulted the other too badly. We have learned to settle for less because we do not expect more.

## What Is Real Listening?

You should not confuse listening to a person with listening to a train whistle, a phonograph record, or even a screeching cat.

These simpler acts of listening require no particular interpretation, raise no concern about hidden motivations, and place no requirement on you to prepare a response. It is too easy to imagine that listening to a person is equally simple, just preparation of your sense receptors for some sounds that will be immediately understood.

Theodor Reik has referred to listening to human beings as "listening with the third ear."[23] This means that we can hear more than what the words are saying. What is this *more*? Don't people say what they mean?

**EXAMPLE**

Janet talked to her husband many times about her work. She complained of the long hours, the constant squabbling with legislators (she was a lobbyist), the intricate nature of written legislation, the necessity of making deals with everyone in sight. Her husband heard all this, but watched her feelings as she talked. He said to her: "Yes, there are a lot of frustrations about this work, but you seem to get a kick out of the whole struggle." Janet nodded her agreement after some thought and thanked her husband for listening.

The husband had listened closely with the third ear to what his wife was saying and had "heard" her feeling for the work.

At first glance the term "listening" implies a passive act of taking in the content of the [person's] communication, but actually it involves a very active process of responding to total messages. It includes not only listening with the ears to his/her words and with the eyes to his/her body language, but a total kind of perceptiveness. . . . It means also that we are silent much of the time. . . . When the [listener] can answer in considerable detail the question, "What is going on in this person right now in his/her life space?" s/he is listening with all his/her perceptual capacity.[24]

## Levels of Listening Behavior

Seldom is effective listening as simple as the previous example suggests. The example illustrates how accurate a listener can be when tuning in to the other person on all wavelengths. Listening begins with wanting to hear what another person has to tell you.

In terms of the previous example, let's take a look inside the husband's mind to see what he was attending to as his wife spoke about her work.

- *Identity.* This is my wife talking; I'm interested in listening to her because her work is important and I want to help her reflect on what it is doing to and for her.
- *Voice.* Her voice is sometimes tense as she talks, though almost always excited as well. She talks hurriedly, trying to get everything in, but always volunteers more than I ask for, gets carried away, voice goes to a high pitch. Her voice is strong and confident as she talks about this.
- *Body.* She is physically animated as she talks, yet does not seem unusually tense. Her body expresses involvement with the topic and willingness to continue because she faces me, leans forward, and talks in a relaxed way.
- *Words.* She is describing problems, struggles, conflicts, but they usually seem to resolve themselves in ways that give her satisfaction. If I connect all the words over several conversations, I get the picture that she has this job under control and needs to ventilate its frustrations.
- *Feelings.* Some feelings escape her words, but are there in her attitude toward what she is saying. In keeping with her voice, she feels excited by what she is talking about, shows this in her general state of body excitement, and seldom seems discouraged or beaten by the conflicts she is describing.
- *Values.* I suspect she feels very deeply about what she is doing, that the involvement in this political process would keep her motivated despite a steady stream of frustrations. She renews herself for this work without prodding from me or anyone else; must be something inside that keeps her going.

I have been focusing on listening as psychological attending thus far. Such mental attentiveness must always be accompanied by physical attending that enhances the overall message: "I am in touch with you, am tuning in to what you are saying." Gerard Egan, in *The Skilled Helper*,[25] writes that effective physical attending includes the following characteristics: (1) facing the other person squarely, (2) maintaining good eye contact without staring unnecessarily, (3) using a posture that is open to the other person, (4) leaning toward the other person as a sign of involvement, (5) being physically relaxed during the conversation.

## Nonverbal Communication

Much of what you are seeking in effective listening will come to you through nonverbal channels. Here are a few cues that suggest what you can look for:

- Is he smiling at me?
- Does she fidget while I am talking?
- Is his body posture relaxed and facing me?
- Are her hands wringing while I talk?
- Is he giving cues that he wants to end the conversation?
- Does she watch me closely?

"Non-verbal behaviors are often carriers of the emotional dimensions of messages (for example, the client kicks his feet, maintains a half-smile, wrings his hands, grimaces, or folds his arms over his chest) and, as such, constitute a more primitive and less easily controlled communication system."[26]

Nonverbal signals can be the individual's unconscious effort to tell you what cannot be put into words or is difficult to describe in rational terms (because, perhaps, it does not feel reasonable). Such signals far more frequently refer to feelings than to ideas and as such tell you more about the person's inner experience than what is being put into words. Eyes, hands, feet, and other body parts are all mirrors of the soul; words are sounds we sometimes use to fog that mirror so that you are not sure what you are seeing.

Though your concentration in any conversation should be focused on the person talking, you must also be alert for cues within yourself, both when you are listening and when you are talking. Listening to yourself with the third ear means attending to your own nonverbal cues:

- Why do I feel relaxed with her?
- Am I getting sleepy?
- He raises my energy level.
- She makes me edgy when I listen to her.
- My voice is less confident.
- I avoid looking at him.

# How to Become an Effective Listener

Your total effectiveness as a listener depends on what you see, what you say, and how well you integrate the two. I have described the key elements of effective listening below. Before you focus on them, however, you should recognize that your personal *attitude* must be the foundation upon which your listening behavior rests. The attitude with which you must begin any communication is that you care to hear everything the other person is saying, knowing that he will say more to you than words, and that you must concentrate to hear his messages at all levels. You are not interested in simply facilitating conversation, but in absorbing as much meaning from the speaker as you possibly can.

**Distinguish Content from Feeling •** You must learn to distinguish between what the other person tells you has happened and how he feels about it, the emotions he attaches to the events. As noted before, much of the feeling that lies underneath the events is carried by the speaker's nonverbal behavior. Does he fidget when talking about that job? Do her eyes widen with joy when describing a project she did last week?

**Listen to the Voice •** In *The Voice of Neurosis*, Paul J. Moses claims that the voice is a highly reliable index of a person's emotional state.[27] The voice is much more difficult to control than the words it is uttering, and you should look closely for clues regarding the person's inner emotional state. Hitches in speech, tiny stutters, voice cracking, the high pitch of tension, the rich sound of excitement and confidence—all these tell you feelings you'll want to know.

**Notice Body Movements •** Though we cannot claim hand, facial, and body gestures can be read for total accuracy, you should recognize that these communicators are powerful and that people tell you many things from their gestures that their words do not reveal. A shrug of the shoulder, a wink, a posture of utter dejection, or a wild gesticulation of excitement—such gestures constitute a universal language and must not be taken lightly, especially in view of how effectively people use words to mask their inner attitudes.

**Give Encouragement** • The easiest signals you can give to indicate you are a willing listener are those that urge the speaker to continue. These can be nonverbal signals or brief spoken cues, such as "tell me more about that" or "go ahead." Without these simple cues, the person speaking will take the more cautious view that perhaps you really don't want to hear more. With them, you can trigger the speaker to continue.

**Allow Silence** • Little empty spaces between bursts of talking are the all-purpose oil that lubricates any conversation. Your careful silence following the other person's talk tells him you are not sure he is finished, that you want to be sure he's completed the thought. Since most of us think and speak in fragments anyway (we do not speak in paragraphs), silence from the listener allows us to piece these fragments together. Silence tells the speaker you were actually listening, not mentally rehearsing yourself to speak once his lips have stopped moving.

**Use I Statements** • You should be amazed to discover how often people use *we, they,* or *people* instead of *I* to describe how they feel about a particular situation, person, or event. Any such pawning off of your ideas or feelings on other sources distorts the personal quality of the interchange because it suggests you don't want to own what you are saying. It leaves the other person wondering what belongs to you rather than others.

> **EXAMPLE** _____
> YOU: They say that working in advertising involves a lot of pressure.
> INTERVIEWER (TO HIMSELF): Does he mean he doesn't like pressure?

**Paraphrase** • While silence and verbal encouragements facilitate the flow of the person's conversation, they do nothing to demonstrate that you have actually heard what the person told you. You must use your own words to give evidence of what your facial expression, body posture, eye contact, and other nonverbal clues have said—that you were really listening. A paraphrasing response attempts to capture the person's basic message in a much smaller number of words. ("You mean that you really like dealing with the customers.") A simple paraphrasing response usually expresses feeling as well as content in its attempt to hear the person as fully as possible.

**Check for Meaning** • The most powerful form of listening behavior you can employ is asking whether your summary of what you have heard is correct. It is your way of saying: "I want to be really sure I am with you, so I will check my perception to see if I am on the right track." This response, which can also be called "clarifying" in nature, is more complicated than the paraphrase in that it seeks not simply to repeat, but to capture an essence that may not be explicitly verbalized.

**EXAMPLE**
It sounds to me as though you would like to move away from the profession you are in. Is that right?
I wonder whether you feel torn in several directions by your various interests. Is that true in what you're saying?

Listening is a skill you have countless opportunities to practice, in terms of both the listening you do in the presence of others and the quality of listening people exhibit when you are talking. There are as many opportunities for practice as you are willing to seek. Furthermore, you have direct feedback available to you in terms of how well the individual responds to you. You can practice your skills and observe the results without resorting to anything more elaborate than a simple dinner conversation.

Finally, you will find many opportunities to sharpen your listening skills because most people prefer to be listened to, will regard your attention as a compliment, and will probably reward you with more conversation.

## Listening Exercises

Select a person you know, but one who has been relatively difficult to talk with. Don't take the extreme of choosing a recluse, but simply find someone you regard as a challenge for your listening skills. Engage this person in conversation on an informal, non-threatening topic (sports events, how the car is running, pets) and use the following guidelines:

**1)** Give small verbal encouragements each time the person says something.

**EXAMPLE**
How did you like that game?
What makes your car run that way?

**2)** Allow three to five seconds of silence each time the speaker finishes talking.

**3)** Paraphrase or clarify (check for meaning) in *one sentence only* what you believe the person told you at pauses in the conversation you are pretty certain finish a thought.

**4)** Look for contradictions between content and feeling (often expressed in nonverbal cues) and let the other person know you have noticed this when appropriate.

**5)** Don't practice the above skills to such excess that it all sounds phony. Intersperse your listening skills with natural comments of your own.

Choose another person of similar shyness and direct the conversation in the following ways:

**1)** Interrupt at various times.

**2)** Change the subject whenever he or she is done speaking, rather than adding any comments of your own.

**3)** Don't clarify anything that has been said. Assume you heard correctly and move on to a different topic.

Compare the two conversations. How long was the first person willing to continue talking? The second person? What nonverbal expressions of pleasure, boredom, frustration, or other emotions did you receive from each of the other persons? How willing was each person to speak with you again on later occasions?

# · chapter sixteen ·

 # Questioning

RED QUEEN: *Speak when you're spoken to.*
ALICE: *But if everybody obeyed that rule, and if you only spoke when you were spoken to, and the other person always waited for you to begin, you see nobody would ever say anything, so that . . .*
         • Lewis Carroll
         *Through the Looking Glass*

Your right to gather information is represented largely by your right to ask questions during an interview. In this chapter I shall discuss the skill of questioning within the context of the formal job interview; you should recognize, however, that all these principles and ideas apply equally well to any variety of information interview (see Chapter 12).

Questions take the lid off the interview. They give you a chance to free the interview from a rigidly structured format that may have been used a thousand times before. You will be thanked for this, and you shall get your reward in heaven. The unpredictable nature of questions makes them enjoyable for the interviewer; you may be even asking something new, or at least something not heard in the past few days. Try to make the interviewer happy in this way. Is your question the one that will make him or her wonder how much thinking and background research you had to do to come up with it?

## The Purposes of Questioning

There are three major purposes of questioning. The first is to gather information. Most frequently your inquiries will serve this purpose, as you acquire information you need to clarify your view of what the work will be like.

180

**EXAMPLE** _____

How do you train new management people?

In what ways is your product different from your competitors'?

What new programs is your department planning for next year?

The second purpose of questioning is to clarify. You will often use a clarification-seeking inquiry in conjunction with an information-seeking question. Your intention is to remove your confusion about a particular matter, clear up a misinterpretation, or illuminate an issue that is important to you. This purpose of questioning is very similar to what I called "checking for meaning" in the previous discussion of listening skill.

**EXAMPLE** _____

Do you mean that the company is planning new foreign offices?

I don't understand the stock option plan. Could you explain?

I am confused about what you mean by editorial responsibilities.

Third, questioning is used to elicit feelings. Not all questions are used to acquire factual information. In some instances you may want to know the interviewer's personal reaction to a situation. This is an effective way to move the interview to a more individual level, though you must be careful to sense whether the interviewer feels comfortable with your question. Try nonthreatening, feeling-oriented questions first.

**EXAMPLE** _____

Did you want to know more about my managerial experience?

Would it be helpful to you to know where I learned about supervisory techniques?

What other information about my public relations background would you like to know?

The word _question_ is derived from the word _quest,_ "a search." Let this be a reminder that questioning should not be a search and destroy mission. If you use questions too boldly, too frequently, or too insistently, you risk alienating the affections of your interviewer.

Questions can be lethal weapons. They can be used to hammer people, bludgeon them, or at least make them a little uncomfortable. Use questions sparingly. A few well-chosen inquiries can be a positive index of your curiosity and intelligent forethought; too many questions can create a dynamic of interrogation from which you will find it hard to extricate yourself.

Questioning skill keeps you from entering an interview flat on your back. It forces you to prepare questions in advance, to decide what is important for you to know. It pushes you to rank your information needs according to priority and decide which questions you must ask first, given the limited time available.

Questioning keeps you in the role of chooser. It reminds you that you are the person who has the most at stake in this search process and that your questions will help you decide whether you will accept an offer if it is made.

Coming prepared to ask questions forces you to concentrate more closely on the flow of the interview because you must look for suitable places in which your questions can be posed. Questioning keeps you from lapsing into a passive stance that might imply: "Go ahead and interview me." You have as much responsibility for the conduct of the interview as the interviewer does, and questioning allows you to assume this role.

Every question you ask requires an act of initiative from you. Do not make the mistake of waiting for the interviewer to ask: "Now, do you have any questions for me?" If you wait for that permission, it will probably be a cue that the interview is just about over, far too late for you to get substantive responses to your questions.

When your question relates to something the interviewer said, don't delay your inquiry; ask as soon as possible. Occasionally, you may even interrupt if necessary, if the question is vital enough to your plans. If you don't want to leap in at once, intervene with: "May I ask you a question?" Such interrupting, however, is less desirable than tagging your questions on to the flow of the conversation. Insert them naturally, as issues arise, if possible.

## **Effective Questioning**

After perhaps one or two warm-up questions—though these are not always necessary, especially if you have had previous contact with the person—be sure to pose the questions you regard as most important early in the meeting. This lets your listener know your priorities and minimizes the possibility that you may not get to ask your crucial questions at all. Questions asked in a hurry toward the end of the interview usually get short shrift; they are answered in a cursory manner because the respondent simply does not have time to think about them.

Here are some of the ways to ask questions most effectively.

**Ask Open Questions •** The open question is highly recommended because it encourages a respondent to answer in the broadest terms possible. It gives him the freedom to say whatever he pleases, does not restrict the boundaries of the responses. Open questions most often begin with *what, how,* or *in what ways.*

> The open question is broad, the closed question is narrow. The open question allows the interviewer full scope; the closed question limits him to a specific answer. The open question invites him to widen his perceptual field; the closed question curtails it. The open question solicits his views, opinions, thoughts, and feelings; the closed question usually demands cold facts only. The open question may widen and deepen the contact, the closed question may circumscribe it.[28]

Closed questions usually call for a yes or no response. Compare the way in which a single inquiry can be posed in both open and closed ways:

Closed: Did the college decide to expand enrollment?

Open: What future plans does the college have for its enrollment?

Closed: Is the company going to seek new markets?

Open: In what ways does the company anticipate seeking new markets?

**Ask Answerable Questions •** Be sure you ask a question you believe can be answered without difficulty. It makes the interviewer feel good to have the answer, and you can smile appreciatively at the information you receive. However, if you unwittingly ask a stumper, be careful to express your concern and stay clear of that area for the rest of the interview.

Be sure your questions actually have answers. Don't ask an impossible-to-answer question just because it sounds clever. The interviewer will regard you as pretentious, and you will deserve every bit of displeasure.

**Ask Nonthreatening Questions** • Questions that are low in emotional content and do not require deep thought can be used early in the interview to warm yourself to the task of more serious inquiry and to cue the interviewer that you will be active in the process:

> **EXAMPLE** _____
> I'll bet it's been a long day for you.
> How many people have you spoken with today?
> When did the company acquire this property?

**Express Puzzlement** • A good interviewer usually reads the puzzlement on your face before you express it in a question; therefore, you should speak up when something is said that you didn't understand. Interviewers appreciate your giving them a chance to clarify some of the more difficult topics or issues.

**Ask Well-Informed Questions** • Often the best use of a question is to show you have done some homework on the organization. Ask a question that demonstrates your knowledge. Generally some questions not only yield good information but also remind the interviewer that you are well organized and self-motivated. Be careful, though, not to push the well-informed question too far. In your haste to prove yourself, you may mistakenly ask a probing question that should have been avoided. A well-informed question, for instance, might be: "How does the company plan to market its new line of ski equipment?" A probing question, on the other hand, is something like: "When did the company decide to take over the southern markets?"

**Use Indirect Questions** • This method allows you to ask a question without insisting that the person answer it. As Benjamin says: "The indirect question usually has no question mark at the end, and yet it is evident that a question is being posed and an answer sought."[29]

> **EXAMPLE** _____
> I'd sure like to hear a little more about that project.
> You must really be busy with these new departments.

## Poor Questioning

It is easy to fall into the trap of thinking that any question asked is a point in your favor because it displays your initiative. An interviewer can usually detect when you are asking a question simply to sound impressive; you swing rapidly to another topic and usually string one nonsensical question after another. Stick to the questions that matter. Anything else will expose your tactic as superficial window dressing.

Here are some other kinds of questions to avoid.

**Use of Why•** Though *why* is a perfectly legitimate word in our language, it carries an unavoidable risk when it is used in an interview questioning process. Simply put, it is threatening and should be used with greatest care.

> Today the word "why" connotes disapproval, displeasure. Thus when used, it communicates that the respondent has done "wrong" or behaved "badly." Even when that is not the meaning intended . . . that is generally how the word will be understood. The effect . . . will be predictably negative.[30]

**Loaded Questions•** Loaded questions imply that you have an attitude or strong feeling about the subject and know or suspect what the answer is. They are asked to elicit a particular response. They insult the interviewer's intelligence and put him or her on the defensive.

> **EXAMPLE** _____
> Did the company decide to close that office because they didn't want to pay the high wages being demanded?

**Double Questions•** Probably one of the most common blunders, the double question reveals your desire to get a lot of information fast. You ask the interviewer to answer several things at the same time. Make it easy on your respondent, even if it means you may forget one of your precious questions entirely. Choose the most important question first and trust you'll find a chance to ask the others later.

**Curiosity Questions•** Don't waste time with questions about things that have piqued your curiosity but have little relevance or importance. It is easy to get sidetracked by something that "crosses your mind," especially in your anxiety to fill the time. That is precisely why you must have your important questions prepared in advance.

**Machine-Gun Style•** Avoid like the plague asking questions in series; the interviewer feels he or she is in the path of a dangerous weapon and must find a way to divert it. Each question should be followed by nonquestion interchanges. Wait for the interviewer to say something, make a comment based on the response, volunteer some new data about yourself, and then perhaps come back with another question.

**Shifting the Subject** • Be careful not to let your questioning move away from a topic area that interests the interviewer. It may seem that you are deliberately avoiding the topic. As noted later, abrupt shifts of topic are less desirable than questions that flow naturally from the previous response.

**Intellectuality** • This is probably the first cousin of the well-informed question, but it reaches too far. In your effort to display the depth of your thought and the way you can tie a contemporary question to a universal concern, you go too far, perhaps off the deep end. Avoid such pretensions, even if you *are* an intellectual, because most interviewers are not.

**EXAMPLE** _____

Could you tell me how Herzberg's theory of internal and external motivators relates to the distribution of work incentives among your professional staff?

**Probing** • The brother-in-law of the loaded question, this one will hurt you most dearly if you fail to see you are putting pressure on the poor fellow. No interviewer wants to be called to task by a job seeker, so if you are in doubt about whether your question touches a sensitive area, drop it. If it even *sounds* probing to you, in all likelihood it will land on him like a bombshell.

## Speech

Highly correlated with poor questioning are the ways in which your manner of speaking can intrude upon a free exchange of information. These are some of the key things to keep in mind.

**Speak Clearly** • If your natural speech pattern is too fast, slurred, garbled, or otherwise fuzzy, give it some attention. No one expects you to be number one on the diction or elocution list, but others have a right to understand what you are saying. Practice with your friends, people who will be honest with you. Play back a tape recorder if you need further evidence. You won't like the sound of that strange voice you hear, but you'll know whether it's understandable or not.

**Natural Tone** • Within the limits of reasonably good diction and clarity, stay with the voice that is your own. Any effort you make to assume a different persona through adopting a voice that *sounds* better will reach the listener's ear as phony, and you will be caught up in your own duplicity when you drop the new voice and return to the natural.

**Modulation** • Some people talk too loudly; others much too softly, so that they cannot even be heard. Speech volume is important because energy devoted to adjusting ears and body to your abnormal vocal level is energy subtracted from attending to what you are saying and feeling.

**Vocal Flatness** • Some people believe that it is "professional" to be even-toned, carefully modulated in their talk, not excited about anything because that would sound so childish. Rubbish. If you have feelings associated with what you are saying, it is vital that you express them. Of course, this can be overdone by a screaming cynic or a laughing hyena, but you get the idea. There is nothing professional about vocal flatness—it is simply boring.

## You Are Your Questions

The questions you ask are a Rorschach of your career personality. By these inquiries shall ye be judged. If you ask a lot of stuff about salary, fringe benefits, vacation time, you will be spotted as a person who is clearly motivated by the external rewards and less driven by internal needs. You may not have intended this impression, but your questions will reveal it. If you ask about the company's future plans, you will be tagged as a person who thinks in terms of the big picture. Let your questions create an impression of yourself that accurately reflects your attitude. Imagine that you have only three questions to ask. Which three best reveal the self you would like the interviewer to remember? Avoid the temptation to be pretentious. Choose those questions that clearly represent your highest priorities.

## chapter seventeen

#  Assertiveness

*No one can make you feel inferior without your consent.*
· Eleanor Roosevelt
*This Is My Story*

To the job seeker, darkness seems to cover this world of work. Imagine a huge pasture in which a thousand people are wandering around at nighttime trying to find each other with lit matches and you have an idea of the perspective of both employers and people who want better work. Employers have little idea where the right candidates are, and people who want to improve their work situations have even less idea where their talents can be used. Occasionally someone comes along and shines a spotlight on this pasture for a moment, foolishly believing he has illuminated The Job Market. Two minutes later he is gone, people shift their positions, and his picture is already out of date. Such feeble efforts to throw light on the process of work patterns may be called job clearinghouses or job banks; they fail to capture a restlessly shifting scene.

Most of your self-assessment will be wasted effort, done for naught, if you fail to make connections with employers who need you. Assertiveness is the skill that permits you to make these connections. This vital skill enables you to plug in a number of lights that will illuminate your place in the world of work, allowing you to stand out in the darkness that pervades so much of the hiring process. Assertiveness allows employers to see who you are and permits you to discover what they are doing. Keep in mind that there is no central control switch in this blind-finding-the-blind process known as hiring. If you do not make the connections yourself, you leave the employer cruising the pasture with a flickering match, trying to find his way to wherever you are hiding.

# What Is Assertiveness?

Assertiveness is not, contrary to popular belief, walking up to a bull elephant and asking him to whistle "Dixie" for you. Nor is it bulldozing your mother-in-law into changing the TV channel from her favorite show. These are examples of *aggressive* behavior, which can be defined as taking away the rights of another in order to satisfy your own. People frequently confuse aggressive with assertive behavior.

*Assertiveness* can be defined for our purposes as (1) expressing what you feel about the work you are doing and the work you would prefer to do; (2) taking those actions necessary to put you in touch with the people and situations that appeal to you; and (3) asking for their advice, insights, information, and referrals to others.

Bower and Bower, in *Asserting Yourself*, their detailed treatment of the subject, remind us:

> Some people believe that assertiveness training must turn a nice person into a constant irritant, a rebel, a complainer, and a general all-around pain. Others charge that assertiveness training teaches people to be calculating and manipulative, and helps them control others for selfish ends. Views like these are based on a misunderstanding of the goals of assertiveness.[31]

Assertiveness is the simple act of asking for what you want. It is not a matter of winning, outwitting, bludgeoning, controlling, or even manipulating your foe. The person from whom you seek assistance in your work search is not a foe at all, but a willing accomplice.

Nearly all the work search activity in the detective and research stages can be stunted if individuals believe they have no right to do what they are doing. "Why would anyone want to talk to me?" "What makes me think others would want to help me?"

There is an old story about the man whose car has broken down on a deserted rural highway. He walks a mile to a farmer's house to ask for help. During the walk, he ruminates about the farmer's possible responses to his plight. Being of pessimistic bent, the driver creates a scenario in which he imagines that the farmer will be reluctant to help. Thus, by the time our poor beleaguered driver reaches the farmer's door and the door opens, he says: "You can keep your automobile tools to yourself, I didn't want to use them anyway!"

Many of us concoct scenarios of this kind before we approach people to ask them for help with the job search, and these anticipations prevent us from acting. Though there is never any guarantee that an individual will assist you, you always have the right to ask. There is nothing in anyone's code of professional or ethical behavior (confidential matters excluded) that says a person is prohibited from talking about his or her work or from referring you to others in similar positions. Furthermore, there is every reason to believe that people will do so willingly because people generally *like* to talk about themselves and their ambitions, frustrations, accomplishments. And they like to be helpful in ways that enable them to feel potent.

## Passive, Aggressive, and Assertive Behavior

Let's settle once and for all that assertive behavior is neither passive nor aggressive in intent. Passive behavior will kill your work search because there will be no search at all; you will snuff yourself out before you start. Aggressive behavior will kill your search because you will stifle your listeners, attempt to railroad them into giving you information and leads you require, no matter what their objections. Assertive behavior permits you to ask for help in a way that respects the rights of respondents to satisfy you or refuse, as they please. Since you are not asking for the keys to the safe, the secret formula for Coca Cola, or a seat on the New York Stock Exchange, you can reasonably expect that most people will try to help you.

**EXAMPLE**

Passive behavior: I'd better not go in here; they will think I am disturbing their workday.

Aggressive behavior: I'm going to find out what they do with their used nuclear fuel, or they'll have to drag me out of here, kicking and screaming.

Assertive behavior: Would you mind if I asked a few questions about your job, only those you feel comfortable answering?

There is a delicate balance between asking for what you want and intruding your needs upon the rights of others. What I call assertive boors believe they can make requests any time as long as they preface them with "I would like," look directly at the person, and speak in a clear voice. Assertive boors fail to observe cues supplied by the respondent: that he has not yet finished speaking, that his nonverbal leave-taking behaviors indicate he has no more time to talk or listen, that he shows nonverbally some discomfort with the last question asked. And boors fail to recognize the needs of others in a group to be heard. It is always important to watch anticipatory nonverbal behavior in the people to whom you are speaking; assertive boors usually miss most of it.

Failure to observe your respondent's nonverbal cues can be disastrous for you. If you trigger in your listener a "get this person out of here" feeling, by virtue of your insensitive assertion, the feeling will undo any progress you have made, and you may not even get a decent referral to another person. Accurate observation of cues from others and respect for their time and their needs to be heard will not prevent you from saying or asking what you desire. They will facilitate the process.

## Assertiveness in the Work Search

Any active step you take beyond the mental gymnastics of self-assessment requires that you be assertive. You cannot survive without this skill; you can take giant strides ahead of your competition by learning to use it. Assertiveness is required, for instance, when asking a person for an information interview, declaring that you want to get out of your present work, requesting a firsthand look at the work site, asking for a personal referral for another information interview, and expressing your creative ideas to a prospective employer.

There are three levels of assertive work search behavior.

**Public Request •** At this level, you are making ordinary requests anyone might make, so you can expect an answer from the secretary, receptionist, or representative of the organization without any difficulty. Any citizen, individual, or information seeker has a right to ask such questions; your respondent provides such information routinely.

**EXAMPLE**
Who is head of the accounts receivable department?
Could you send me a copy of your annual report?
Where are your branch offices located?

**Do Me a Favor** •  At this level, you are asking friends or people to whom you have been referred to give you information that they have available, but that is not necessarily a part of their everyday responsibilities. However, you will discover that most people are more willing to do favors than you would expect because people generally like to be helpful if your requests are manageable, if you present them in person, and if you have established a comfortable relationship.

**EXAMPLE**
May I see a copy of the organization chart?
Could you refer me to someone else in your field?
How might I get a tour of the plant?
Is it possible that I might do some volunteer work here?

**Cold Turkey** •  At this level, you are approaching people who do not know you at all, and you are making requests without prior introduction or preparation. This is not as difficult as it sounds if you keep in mind that the person has the right to refuse, but that you also have a right to ask. If you are willing to endure a few refusals, you will get some unexpectedly good information this way.

**EXAMPLE**
Approach a person in his or her office and ask for an information interview.
    Sit next to a stranger on a bus and ask about his or her work.
    Ask another customer's opinion of the store where you're shopping.

When using assertiveness skills in your work search, try the easiest level first, so that you get practice in making contacts with people you do not know and in being the initiator. Assert yourself with the least threatening people at first—your neighbors, relatives, and friends—so you can practice the skills without unnecessary risk of rejection. And remember that as you develop personal referrals and accumulate contacts from your various interviews, you will have less and less need for level-three assertiveness and probably can dispense with cold-turkey initiatives after a while.

# How to Be Assertive Without Muss or Fuss

How do you steal a piano? By behaving as though you have every reason to be there in the first place. You act in a way that leaves no suspicion about your purposes or your right to be engaged in what you are doing. You walk in the door, enter the appropriate room, set up your moving equipment, and remove the piano with dispatch. Although the ethical dimension is twisted in this analogy, the *attitude* is one that should pervade your assertive behavior. You have every right to explore, question, inquire, volunteer, and be assertive in other ways toward your vocational objectives. There are four rules you should follow.

### State What You Want Without Hesitation

EXAMPLE _____

I want to know what kinds of public relations work your firm does, how you go about completing your contacts, the methods you use, and the ways in which you are usually successful.

In speaking, face the other person with your body, so you are not turned away at an angle and do not appear to be looking in another direction. Look at the person directly; your eye contact should be direct and steady but not so fixed that you are staring; occasional glancing away is fine. Speak with a tone of voice and diction that are clear, and speak slowly enough to be understood but not so slowly that your listener becomes impatient.

### State What You Do Not Want • Anticipate any misinterpretations that might stem from what you are saying.

EXAMPLE _____

I am not interested in asking you to hire me, and I have no intention of trying to sell you anything.

### Be as Specific as Possible

EXAMPLE _____

It would help me to know how you recruit your staff, what skills you believe are most important in effective work here, and what kinds of training and experiences are most beneficial.

## Adjust Your Requests as Necessary

**EXAMPLE**

I understand you have less time than we'd originally planned for. Would it be okay to ask you just the few questions I have regarding how you get your contracts and the methods you use to fulfill them?

This last step is particularly important. A juggernaut style of assertive behavior will quickly backfire if you do not pay attention to how the other person is receiving your requests. Each request you make or question you ask must be modified by the willingness of the respondent. Assertiveness engages you in a friendly negotiation process that yields results because you have no intention of alienating the other person.

Here are some examples of how assertive language is used with a wide variety of people.

- *To a secretary.* I would like to speak personally with one of your editorial assistants so I can gather some information about that job.
- *To an employer.* I would like to know more about your branch services; could you give me the name of one of your branch managers so I can ask a few questions?
- *To a public relations department.* I would like a copy of your annual report.
- *To a receptionist.* I would like to know who does the long-range planning work in this company. Could you direct me to his or her office?
- *To a referral source.* I am interested in speaking with other people who do work similar to yours. Could you recommend a good person?

## Self-Putdowns

Sitting around trying to screw up the courage to ask a stranger for advice or information, how many times have you said to yourself: "She really wouldn't want to hear my silly questions." "I'm not interesting enough for anyone to talk with." "He couldn't possibly have enough time for me." "She won't understand what I am looking for." "I know he gets bothered all the time by people like me."

Though there is no guarantee that you will get what you want, you can succeed in eliminating yourself from the game if you let self-putdowns dominate your thinking. Rather than assuming the worst, *let the other people decide.* Don't you decide for them whether a conversation should take place; they have a right to make that decision without your assistance. Ask yourself: "What's the worst thing that could happen?" The most severe consequence of your rash, impatient act would be a simple no, a polite request that you come back later. As my wise grandmother used to tell me: "If that's the biggest problem you have in your life, you'll be all right." And remember, *you don't have to be interesting*; the target people are interested enough in themselves. You don't have to provide the entertainment; just be prepared to listen.

## Shy People Can Be Assertive Too

Philip Zimbardo, in *Shyness: What It Is and What to Do About It*, reports:

> The most basic finding of our research establishes that shyness is common, widespread, and universal. More than 80 percent of those questioned reported that they were *shy at some point in their lives*, either now, in the past, or always. Of these, over 40 percent considered themselves *presently shy.* . .[32]

Let's assume you are shy too. You are generally afraid of people in positions of authority, feel intimidated by secretaries, fall over at the sight of a business suit, and would faint if you had to approach three strangers at the same time.

In the long run, you might resolve to read Zimbardo's book and practice the behaviors he recommends. For now, try these three simple rules.

**Don't Be the Life of the Party •** It is never necessary for you to laugh a lot, tell jokes, or otherwise entertain your hosts. Your quiet, unobtrusive attention to their work and lives will be enough to excite their sensors and keep the conversation moving.

**Bring Along a Scrap of Information •** An easy way to stimulate conversation is to scrounge a morsel of information about your target person, offer it, and let the conversation carry itself from there.

**EXAMPLE** _____

I heard your agency is planning to move into a new building.

I saw the new store that opened up across town; it has a lot of merchandise I've seen in here before.

**Use Your Observational Powers** • What kinds of materials are displayed on the work desk? Trophies, plaques for some kind of service, diplomas, copies of new books you can ask about? What pictures are there on the wall? What do they represent to this person? How is the office decorated? Who decorated it?

## Assertiveness on the Job

There are applications of assertiveness that can relate to your current work situation. Your failure to be assertive in your present job may account for much of the unhappiness you feel. Do not assume there is only one way your job can be accomplished. Use your imagination to suggest to yourself ways you might use different skills to accomplish the same objectives. And use assertive behavior to make requests for changes on the job. Here are a few examples of assertiveness and some effective and ineffective ways of expressing it.

**EXAMPLE** _____

Ineffective: I would like to do more writing in my job.

Effective: I would like to prepare a set of publications describing what the department does, so that field offices could use our services better.

Ineffective: I feel I am not learning enough on this job.

Effective: I would like to know more about insurance tables, how policies are underwritten, and the criteria that are used to make these decisions.

Your boss's job is to say yes or no; your job is to ask him. Many workers make the fatal error of assuming that the boss, in his or her infinite wisdom, will _know_ when your job should be different. In fact, no one knows your job as well as you do. If you want different responsibilities, you must spell out what you want in enough detail so that the boss is faced with the simple task of saying yes or no. Bosses are far more likely to say yes when they don't have to do any background work to discover what you are asking for. If you simply complain about your current work without detailing to the boss how it might be different, you place the maximum burden on him or her. The boss must then wonder in frustration: "What does this guy want? Why is he complaining? How can I get him to shut up?"

Assertive behavior lets others know in the clearest possible terms what you want. It takes the pressure off them because they no longer have to guess about your intentions. Assertiveness erases misconceptions. It has the same comforting function that the handshake did when it was originated as a way of showing your guest or visitor that you had no concealed weapon.

# · chapter eighteen ·

# Self-Disclosure

Dear Howard:

I don't know how to talk about myself. I'm terribly self-conscious about saying anything complimentary about myself because I know how conceited it would sound. It seems to me that the interviewer who asks me about my strong points is just testing to see whether I will trip up and make excessive claims about my abilities. So I feel better playing it safe and not claiming any great talents that I would not be able to defend under more intense questioning.

*Signed,*
*Modesty Becomes Me*

Dear Mod:

Contrary to what you may think, interviewers are not waiting to pounce upon your self-revelations with demands that you prove yourself immediately or never darken their doors again. And, you will discover from bitter experience if you stick with your self-effacing stance, modesty gets no points when a potential job is on the line.

Rather than think you are shouting, bragging, or otherwise falsely representing your qualifications, follow these simple guidelines. First, be as *specific* as possible about your abilities. Don't say "I am a quick learner" or, worse, "I can deal with a variety of situations." Instead, tell them concretely: "I organize detailed paperwork well" or "I can do numerous computations quickly and accurately." Second, back up your statement with a specific life experience. For example: "I learned how to work with numbers when I was a kid by figuring out batting averages in my head and computing all the statistics for my team" or "I learned how to organize data when I was leader of a new department in my previous job; we had to draw up budgets, select new employees, and write the job descriptions within a month." Third, don't ramble to excess in describing your strengths. Take one sentence to tell what the skill is, then one or two sentences to back it up with life experiences. Finally, don't hedge your self-statements with words that permit you to back off from what you've just said: "I really wasn't the greatest at this" or "I could've done a better job." A hedge remark does nothing to further convince the listener of your sincerity.

*Signed,*
*Howard*

One would imagine it is the easiest thing in the world to talk about yourself, to reveal lovingly and fluently the person you know best, but most of you who read this know better. The beast that lives within you tells you to keep under cover, protect against injury, show only the better side. Or it whispers: "Who would want to know anything about me, anyway?"

Perhaps you prefer to rely on paper credentials, recommendations from others, or the power of sheer happenstance to get you a job, because these devices minimize the extent to which you must reveal yourself. Once you let the beast out of its cage, the jig is up.

We live in a time when all but the most outspoken of athletes and entertainers are loath to declare they are good at anything or to stand for any particular value or point of view, lest they face ridicule from others. Better to be quiet and unassuming than to be the target of barbs or angry witticisms or, worse yet, to have to live up to something.

Shyness, reticence, self-protectiveness, and defensiveness are rampant in our lonely society:

> Shyness is an insidious personal problem that is reaching such epic proportions as to be justifiably called a social disease. Trends in our society suggest it will get worse in the coming years as social forces increase our isolation, competition, and loneliness. . . .

> Hawthorne may have been thinking of the shy person when he wrote: "What other dungeon is so dark as one's heart? What jailer so inexorable as one's self?"[33]

Of course, you are not self-protective with everyone. You tell your little brother how great you are or share your deeper aspirations with your friends. But when it comes to sharing yourself with a stranger in a situation in which you are being evaluated, you are understandably cautious. It matters who is doing the listening, because an interviewer is more likely to make you prove what you are saying.

You're not sure whom you can trust with revelations about yourself. Is this person going to use it against you, put what you have said in a record somewhere, perhaps embarrass you by reporting it to someone else? Do you have enough time and does the other person have enough patience to listen to the supporting evidence for what you have just said?

All these thoughts weave through your mind as you try to decide whether to reveal yourself. Given the fears and the uncertainties, it seems the prudent course of action to play safe, tell only as much as you have to. Like folding your cards before the betting gets heavy, it seems better to avoid the big blunder, the genuine faux pas, and hope your paper credentials will deliver you safely to your goal.

Set in the context of the job interview, your self-disclosure includes talking openly and fully about your chief strengths, skills, abilities to perform certain functions; the values you regard as most important in your choices of work; your private ambitions, what you hope to accomplish with your work; experiences you have had that reflect your unique work history.

All the most common questions employers and interviewers ask call for some measure of self-disclosure. These questions are designed to draw you into the open. They are not meant to engage you in a fencing match to which your response is: "Let's see how I can dodge this one."

When asked a self-disclosure question, you cannot say "I don't know" because there is no excuse for not knowing yourself. Self-protection is characterized by filtering, screening your responses, planning what you will say and what you will try to hide. As you learn self-disclosure, you will discover that it creates a state of mind in which you feel little need to filter because you are pleased to tell who you are without any need to alter the script to suit the listener.

Of course, it is unrealistic to suggest that you talk about anything and everything in a work-related conversation—or in any conversation, for that matter. Your private personal concerns are off limits if you choose to protect them, and you can be carefully selective in what you say. You can feel free to defend yourself against invasion of privacy or the risk that your words will be misinterpreted by choosing your language judiciously. However, if you are comfortable with your career aspirations and enjoy talking about them, you will not often need to use defensive tactics to screen or modify what you are saying.

If you cannot reveal who you are, then certainly no one else can do it for you. There is nothing earthshaking about that statement; it seems the most self-evident of principles. But we have become so accustomed to letting paper credentials (résumés, application forms, and so on) tell our stories that we depend more heavily upon these so-called legitimate sources of data than we do upon accounts delivered in our own words.

If you are a soft-spoken person, you need not feel this message is inappropriate for you. In revealing yourself to someone else, it is not necessary to be a bubbling personality, the life of the party, or an effervescent talker. Many people prefer understatement as a style of conversation because it makes fewer demands on them and is generally easier to take. Be yourself, but show yourself, and the other person will respond warmly to your genuineness.

Don't rely on your work history to speak for you. Paper summaries of your existence are sterile, past-oriented documents. They fail to capture the flavor of what you are doing now, what you feel ripe for at the present moment.

Increasingly, employers have little personal knowledge of the people who apply to them for work. It has been estimated that 40 million Americans change their residence every year; hence, it is increasingly rare that an employer has seen you before or even heard anything about you. This makes it doubly important that you tell him in your own words about yourself, instead of letting him make erroneous judgments from the labels and categories squeezed onto a piece of paper.

## When to Let Out the Beast

Is self-disclosure a pell-mell rush to declare who you are, delivered as a soliloquy to the breathlessly waiting interviewer? Not necessarily. Your choice of a moment to speak about yourself depends on the format of the interview.

If you are the one who requested the interview, it is your responsibility to make a *brief* opening statement about yourself to explain why you are there:

**EXAMPLE** _____

I want to talk with you because I feel I can offer the sort of experience and abilities you need to keep this greenhouse running and expand its business.

Your opening statement declares the purpose of your meeting and gives your listener a chance to say whether he or she wants to hear more. A long opening statement, replete with your numerous skills and experiences, is not going to help you because you have little idea what the other person would like to know.

If the interviewer has called this meeting, which is more likely to be the case, you should ordinarily wait for appropriate cues that you are expected to tell about yourself.

**EXAMPLE** _____

Tell me why you decided to apply here.
What have you done before that relates to our operation?

However, if the interviewer fails to ask you questions that allow you to talk about your chief qualities, you must volunteer the data you want heard.

**EXAMPLE** _____

I would like to tell you why I believe I could do this job.

I have some experiences that relate closely to what you are doing. I would like to tell you about one of them.

---

## How to Practice Self-Disclosure

Self-disclosure questions in the job interview generally reduce to one of three varieties: (1) Why us? Why have you chosen to apply here? What interests you about our organization? (2) Why you? Why should we be especially interested in you over others? (3) Why now? What makes this the right time for you and us?

There are three parts to any self-disclosing response that characterize the best statements you can make: (1) the basic self-statement in response to one of the three types of questions noted above, (2) evidence to support that statement, (3) an evaluation that you use to summarize your view.

**EXAMPLE** _____

I want to work here because there is more opportunity to grow with a company that is creating new product lines (self-statement). I have read articles about your product changes and your interest in creating new customer service (evidence). I welcome the challenge of trying new markets, and feel the risk is worth the potential gains (evaluation).

Self-disclosure may seem dangerously close to bragging, but it is not. The braggart attempts to convince his hearers that he is a little bigger than life; your self-disclosures are plain revelations of what is you. To become comfortable with self-disclosure, you must practice it according to these guidelines.

**Support with Evidence** • Any statement about yourself should be accompanied by evidence that you can support what you say ("I did this before").

**Focus on the Present** • Show how your past experiences culminate in the present, in terms of what you can and want to do now. Past experience can also be leavened with a strong dash of future imagination.

**Use One-Sentence Bites** • Avoid rambling at all costs. There is no value in setting endurance records for talking about yourself. Listeners appreciate concise self-statements that can be remembered easily. If they want more, they will ask for it.

**EXAMPLE** _____

I believe I am ready to take over a managerial position because my supervisory experience at the mill taught me about handling personnel problems and planning an efficient operation.

I feel I can offer your school some competencies that you don't currently have— namely coaching for soccer and directing a performing theater troupe.

**Serve Them, Not Yourself** • Though self-disclosure grows from your knowledge of yourself, it should be oriented toward the needs of the potential employer. Focus on what you have done that would serve his interests, not on what the employer can do for you.

**EXAMPLE**

Since you want someone who can take over the programming functions, let me say that my work with the radio station will enable me to do the job. I feel I can give you the popular style of programming you need.

## Revealing Weaknesses

Though honesty is the best policy and full self-disclosure means not having to engage in a hiding contest with the interviewer, your primary objective is to show what you are capable of doing and why you can do the job, not to provide reasons why you cannot do it. Thus, there is no value in admitting your liabilities as an exercise in honesty. Think of it this way. Any interview is brief enough so you can fill it talking about your strengths, your experiences that support these strengths, and your high interest in this particular opportunity. Why save time for the liabilities? If you are pressed directly to talk about your weaknesses, remember (1) that the interviewer is probably more concerned about how smoothly you deal with the question than about the content of your reply and (2) that a weakness can usually be coupled with a strength, if you anticipate this possibility in advance.

**EXAMPLE**

It takes me a little longer to do a project than most people, but I make sure it is done thoroughly, without slip-ups.

## Other Forms of Self-Disclosure

Talking about your strengths and expressing your belief that you can do the job are not the only forms of self-disclosure. Other kinds of self-disclosure call attention to a particular feeling you have about the work being discussed, rather than to the work itself. These feelings are important to introduce, but you must use them with care lest you risk being labeled a "complainer," "overly emotional," or some such epithet. Choose your spots carefully, but say what you feel you must say. Here are some other ways self-disclosure can be used.

- *Admit conflict.* I believe we have different ideas about what the manager of this department is supposed to do.
- *Express confusion.* I do not understand how the purpose of this department differs from that of the production department.
- *Share opinion.* I believe that this agency could be directing more of its attention to older people.
- *Share values.* I feel strongly that teachers in this school should be given the chance to broaden their knowledge by teaching different courses each year.
- *Reveal anger or disappointment.* It bothers me that this job is saddled with so many trivial duties.
- *Express concern.* I am concerned that most salespeople who deal with pensions and annuities do not have knowledge of estate planning and cannot handle investment portfolios.

## Self-Disclosure Exercise

Practice during your daily routine any three or more of the activities listed below. Note how you feel when doing each of them. Awkward? Shy? Happy? Keep a chart of how you feel from week to week to discover changes in the self-disclosure activities you are able to perform and how you feel about doing them.

**1)** Tell a friend about something helpful you did.

**2)** Describe a strong personal trait you possess.

**3)** Name an experience you felt excited about.

**4)** Reveal an experience you had previously kept secret.

**5)** Talk about something you do that you feel is superior to most other people's similar efforts.

**6)** Describe a strong attraction you have to a certain kind of work or career.

**7)** Talk about your fantasy ambitions for the future.

**8)** Describe a career you've imagined for yourself that doesn't even exist yet.

## chapter nineteen

#  Writing

Dear Howard:

I am tired of all this traipsing around the streets, talking to everyone in sight, peeking in stores, sneaking around corners trying to catch somebody in the act of working. Maybe it isn't all that bad, but I need a break. Can I just sit in the comfort of my room and write to somebody for a change? I know you said people don't answer letters too fast, but I'm willing to wait.

> *Signed,*
> *Pen in Hand*

Dear Penrod:

Off with your shoes, feet by the fire. Up with the pen; there is method to your madness. You have a right to retreat from the madding crowd, and you can take comfort in the fact that writing still counts. In fact, good old-fashioned letter writing may achieve a breakthrough door knocking has failed to attain.

If you like writing to people, translate that urge into making pen pals of prospective employers. Forget the hogwash that says applying for work is a formal process and you shouldn't let your silly old informal self gum up the works. An employer is a human being just as you are. Treat him almost like a prospective lover. Let him know you've been thinking about him, that he's the only one for you, that it matters a lot that you get together. This approach can be stretched out of shape and distorted to be more ludicrous than beneficial, so use your good sense. Employers like to be courted like anyone else.

Letters to your intended employer must be done with taste and a sense of what is believable. Selling yourself is not appropriate in letter form; your objective is to establish a relationship and build a bridge to in-person meetings.

The letter is a subtle wand. It requires only a few moments of reading time, but can leave an indelible impression on the person who likes to be appreciated. Write on, Macduff.

*Signed,*
*Howard*

Words give shape and substance to your thoughts; they bring your feelings to life and create pictures where before ideas were scattered and fragmented. Writing forces you to make coherent sentences of your unshaped flashes of insight. It puts flesh on the bones of your ideas and allows you to capture images that dart to and fro in your mind.

Can the pen be mightier than the tongue? Yes, on many occasions your written communication to an employer can be quicker and more effective than an in-person interview. During the days or weeks (if you are far away) that you wait to see an individual personally, you can penetrate his consciousness with a well-timed note. I will confine my discussion of writing skill to the personal letter because I believe traditional forms of written communication in the work search encourage passive behavior and are ineffective if used without more active methods of inquiry.

The warlords of the working world seek to standardize your written communication in the form of business letters, the résumé, and the formal job application. These are tools you must be familiar with, but you should note that they give you limited opportunity to set yourself apart from the crowd. Thus, I shall leave discussion of formally written job-seeking materials to other publications and attempt to persuade you that your ability to use writing to your advantage depends largely upon the *personal* and *informal* qualities of what you say.

We are all egotists. We wait by the mailbox for letters to arrive and remind us that someone remembers. The mailbox game never loses its excitement because it offers a pleasant surprise, an unexpected compliment, a voiceless hello that you prize because the sender took time to remember you. Don't you still sort through your office and home mail, looking hopefully for an envelope that is personally typed or handwritten to you?

No matter how resolutely and tightly the employment world attempts to depersonalize itself, there will always be individual egos. People will be proud of what they have done and will generally appreciate another person who notices. In view of the numerous impersonal communications that are enforced in a hiring process, the *personal communications* stand out because they escape the trap of formalized language and structure.

The written medium is made to order for those of us who like to think slowly and carefully and say things in just the right way. No one asks you to defend yourself while you write; nor do they hurry you along with their own restless needs. You can talk to your target person at your own pace. Moreover, you can control the agenda by organizing your thoughts in the order that seems most likely to make an impact. The best quality of the written word is that you can take as long as necessary to get the desired result. You can make countless mistakes without reprisal and show your audience only the finished product.

A letter affords the receiver the same degree of freedom. He or she can imagine the reply a hundred times, reflect upon your words, turn them over and over, and savor them if they are complimentary. And whatever effect you achieve with your written communication, you have the pleasure of knowing that it lasts and lasts.

## Getting Personal

The résumé, application, and other standard forms of written communication are impersonal; they lack the single most potent quality in any writing—a direct connection between one human being and another. Even personally addressed letters can lack this quality. Of the two following letters, both personally addressed, the second— more specific and personal—is far more likely to evoke a positive response and be remembered.

**EXAMPLE** _____

Dear Ms. Jones: I have been reading about your company and would like to know more about its operation. Could you send me literature describing your overseas branches?

Dear Ms. Jones: I have read about the Universal Company in a recent article in *Business Week* magazine. Your work with new metal alloys in foreign markets interests me. Could you send any literature that describes these operations?

I believe a job is a very personal matter, second only to family relationships in its intimacy and demand for interpersonal cooperation. Therefore, I will focus this chapter on methods that will help you cultivate the personal touch in your writing. The more you depend on stiff, aloof, and structured forms of business writing, the more you surrender your chance to reach your correspondent and be remembered, because your letter will sound like everyone else's.

The personal quality can be established by a combination of three approaches in your writing:

**1)** Comment directly about the person to whom you are writing.

**EXAMPLE** _____
I have read your study of the ecology of local wildlife.

**2)** Comment about the organization for which the individual works, even if you don't know the particular function of the person to whom you're writing.

**EXAMPLE** _____
I am aware that your agency has been studying local wildlife and would like to know more about your findings.

**3)** Tell something about your own background that relates to the purposes of the organization to which you are writing.

**EXAMPLE** _____
I have done a study of deer in the local area.

A combination of knowledge about the individual or organization to whom you are writing and reference to your own experiences is best because it establishes a basis upon which you can meet for a mutually profitable discussion.

## Behind-the-Scenes Writing

There are several ways you can practice your writing skills without having to take the risk of exposing your words to target employers. Any of the following kinds of writing sharpen your prose and build your confidence for future writing in the job marketplace.

**Letters to Friends** • Perhaps the best way to begin putting yourself into print, the informal letter provides you with the protective cover of a friendship and allows you to be free with your language, convey feelings without embarrassment, and make mistakes without consequences. If you can tell a friend why you want to get into a particular line of work, why you believe you ought to be hired, and what you value in this kind of work, then you can say the same things to the employer when that opportunity occurs. But practice first without the threat of being evaluated. As Ernst Jacobi points out:

> Writing in the form of a letter to a friend gives you several immediate advantages. It forces you to focus on one specific person, preferably one whom you respect and especially like; this immediately influences your communicative attitude. You will tend to be warm, direct, informal, and spontaneous. You will instinctively take care to stress why you are writing and why you think that what you are writing will be of interest. And you will probably avoid being pompous, stiff, and self-important. You are, after all, writing to a friend. You are not trying to impress him. You know he knows you're not stupid, and you need not be afraid of his criticism.[34]

**Fantasy Letters** • What would you write to a fantasy employer if you had the courage to send this person or organization a letter expressing your loftiest ambitions? Try a letter of this kind, with no intention at all of ever sending it. Assume instead that you have an imaginary reader who will accept and welcome anything you say and believe it as well. Make sure you tell the letter's receiver what you feel about the work but are embarrassed to tell a real person ("I really want to be the sort of insurance salesperson who sells a policy only when I believe the family needs it and who looks after the family's entire financial program").

**A Letter to Yourself** • Your inner conversations flicker in and out of your consciousness hundreds of times a day. Try putting these exchanges into more coherent form by addressing yourself directly and attempting to convince yourself that your course of action in the work search is justified. Take it even a step further and imagine you are persuading yourself to hire yourself. If you are your own worst critic, this may be a useful crucible in which to test your aspirations.

## Writing Employers Informally

It is a good idea to make written contact with target employers before you formally apply with letter and résumé. Three informal categories of writing can be used to great advantage.

**Thank-You Notes •** These subtle little devils offer you ways of getting across your interest and enthusiasm for the work without professing to be bargaining for a job. Usually the thank-you note follows an information interview. In such a note, you can tell the person how much your talk reinforced your interest in the work, perhaps set the stage for future contacts, and express personal interest in the individual, all in the context of showing gratitude for assistance.

**Note from Admirer •** If you have done any measure of research on an individual or an organization, you are in a position to write this kind of note. For example, an aspiring advertising executive who researches a particular ad agency can identify the name of an account executive, study the ad campaigns for an account he or she handles, and write a letter of admiration for the way in which the campaign has been formulated. Such letters out of the blue are so rare in business communication that the receiver will be flabbergasted to realize that someone actually noticed and thought enough to comment. Be careful not to overdo this kind of letter; make sure you are speaking with definite knowledge and sincerity and that you are not effusive.

**Portfolio •** In any profession where the work you have done can be shown in writing, this form of communication is an excellent supplement to the résumé because it gives evidence of your résumé's claims and demonstrates that you had the foresight to prepare yourself. Articles, reports, memoranda, advertisements, newspaper copy, training manuals, sales reports, or anything else you have written provide proof of the work you have done. If you do not currently keep a sample book of such materials, now is the time to begin collecting and organizing them.

# Warning: Writing Can Work Against You

Like a piece of spinach stuck in your teeth while you are talking, poor writing can distort the quality of your essential message. J. Mitchell Morse cites examples of the written communications he gets from college students: "What is needed is the restorement of confident in fair taxes. The fairest are the sail tax which the rich pay more than the poor because they buy more and are not discriminating against them they feel."[35] The Public Relations Society of America reports:

> Now, bear in mind, the following excerpts are from real letters written by real applicants seeking a real job as editor. Most possessed graduate degrees, many in English! ... "My doctoral program provided an interdisciplinary continuation of the Master's program emphasizing research, management and organization theory and practice, decision making, theory, personnel and business administration, and directed institutional communications." You can't help but like a guy who gets right to the point.
> Another Ph.D. in English wrote, "I have become proficient in quick but competent research and apprehension of complex matters." Well, at least he writes shorter sentences.[36]

If you want to use writing skills in your work search but have always been afraid of making errors like these, here are a few suggestions for you. First, write as much as possible in the same style you use in talking. Don't adopt one style for writing and a different one for talking. Use a tape recorder if necessary to hear your conversation or that of others, and do what is necessary to make complete sentences of it. Second, ask a friend or teacher to serve as editor for your writing; accustom yourself to hearing criticism and learning from it. Most people who are good editors love doing it for their friends occasionally because they like to show their proficiency. Third, practice, practice, practice on nonthreatening targets. Write letters to your sports heroes, politicians, the television networks, and any other people or places you know are not likely to be offended by what you say or how you say it.

# Guidelines for Effective Written Communication

Ernst Jacobi, in his excellent book *Writing at Work*, urges that every piece of writing can be improved by attending to several important guidelines. Though his guidelines apply to writing that would be done after you are hired, I feel these recommendations apply equally well to the writing you do in your career search.

**Make Every Word Count •** Do not write for the sheer sake of writing. Words by themselves are empty shells, signifying nothing, if they are not focused toward a message. Say what you have to say economically. Don't say it again to remind your readers that they might have missed it the first time.

**Adopt a Point of View •** Try to leave your readers with the impression that you have reached a particular conclusion, so that they know how they and their work have affected you.

> **EXAMPLE**
> It is clear to me that your organization is trying to reach the youth who need help but do not use traditional helping services. This is the kind of effort I am interested in joining.

**Watch the Mechanics •** Everyone who has ever made a spelling error or a mistake in grammar or shown sloppy syntax will hate me for bringing up the subject, but errors of this kind distract the reader from your intended message. Hence, you are unwise to let them occur. Even typos jar some readers and leave the impression of carelessness. Proofread your writing. Enough said.

**Use Strong Verbs •** If you want to tell a person you were impressed with his work, try to say a little more than that you "liked" it. Say the work "stimulated" you or "encouraged" you to do additional reading. In describing your own work experience, choose such verbs as *managed, directed,* or *organized* over weaker verbs like *coordinated* or *compiled*.

**Give Specifics** • If you make a complimentary comment, do your best to back it up with specifics, lest the reader think you are pulling phrases from thin air.

> **EXAMPLE** _____
> I will remember your presentation on the new laser show because it reminded me of the relationships between physics and art.

**Read It Aloud** • It has been said that Guy de Maupassant read all his stories aloud to his cook, and if the cook couldn't understand their themes easily, he threw the stories out. Test your writing on a friend, preferably one who has no familiarity with the specific content of what you are saying. See if your writing stimulates interest.

**Use Your Own Vocabulary** • I cannot emphasize this strongly enough. If you try to adopt words that sound lofty and impressive, your phoniness will be detected. Speak in your own familiar words, as long as they represent plain English, so that you can retain the informal, personal quality of your writing.

## Sample Letters

The following sample letters to an employer whom the job applicant has never met show the contrast between an impersonal, business style of writing and a more personal, informal style. In both cases, the applicant has done appropriate research and feels it is possible to create enough interest to obtain a formal job interview.

First, the business style; note how dry it seems.

Dear Ms. Beaumont:

In your capacity as personnel manager of the Robinson Crusoe Company, you have many occasions to talk with people about the responsibilities of your office. In this regard I would like to request that you let me know whether I could meet with you on an appropriate occasion to discuss matters of some importance to me.

I am interested in requesting information about the nature of your operations, key personnel, organizational structures, and institutional policies. This information would assist me in expanding my knowledge of facilities similar to that which you direct.

I have collected certain background information about your organization that would provide suitable preparation for my visit with you. In my efforts to conserve your time, I have prepared a formal agenda that will not make undue demands upon you.

Could you reply to me at your earliest convenience, so that we can arrange this meeting for our mutual benefit? Thank you kindly.

Now the informal style. Note how the writer uses specific terms about his or her qualifications and language that is personal and direct.

Dear Ms. Beaumont:

I have learned from contacting your office that you are personnel manager for the Robinson Crusoe Company. I am writing to you because I have read about personnel work in the business world for the past few months and would like to meet a person who does it as a professional. I have read several books on the topic and have spoken with relatives who work for International Tool and United Ball Bearing. These relatives told me that personnel work involves a lot of activities similar to what I am doing in college. I am social chairperson for my sorority and look after the staff of the school newspaper. I like these responsibilities and would like to hear what you have to say about personnel work before considering it as a career.

Perhaps you could tell me how you got into this work and why you feel it is the right field for you. I would benefit a lot from the insight you could give me. I have prepared a small number of key questions I would like to ask you. Would you be willing to see me for thirty minutes?

I have known several people who have applied for and worked at the Robinson Crusoe Company, and they have told me how pleased they are with their jobs. One, John Meharry in the automotive department, even wrote you a note of thanks a few months ago, I believe.

I suspect it must be frustrating to be concerned about the welfare of every employee in the entire company. I am interested to hear how you deal with this responsibility and why you like it.

I will be graduating from college within the next year and a half, so your views will be a great help in shaping my own plans. Thanks very much.

Finally, here is an example of a good letter to an employer with whom you would like an interview.

Ms. Carolyn Randolph
Editor and Publisher
**Outdoor Education Press**

Dear Ms. Randolph:

I read about your publishing company in a recent issue of *Printer's Ink* and was very much intrigued with how you started the business with only one title (your own book) and used your advertising experience to generate contacts with authors so the business would grow. I noticed that you have a particular interest in encouraging authors whose books might be turned down by the publishers who seek mass-market potential. I appreciate this sensitivity on your part to the need for helping good books to appear despite marketing constraints.

Since reading the article in *Printer's Ink*, I have read many of the books you currently list because I have considerable experience with outdoor matters and would like to become more closely involved with this kind of publishing. I noticed from the article that you market your books by direct mail and coupon advertising and do not use a sales force to enhance your efforts. I would like to propose that you experiment with the direct sales approach by considering my services. I have a particular preference for marketing your products on college campuses.

Before writing to you with this proposal, I tested my idea by phoning or contacting personally twelve different college bookstores in our local area. Each told me it would be willing to stock your books if they were more readily available. Hence, I am encouraged to believe that there is sales potential that has not been tapped.

I believe I can help your sales for several reasons: (1) my previous experience (résumé enclosed) as a graduate school representative taught me how to make contacts on large university campuses and the value of the personal approach; (2) I sold computer equipment during my college years and thus learned to be comfortable with selling skills; (3) my experience with outdoor activities includes ten years as an active supervisor of the Appalachian Trail, a term as president of the local hiking club, and occasional articles for the Sierra Club (see enclosed sample).

I believe we should get together to talk about this idea, if you feel it has some potential for you. I will call you during the week to discuss a time we might meet.

*Sincerely,*
*Chris Jones*

I have chosen to emphasize writing as a separate communication skill because I believe you can enhance your career search greatly with a personal letter on those occasions when the written form is most convenient and appropriate. A clear and personal writing style is the natural complement to an effective set of interviewing skills. Often the potent and readable letter creates invitations to interviews that would not have occurred otherwise.

part

5

Transition
Skills

## · chapter twenty ·

# Support Group

*No man succeeds, unless by hook or crook or threat he
forces or bribes other men to assist him.*
  • Elbert Hubbard
  *A Message to Garcia and Other Essays*

A companion of mine used to say: "What good are your friends if
you can't use 'em, because if you can't use 'em, they're not your
friends." This chapter deals with how best to use your friends,
relatives, and neighbors as a supporting cast without making undue demands upon them and with the assurance that a good time
will be had by all. You may wonder how others can be enlisted to
help in your work search, when finding work has been portrayed as
such an individual process. You may mistakenly envision the entire
work search in terms of the final encounter, when you are one-to-
one with the prospective employer. You cannot carry your friends
with you to this meeting; however, they can help you in *all* other
stages that precede the formal interview—self-assessment, data
gathering, information interviewing, participant observation, and
others. As this book demonstrates, at least 80 percent of the work
search can be accomplished before formal interviews.

It may surprise you that the support of others can be enlisted in
the work search. This is largely because you have a jewel-thief
mentality about looking for a job. You suspect that you are doing
something underhanded, that as few people as possible should
know what you are doing, and that the more secretive your operation the better. On the contrary, you should design your work
search so that as many people as possible know what you are up
to, instead of keeping the operation under wraps. Treat the whole
matter as though you are making a trip down the Amazon River.
Keep people notified at all times of your whereabouts, make sure
sources of help are available in case things go wrong, and never
travel anywhere without assistance.

Loneliness, Lonesome Polecat, Lonely Hearts Club, Lone Wolf, Alone by the Telephone—all these are images of sorrow associated with the word *alone*. Why inflict this sort of punishment on yourself in the work search? Only the Lone Ranger salvages any satisfaction or respect from working in solitude. Get yourself involved with other people or you will build a cocoon from which it may be difficult to emerge when you are called upon to show your interactive qualities with a prospective employer.

Work searching by yourself will grow warts on your psyche, cause an ache in your metatarsals, and perhaps give you indigestion too. You have every reason to develop a support group and no reason to avoid it. Anyone willing to lend support and encouragement to your efforts is highly unlikely to be critical, deflating, or counterproductive to your efforts. Too many folks think that having to look for work is like being banished to the back of the classroom or being punished for misdeeds. The résumé, or whatever piece of paper you use announcing your availability, is not a badge of shame, but a ticket to adventure.

## Sources of Support

You can organize your support from any of several convenient pockets of people in your daily life: immediate family, extended family (cousins, uncles, aunts, and so on), professional colleagues or others who do work similar to yours, friends and acquaintances, and fellow sufferers—that is, others who are seeking better work at the same time you are.

Choose whichever of these groups seems most convenient to you and most likely to derive enjoyment from lending you support. Of course, it is possible to create a mixture of people from several of these groups. These people—you can think of them as your own private commandos, raiders, or henchmen—can assist you in many ways.

- They serve as the gyroscope for your self-esteem. Whenever you feel yourself being knocked off course by an unsuccessful interview or the latest blind alley in your search and say to yourself, "I am really not going to find anything, because I am no good anyway," the support group will remind you that you are your own worst critic. It will counsel you to avoid the trap of personalizing every false trail ("there's something wrong with me"). There's a lot of the roulette wheel in the work search, but the advantage belongs to the person who keeps it spinning.

- They provide feedback whenever you need it, which will be often. You will ask group members to read your letter of inquiry, your cover letter, or your résumé before you send it. You will practice your style of answering questions with them before meeting prospective employers. You will enlist their support in reviewing your self-attributes. Look upon whatever feedback you receive, whether it is totally accurate or not, as data you did not have before, and process it with all the other information you receive.

- They serve as your companions. If they are people with whom you feel comfortable and ordinarily have fun anyway, they will lend an air of "we're taking a field trip" to your work search festivities. They will relieve tension when you are working yourself into a frenzy and energize you when you are growing weary of the chase.

- They provide you with the capability of being in two places at the same time. If you have an information interview across town, but also an opportunity to meet a good contact on the same afternoon, send a friend to gather information for you and pave the way for your eventual firsthand contact.

- They give you kindness and kicks. Your squad of helpers exists to provide warmth and friendship when you need it, but it serves an equally important function as energizer. When your efforts are slacking, and you are backsliding to dependent forms of activity ("I'll just wait to see what turns up"), the team members serve you best when they remind you that the advantage belongs to the initiator.

## Your Attitude

If you view your work search as a trip through a chamber of horrors, this attitude will affect everyone who works with you. A sense of adventure, exploration, and fun is absolutely crucial to your search. It is not written anywhere that you must suffer in looking for better work. Images such as a treasure hunt or detective work are useful. Call your group something that takes the edge off the seriousness of your task—Bureaucratic Demolition Team, Riders of the Yellow Pages, Job Jumpers Juggernaut.

It will also help you to keep in mind that your helpers can benefit from the experience too. Everyone hits the streets for a change of work sooner or later, you will remind them, so whatever information they uncover or skills they learn by working with you will repay them in terms of future benefits. Furthermore, those individuals who job-seek for someone else—in this case you—benefit by being able to practice their work search skills under nonthreatening conditions.

## Materials

It is probably best to choose people who are near to initiating their own career searches so they can help themselves at the same time they help you. To encourage them to become involved, I recommend you provide each with the following items that will assist them in their exploration.

**Telephone Books** • Provide one for the local area and another for a near or distant town where you hope to find future employment. These books give your group members handy references for prospective employers so they can develop target lists on their own.

**Bus Tokens** • Invest in enough low-cost transportation for your co-workers so that they feel they are not being taken advantage of. This small investment formalizes your involvement with them and encourages them to make a plan for investigation.

**Supportive Materials** • Be sure your group members have whatever supportive materials they need, such as a list of sample questions for the information interview, a skills list to help them remember your (or their own) strengths, and so on.

**Food** • There is nothing more universally rewarding than getting together to eat and share the events of the week. Most of us are suckers for a good meal, and your willingness to build your review sessions around food will ensure the continued support of your team members.

# Assignment of Roles

In the ideal situation, you have several people helping out who are highly motivated and willing to let you organize. Their primary responsibility is to aid you in all facets of information interviewing. Depending on their prominent strengths and preferences, you can assign additional specialized roles as discussed below.

**Head Cheerleader** • This is the friend who will give you a boost when you need it, lead the group in a standing ovation whenever you have made a breakthrough, and generate enthusiasm in the group because this is his or her personal style. Every group needs a resident optimist, so be sure you include one.

**Record Keeper** • If you easily tire of keeping track of the names, titles, and functions of everyone you have seen, you need a person who likes doing this sort of thing. Making contacts can become confusing after you have seen a few dozen people. It is best to try keeping these records straight yourself, but having someone around who is a little more organized than you isn't a bad idea.

**Scorekeeper** • This is the person who takes greatest pleasure in keeping a *numerical* tally of everything you have done—how many interviews, how many referrals generated, length of interviews, number of phone calls made, and so forth. You and the scorekeeper may discern valuable insights from such data. Are longer interviews usually better or worse? How many cold-turkey information interviews are necessary before I get a useful referral? How many phone calls must I make before getting through to a target person?

**Role Player** • The actor or actress among you will enjoy taking the part of an employer, feeding you typical questions, and responding in ways you would expect from a prospective interviewer. Let your role player act to the hilt, forcing you to deal with the emotions of the situation before you must do so for real.

**Head Snooper** • No group should be without one. This person takes delight in unearthing facts, discovering how to reach hard-to-get target employers, ferreting out inside information about a company, the things the public is not supposed to know. The snooper likes the challenge of the hidden clue, the unexplained relationship.

**Phone Scavenger** • This is the person who loves to see how much can be learned by simply sitting at the phone, asking questions designed to get past the secretary, trying to gather as much information as possible without lifting a pencil or going to a company in person. Acquiring information this way is a challenge, but some prefer it to in-person interviewing, and others try it just for the sheer difficulty.

**Library Rat** • This individual can burrow through printed material, amassing hitherto unknown facts, finding articles that illuminate your target employer and background data that help make you a knowledgeable applicant. These talents should not be wasted on the phone or in the streets.

# Methods

In working with your support group, you should expect to follow a sequence of informal meetings that might be as described below. Of course, you can vary this as your needs and the preferences of your group members dictate, but the sequence is suggestive.

**1. Truth Session** • In order to generate material for the self-assessment phase of your work search, brace yourself, gather the group, and ask the members: "What are my strengths, the qualities you believe I should use most? What do you believe motivates me? What kinds of payoffs make me work the hardest and most energetically? List as many attributes that describe me as you can—personality traits, nervous habits, defense mechanisms, style of operating, anything you can think of."

**2. Brainstorming** • You should probably do this at the same time as you conduct the truth session. It is a good idea to break bread at this session, then ask your group members to use the self-assessment material they just produced to generate ideas about the kinds of employers who would want a person like you. In brainstorming, follow these rules, which are adapted from Alex Osborn's excellent book, *Your Creative Power.*[37]

First, defer judgment. Make sure no one is allowed to say anything evaluative or judgmental about the ideas anyone else has generated. Second, aim for quantity of ideas. Produce as many different employer possibilities as your group can think of, without regard to quality or eventual suitability. Later you can assign priority to the ideas and use your judgment about them. Third, build on ideas of others. The open secret about brainstorming is that one individual gets new ideas from hearing what the others have to say; thus the creativity accumulates as a function of your being together. Fourth, be ridiculous. The more ridiculous the ideas of group members, the better your brainstorming session will be. Try hard to be outrageous, and you may find the nugget of a good idea. Try "Salami Designer, Lab Rat Midwife, Fish Counselor, Jailhouse Accountant, Cucumber Waxer, Succotash Supervisor."[38] In a more productive sense, being ridiculous means suggesting ambitious possibilities for you, even though they may seem unattainable or the jobs you seek may not have even been created yet.

**3. Setting Objectives** • Following the truth and brainstorming session, your next meeting should focus on setting specific objectives so that your work search will have direction and purposefulness. Make sure your objectives are generally measurable ("We will contact at least ten target individuals this week"). Set a deadline that is in the near future ("We will meet next Tuesday night to see what progress we have made"). Form a scouting party and assign the roles: who will gather the printed information, who will seek the initial information interviews, who will make the phone calls to discover what these employers are really about.

**4. Role Playing** • Each succeeding session should consist of some role playing in which any group member who has met or knows something about a target employer gets you ready for an eventual interview by asking hypothetical questions, imitating the employer's style, and generally having fun prepping you for future encounters.

## Group Job Hunting

Misery does love company, they say. With a little effort, you can find at least a few other people who are looking for better work at the same time you are. These folks probably represent your best potential support group because their motivation is just as high as yours, and they will probably agree to share some of your burden if you will shoulder some of theirs. As few as three or four fellow sufferers will do.

To take advantage of your common interests, you might subscribe to the following guidelines. Meet on a regular basis, preferably every week or at least every two weeks, with food and drink available. Agree that everyone will take truth serum. Vow confidentiality, but admit it is important to let each other know what is happening so that no one will feel alone in having troubles. As much as possible, make a game of the information-seeking process.

Agree on a day when all of you will take an information-gathering trip together. Go in pairs if you desire, especially if you or someone else has never done information interviewing before. Start the interviewing with people who are the least threatening, such as those who deal in your favorite hobbies. Who can get inside an organization to see its organization chart, its formal budget, its internal publications?

A trip like this is highly reinforcing in its own right. If you tie it in a neat package by meeting for dinner and sharing the day's experiences, you will develop a natural support function within the group; individuals will cheer each other's efforts because they want to be cheered themselves. As in Alcoholics Anonymous, give loud and clear support to those people who complete their appointed tasks and bring group pressure to bear on those who do not.

Do you want to prove to yourself once and for all that you can manage this work search process, that there is no particular element of it that can scare you? Then take your group out for a field trip in the most demanding of circumstances. Purposely arrange the experience so that you have the toughest conditions possible. Make this your version of an Outward Bound expedition into the wilderness of the working world. Impose the following conditions on yourself and your group: (1) go to a town or city where none of you has any personal contacts or acquaintances; (2) take a minimum of money so you cannot buy your way into employment agencies; (3) impose a time limit on yourselves; (4) don't take any formal paper credentials, such as a résumé; (5) read no classified advertisements or other readily available sources of information;

and (6) seek work in a field that is clearly different from your present occupation.

If you can obtain valuable job-related information and make contacts under these conditions, you will have proved to yourself that you can do it anytime, anywhere, with a minimum of resources. Every work search thereafter will seem relatively easy.

## chapter twenty-one

# Self-Marketing

If the work search were simply a matter of having certain credentials—academic degrees, certificates of experience, and the like—and a résumé detailing your work history, there would be little debate about hiring decisions. Your fate would be in the hands of the technocrats, and there would be little need for a book of this kind.

Fortunately, there is still considerable debate about the appropriate preparation for most jobs of responsibility, except those that are highly structured and technological. The flexibility regarding appropriate background for a particular job stems from the transferability of skills, our recognition that experience in one context can be applied to a different context once the person acquires a necessary base of knowledge. For example, many military officers who have managed supply operations can transfer their skills to inventory control in private corporations.

I shall use the term *self-marketing* to refer to your ability to see and use transferability in all your life activities. With a little practice, you will recognize that everything you do allows you to cultivate certain skills that can be used profitably in future employment settings. Self-marketing is the ultimate transition skill to carry you from one job to the next because it allows you to see links between what you are doing now and the work you will choose tomorrow.

Most successful work search campaigns proceed on a hurry-up basis; an individual hears about a job opening or perhaps decides to enter a different kind of work, and then engages in a crash program designed to prepare for the new work. In the rush to acquire necessary credentials and obtain knowledge about the desired profession, the person forgets about transferable skills and assumes it is necessary to know everything "they" know before applying for the job. The individual forgets that knowledge can be acquired on the job. An employer looks for certain skills, and once he finds a candidate with them, he assumes he can teach the person the information base without too much difficulty.

Self-marketing is important because you must make the fullest possible use of your past experience when seeking a change of work; otherwise you are judged on the basis of superficial credentials and other external criteria, such as test scores, manner of dress, and prestige of previous employers. Your ability to communicate your worth is a function of your ability to recognize value in your own experience and see how it can be translated into new capabilities.

## How to Cultivate This Skill

You probably possess a great many more skills than you think you do, and they come into play in any number of activities. Learn to recognize them in everything you do.

**Voluntary Service** • Perhaps the last great secret of the work search is that voluntary community activities are highly marketable in employment settings. You can view your volunteer responsibilities in ways that have direct relationship to future possibilities of paid employment. Because you undertake community service for a different purpose—the nobler goal of providing your service to others—you may forget that these tasks provide many opportunities to nurture your transferable skills. Note how each of the following community activities requires or fosters employment skills.

> **EXAMPLE**
>
> Fund raising for the United Way (persuading, selling, organizing)
> Political campaigning (planning, speaking, record keeping)
> Police Athletic League (coaching, teaching, human relations)
> Youth center (counseling, programming, supervising)
> Senior citizens center (programming, planning, entertaining)
> Historical society (researching, writing, promoting)
> Scouting (teaching, planning, human relations)

**Extracurricular Activities** • If you are a full-time or part-time college student, there is a gold mine of potentially transferable skills waiting for you in volunteer activity, clubs, campus organizations, and the like. Note how each of the following out-of-class activities requires skills you can transfer to the employment arena.

**EXAMPLE**

Work as a food service supervisor (listening, directing, supervising)

Organize a college-wide program (managing people, handling a budget)

Plan housing assignments (analyzing a system, managing details)

Arrange an outing club expedition (planning, human relations)

Work with a dramatic stage crew (resource grubbing, building)

**Career Seminars and Courses** • If you investigate programs at your local college or university, regardless of whether you are an enrolled student, you will discover that many of them offer structured opportunities for career planning in which you can participate. Use such a seminar or course as an opportunity to identify your marketable skills and learn how to package them so you become conscious of future career possibilities.

**Market Analysis** • Once you have developed a reasonably sharp picture of your unique abilities, you must begin thinking about the needs of the marketplace. What new products, new services, or perhaps even entire new industries are likely to occur? Will population shifts within our country have any effect upon need for products or services? Solar energy? Leisure products? Physical fitness equipment? You don't have to be a professional marketing analyst to think this way. Just ask yourself: "What do I have that other people might want, and how can I add something unique to it that my competitors will not have?"

**EXAMPLE**

Pete was a moderately successful insurance salesman working with a reputable company, but engaged in fierce competition with dozens of others representing similar insurance plans in his town. He noticed in his routine calls on clients that many asked questions about how to manage their other financial affairs, questions that were only peripherally related to the purchase of insurance. It didn't take Pete long to realize that his ability to serve as a complete financial advisor would greatly enhance his sales of insurance. He boned up on investments, trusts, mutual funds, and estate planning, taking courses whenever he could, and offered these services to his clients as a part of his "package" of services. He understood what the market wanted and used his salesman's skills to talk with equal comfort about stocks, bonds, and insurance.

## The Ten Hottest Transferable Skills

Some skills are more equal than others. I have been encouraging you to identify your most powerful talents, with the implied assumption that every skill can find a home somewhere. While you can expect all functional and adaptive skills to have definite value, you must recognize that certain skills are universally greeted with enthusiasm by almost every employer because these skills occur with some regularity in every job having responsibility and requiring decision making and good judgment. You should pay special attention to them in the work you are now doing, look for them in the nonpaid activity of your spare time, and comb your past experiences for evidence of them.

**Budget Management** • Get your hot little hands on any budget you can find, no matter how small, and take responsibility for it. Manage how the funds are dispensed, keep control of the budget, learn what fiscal control is all about.

**Supervising** • Take responsibility for the work of others in a situation in which some accountability is called for. Have direct contact with the work of others; expose yourself to the difficulty of giving orders, delegating tasks, taking guff, understanding the other person's viewpoint. Here is where listening can become a real feat of skill.

**Public Relations** • Accept a role in which you must meet or relate to the public. Greet visitors, answer phone complaints, give talks to community groups, sell ads to business people, explain programs to prospective clients, or even collect taxes.

**Coping with Deadline Pressure** • Search for opportunities to demonstrate that you can produce good work when it is required by external deadlines. Prove to yourself and anyone else that you can function on someone else's schedule, even when that time frame is notably hurried.

**Negotiating/Arbitrating** • Discover and cultivate the fine art of dealing openly and effectively with people in ambiguous situations. Learn how to bring warring factions together, resolve differences between groups or individuals, and make demands on behalf of one constituency to those in positions of power.

**Speaking** • Take a leadership role in any organization, so that you are forced to talk publicly, prepare remarks, get across ideas, and even motivate people without feeling terribly self-conscious. Good public speaking is little more than the art of dramatized conversation, but it must be practiced so you can discover your own personal style.

**Writing** • Go public with your writing skills, or even the lack of them. There is nothing quite so energizing as seeing your own words in print; exhilarating if they look good to you, and a spur to improvement if they look awful. Practice putting pen to paper. Write letters to the editors of every publication you read routinely. Write a newsletter, however informal, for a club or organization to which you belong.

**Organizing/Managing/Coordinating** • Take charge of any event that is within your grasp. It doesn't matter what you organize—a church supper, a parade in honor of your town's two hundredth birthday—as long as you have responsibility for bringing together people, resources, and events. If nothing else, the headaches of organizing events or managing projects teach you how to delegate tasks to others.

**Interviewing** • Learn how to acquire information from other people by questioning them directly. Start by interviewing the neighbors, your friends, and other people easily available. It doesn't matter what you ask them, but imagine you are a newspaper reporter who needs the information for a story. Discover the fine art of helping a person to feel comfortable in your presence, even though you are asking difficult or even touchy questions.

**Teaching/Instructing** • Refine your ability to explain things to other people. Since most teaching takes place not in the classroom, but in ordinary everyday exchanges between people, you should become familiar and comfortable with passing information and understanding to others. Any position of leadership or responsibility gives you many chances to teach ideas and methods to others.

If you cultivate any three or four of these skills to a high order of proficiency, you are doing quite well. If you practice most of them and feel you are improving in each, you should expect to have positions of decision making and responsibility before long. Conversely, if you anticipate any managerial or leadership job in the future, you will find it difficult to avoid using many of these skills in large measure.

## Making Your Pitch

Once you have identified any highly marketable skills you possess, you must consider how you are going to present yourself to a prospective employer. Usually one or two prominent skills are sufficient to give you a basis for introducing yourself. There are three central things to keep in mind: (1) describe your skills in concise, unambiguous terms; (2) back up your claim to the skills by referring to actual experiences in your life; and (3) make a clear connection between your skills and the needs of the employer.

### EXAMPLE

YOU: I enjoy drawing factual material together into written form. I have written grant proposals for state government, training manuals for a local service club, and newsletters for my church. I believe my ability to do this kind of writing could help your fund-raising department.

EMPLOYER: How could you help us?

YOU: I could prepare proposals for government research money, send news reports to interested citizen groups, write an annual report that would generate positive publicity.

## Physical Evidence

It would seem from our talk about interviews, writing letters, and general conversation that self-marketing is largely a verbal matter, a process in which interpersonal communication must be your chief vehicle. On the contrary, you are not limited to talking about your accomplishments in the work search. In many situations, it can be even more potent to show evidence of the work you have done.

- *Portfolios.* Keep a file of articles you have written, advertisements you have written and designed, stories published about yourself, reports you have written for management.
- *Products.* Show products you have made. These might include furniture, crafts work, musical instruments, mechanical devices, or others.
- *Displays.* Keep photographs of physical displays you have arranged and designed, such as promotion for an arts program, Christmas displays, historical exhibits, and so on.
- *Programs.* Maintain a file of brochures or fliers from programs you have organized—the program of a drama you staged, the program of a conference you coordinated, or the outline of a scouting trip you planned.

## Apply for a Job You Don't Really Want

If you want to practice your self-marketing skills without the threat of being evaluated for a job you really want, get your act together and try it out with an employer who is interesting enough to attract your attention but for whom you really would not want to work. Go through the routine of talking to the individuals who would do the hiring, so that you can practice seeing the relevance of your past and present experiences to work opportunities and learning what skills are desired by employers. Once you have been through this experience a few times in nonthreatening situations, you will know how to talk about yourself effectively when you apply for a job you really want.

If you are offered a job in the process of applying for something you really do not want, you can respond in one of two ways: politely say you will think it over and then write or call indicating you've decided to stay in your present work; or look a little closer at the offer, keeping in mind that you may have unconsciously gravitated toward a field you are interested in without having thought about it in great detail.

# · chapter twenty-two ·

# ✌ Remote ✌
# Control

You are fifty to three thousand miles from where you wish your eventual employment to be and are wondering what exactly to do about this stark reality. Of course, it is very difficult to conduct a work search at a distance. Scattering résumés across the land-scape yields little, and you must wonder what else is worth doing. You cannot expect to receive job offers by mail. There is, however, a considerable amount of preparation you *can* do that will greatly assist your efforts after you make the move.

You may wonder whether it makes any sense to do long-dis-tance work searching. Keep in mind these three things: First, very few people do any preparation at all before they set foot in their target areas. Thus, any advance work you do will put you that much ahead of your competition. Second, every day you are in your target area, you will be hungry and anxious to find work, so you will be sorely tempted to skip much of the recommended detective work and research. Hence, it pays to do as much as possible before you go there. Third, getting an interview by mail and telephone is a challenge. If you succeed in arranging even three interviews this way, you have set the tone for what is likely to be a very successful campaign when you arrive in Target City.

This chapter assumes you have chosen a target geographical area, preferably a town or city, and that you have a goal statement that describes the kind of employment you are seeking (see Chap-ter 6).

### EXAMPLE

I want to work with flowers or plants in Boise, Idaho.

I am seeking administrative work in a college or university in the Boston area.

237

If you fail to target geographically and frame at least a tentative working statement, you will be unable to focus your long-distance attention on specific employers.

## Advantages of Long-Distance Activity

The methods you can use involve three varieties of contact: letter, telephone, and in-person. Each of these has a built-in advantage accruing to the person who operates at a distance.

The advantage letter writing gives you is that people are flattered to receive personal attention by mail. When you receive a letter from someone who is aware of your work and has taken the time to study and think about it, you assume the person is impressed by what you and your organization are doing.

Using the telephone is advantageous because people are generally programmed to be responsive on the phone; it is easier than responding in writing. To increase your probability of getting a good response, use the name of the organization for which you work ("I am calling from XYZ Company") and be specific about your request ("I need some information about your work with low-income housing").

The advantage in-person contact affords you is that since you are going to move to the new town anyway, all contacts you make in the local area can be regarded as practice. You can make mistakes, acquire information without fear of facing an unexpected job interview, and ask people to be sounding boards for your ideas.

Let's turn now to the ways writing, telephoning, and in-person contact come into play.

## Writing

Write letters requesting background information about work available in the area. Direct these letters to the Chamber of Commerce, United Way, or other groups that exist to provide this information.

**EXAMPLE**
Letter to United Way: I would appreciate your letting me know how I might obtain a listing of social service agencies in your area which relate to senior citizens.

Write letters requesting information from a target employer.

**EXAMPLE**

I would like to know about the programs and services of the Community Health Clinic and would be pleased to pay for any publications you may have available.

Write letters to individuals who work at your target employers. You will have gathered these names either from previous literature or from inquiries by telephone. Write to a person whose job title intrigues you, even if you know nothing about the work.

**EXAMPLE**

Dear Ms. McShain: I am writing to you because you are director of programming for the Community Health Clinic and perhaps you can tell me a bit about the kinds of programs you offer in a typical year.

Write follow-up letters to everyone who responds to you. Be sure to research whatever information they have provided in their replies—key articles, books, other information. Include in your reply an example of your work, if possible. Ask for permission to make an appointment when you arrive in the target area. You can enclose a résumé, but emphasize that you are not asking for job help, but are simply including the résumé as convenient summary of your background. You don't want to lose these people as contacts by demanding foolishly that they do your job hunting for you.

**EXAMPLE**

I read your report on the year's programs and was intrigued by the variety of field trips you take within a limited budget. Could I arrange to visit you when I arrive in Minneapolis to ask a few more questions?

## Telephoning

Request printed materials you may have mentioned in your initial letter to the organization. A phone call will probably hasten the arrival of these materials by several days. Ask for the public relations office, the public information office, or some similar department title.

**EXAMPLE**

Would you send me a copy of your annual report and any other publications or brochures describing your activities?

Request the names of key officials mentioned in the annual report, company newsletter, or similar publication. Ask for the personnel or public relations department if the operator is confused about where to refer you.

**EXAMPLE** _____

Could you tell me the name of the vice president for finance?

Speak with a target person, preferably after you have received a reply to your initial letter. Request one or more of the following: (1) an appointment to see him or her when you arrive in Target City, (2) suggestions about additional reading you might do to understand better the individual's profession, (3) recommendations of names of other people in the profession whom you could write to or see when you arrive there.

**EXAMPLE** _____

Thanks for the letter you sent me about investments work in the insurance industry. I read the book you recommended—can you suggest similar titles? Would it be possible to meet with you when I arrive in Hartford? Before I arrive, are there other investment analysts there you would suggest I write to?

## In-Person

Richard Bolles suggests considering your city or town as a replica of your target city so you can do some information gathering before you leave.[39] Your present town or city is like your target city in the following respects: It has many of the same kinds of organizations you're interested in, it has many employers where your skills are needed and values can be satisfied, the process you use to reach employers in your present town is the same as what you would use in your target city. You should (1) obtain printed material—newsletters, magazines, annual reports, and so on; (2) visit these employers in order to practice your information interviewing; (3) practice the process of getting referrals from one employer to another, perhaps even a referral to someone in your target area, and ask about branch offices in other cities or towns—maybe the headquarters of the organization is located in the place where you are going.

## When You Should Move to Target City

You should probably not move permanently to the target area for your work search until you have accomplished the following. First, you need to have accumulated a list of at least fifty prospective employers, using employer directories, telephone books, and other resources. You need this many to convince yourself that there *are* more than a handful of possibilities there.

Second, you should have reviewed enough printed material from the specific employers, the commercial press, and professional organizations so that you are reasonably prepared for a job interview if one should occur the day you arrive. A detailed review of this kind should focus on the top five employers on your prospect list.

Finally, it's not a good idea to move permanently until you have at least five specific places of possible employment in the target area where some individual is personally aware of you as a result of your correspondence, a direct referral from a person in your present area, telephone communication, or any combination of these. Contacts of this kind will assure that you can begin your search on a personal basis as soon as you arrive. These five should probably be the same as the five organizations you have researched thoroughly prior to your arrival.

## When and Where to Begin Your Long-Distance Search

As you must suspect by now, long-distance activity cannot wait until two weeks before you intend to move. You should probably begin six months before you intend to move. This means you will be researching, writing, phoning, and canvassing long before you have resigned your present position.

All the following sources are good places to begin your efforts:

- *Newspaper subscriptions.* Lay out the funds for out-of-town newspapers to be delivered to your doorstep or post office box on a regular basis. This will acquaint you with the newest developments that may have work potential for you.

Such items as "New Plant Opens Up" or "Government Contract Renewed" tip you off about employers you didn't detect in the phone books.

- *Regional magazines.* Currently many regions of the country produce magazines that focus on topics and people of local interest. In the East, for example, you can find *New York*, the *Washingtonian*, *Philadelphia Magazine*, *Pittsburgh*, the *Bostonian*, and others. These publications will keep you abreast of regional currents of change that may suggest employment opportunities.
- *Polk's city directories.* If the phone book for your target city is not available, try the local library and ask for Polk's. It gives you the same information as a regular telephone book, and it locates the people and employers for you by section of town.

Anticipation is important, but it takes time. The more time you allow yourself between long-distance activity and the eventual change of location, the less anxiety you will feel and the more chance there is that "lucky" connections will happen.

## chapter twenty-three

#  Interim Jobs

If your need for reliable earning power is so pressing that you must obtain immediate employment without regard to its suitability to your primary career interests, what you need is an interim job.

An *interim job* can be defined as work that provides you with regular income at a level that permits financial survival. You accept this job as a stopgap without any intention of staying in this line of work on a permanent basis.

You recognize that such a job may have little or no relationship to your more enduring career interests, but you must keep this employment as long as necessary, until you find a position in your desired occupation. This means, of course, that you will continue to search actively for a more desirable career while you are engaged in the interim job.

Ideally speaking, every job of this kind should fulfill four criteria.

- It must ensure a large enough income on a regular basis to allow you (and your dependents) to survive without difficulty.
- It should be obtainable with relatively little or no advance preparation, and more readily available than most types of work. This affords you rapid entry.
- It must be moderate in its demands on your working time so that you have enough time remaining during the week to continue exploration for a permanent career.
- It should afford continual contact with a wide variety of people in the course of the work, so you can make contacts during work time that might be helpful in your career exploration.

243

As you can readily see, an interim job possessing all these characteristics is little short of a fantasy. As the list below suggests, however, it is possible to obtain certain positions that possess at least some of these desirable qualities.

## Interim Jobs Unrelated to Career Goals

If your immediate income needs are not large, there are many interim jobs you can consider that provide relatively easy entry, moderate work demands, and exposure to a wide variety of people. While you are not likely to consider many of these jobs as serious career options, you should examine them first because they make minimum demands upon you other than your devoting the requisite number of hours. They therefore provide the best conditions in which you can save energy for the continuation of your serious career exploration. The jobs listed below[40] also offer you relatively good access to large numbers of people in a variety of work situations.

- *Census taker.* Collecting information most people consider nonthreatening gives you the opportunity to talk with many people about their work.
- *Opinion poll interviewer.* Same as above, with even more opportunity because polls are growing in use and acceptance.
- *Commuter train conductor.* Plenty of opportunity to talk with commuters about their jobs as they ride to and from work.
- *Retail store clerk.* Especially in a bookstore, cigar store, clothing store, or drugstore, people often have time to chat and provide insights into the work they do.
- *Cab driver.* Repeated chances to pick up valuable clues about various professions; businesspeople often chat with cab drivers.
- *Marketing research interviewer.* Obtain product preference information and, in the process, ask people about their work situation.
- *Bartender.* Perhaps the ideal opportunity to listen to people when they are relaxed.

- *Museum guard.* Chance to observe and talk to a variety of people.
- *Security guard.* If you can overcome the barrier of the uniform, there are plenty of people to talk with.
- *Golf caddie.* People who have the time and inclination to play this game usually have rather interesting professions and often depend on you for conversation.
- *Short-order cook.* People are more agreeable when they are being fed, and you would probably serve them at lunchtime, between halves of their working day.
- *Comparison shopper.* You get exposure to a lot of people by visiting a number of stores each day.
- *Receptionist.* You are the first person to meet people who visit the organization. Choose an organization inhabited by employees or customers you would like to meet.
- *Employment agency interviewer.* A good way to learn about job availability from an insider's vantage point.
- *Photographer's helper.* People like to have their pictures taken and do not mind talking with the photographer on a variety of subjects.
- *Travel agent.* Everyone travels at one time or another, often for the purpose of looking for a new job.
- *Advertising space salesperson.* Sell space in newspapers, on radio, in trade magazines, on TV to a wide range of organizations.
- *Mail carrier.* A vital service and an opportunity to visit homes, businesses, stores, government offices, churches, hospitals.
- *Handyman.* Offer a maintenance or repair service for homeowners and you will have a chance to visit with many people about their jobs.
- *Temporary office worker.* An all-purpose interim job available in metropolitan areas; the all-time champ for giving you an opportunity to sample a variety of work situations because you work for a few days or weeks for various employers in different settings.

## Career-Related Interim Jobs

Perhaps you cannot afford to fool around with nonserious jobs, either because they pay too little for your income needs or because they are not challenging enough on a day-to-day basis. Furthermore, you hope to find an interim job that has some inherent connection to your intended career.

If you pursue such a job on an interim basis, please keep in mind that it should still retain two essential qualities: it must give you exposure to potential contacts, and it should not be so demanding that you have to suspend future exploration.

**Sales** • Sales jobs probably represent a decent example of interim jobs in this category. Many sales positions in real estate, investments, insurance, and other fields can be entered with relative ease and give you sufficient freedom to make numerous outside contacts. Often a salesperson can choose to produce only the amount of income required for living purposes. Of course, there are sales jobs that have stringent quotas, and the interim job seeker should avoid these.

**Consultant** • A consultant markets his or her knowledge of a given industry, occupation, profession, or geographical territory to people who pay for such service. For example, a former member of the chemical industry might consult with plastics or rubber products manufacturers. Or a former educator in the social sciences could sell advice to industrial corporations that are developing educational programs for their employees.

**Student** • A temporary return to formal education often provides numerous professional contacts and an opportunity to be a research assistant while waiting for a career opening to occur. An increasing proportion of the enrollment in higher learning consists of people who are either currently employed or have recently been at work; hence, the person who returns to the classroom finds numerous contacts and sources of career information there.

**Apprentice** • A somewhat different example might involve a person who wants to become a carpenter, but must wait for an apprenticeship or suitable position. In this case, an acceptable interim job might be with a lumberyard, in order to become familiar with wood products and the people who use them.

## How Long Is an Interim?

The time lag between your need for immediate employment and the day you find your permanent career may be several months. You should be neither surprised nor disheartened if you must keep your interim job for at least six months, because the career search process can consume that much time if it is done properly. In any event, you should expect to maintain an interim job as long as necessary to discover your more permanent career.

For some, the interim job can last forever if they learn that their intended career is not possible on a full-time paid basis. For example, many performing artists determine that their earning power from stage performances will never be sufficient to maintain themselves financially, so they hold on to their supplemental employment indefinitely.

## The Interim Job in Your Work History

When considering a job that seems marginally or not at all related to your permanent career, you may wonder whether a future employer will discredit you for having worked in an unrelated field. I doubt seriously that this would be to your disadvantage. Most employers recognize an individual's need to make financial ends meet when moving from one career position to another. Furthermore, since the positive publicity afforded John R. Coleman's working-class sabbatical from his college presidency (*Blue Collar Journal*), a new measure of respect has been accorded people who depart from their straight-line career paths.

If you feel there should be some relationship between your interim job and your professional career, choose an interim job that permits this relationship. For example, an investment counselor might spend some months as a marketing research interviewer in order to tap public sentiment regarding certain products owned by public corporations. Or an executive from the transportation field could consider a job as mail carrier in order to sharpen his understanding of traffic problems in the local area.

In the final analysis, you should view the interim job as a device that permits you the freedom to move from one job or career to another without having to arrange for one position to be available the moment another expires. While not necessarily highly rewarding in itself, the interim job nevertheless serves a definite function in the career progress of an individual.

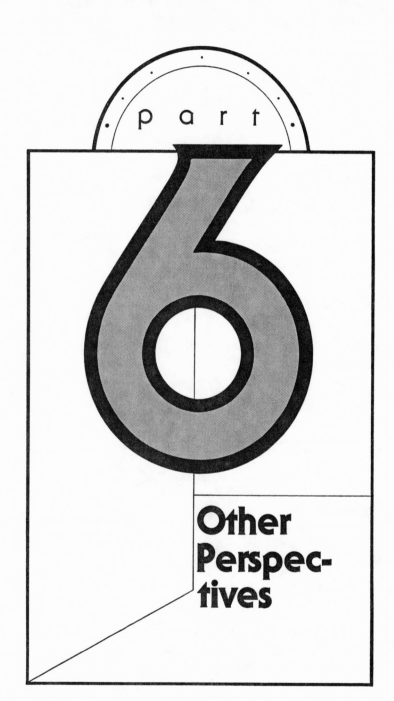

part

6

Other
Perspec-
tives

## chapter twenty-four

# For Shy People

Many of you will protest, however inconspicuously, that all the lessons of the previous pages are lost on a person who is fundamentally afraid of talking to other people, on the shy side, or cowed by the thought of facing anyone in a position of importance, especially a powerful figure in the world of work.

Though it is true that many of the admonitions in the chapters on detective work and research place at an advantage the person who can strike up a conversation easily, you need not disqualify yourself. Since Zimbardo tells us, in *Shyness*, that 80 percent of people feel shy at one time or another in their lives and 40 percent of us feel we are currently shy, I presume a lot of you who read this assign yourself to the shy category. Read on. There is plenty of hope.

## Use Your Other Work Search Skills

In all likelihood, if you feel a bit inferior on the *talking* scale, you are probably a bit on the superior side in one or more of the other modes of getting information—reading, listening, observing, or writing (see appropriate chapters). Begin your work search by playing your favorite skill to the hilt. If you are really crackerjack at using the library and want to get into high finance, read *Fortune* magazine from cover to cover, go to bed with the *Wall Street Journal*, and classify every employer in the *Financial Market Place* before you set foot in the office of a live financial wizard. Let your research skills give you an advantage over the clod who is a good talker but cannot digest and catalog information as well as you can.

Similarly, your listening, writing, or observational skills can be parlayed into a competitive advantage if you use them for their maximum effect. Begin with the skills that come most naturally to you and then progress slowly to the other modes of work search that you find a bit more difficult.

## Go Directly to the Experts

If you want to get in touch with someone who will become a contact, but are afraid to put your ego on the line, take a long step back and place yourself in the hands of a resident expert in the field you are researching. You need not imagine you are applying for a job; begin by soliciting advice from whoever is in the best position to give you expert opinion and counsel. Any approach to an expert is easy if you simply inquire on the basis of "I need some advice from you, kind sir or madam." You will not be evaluated in such a situation, because you are only asking for help. Let's say you'd like to open a crafts shop in your town. Who would be most likely to know about that? Other crafts shop proprietors, crafts teachers at the schools or colleges, craft suppliers, crafts salespeople in the department stores, camp owners who specialize in crafts activities. Any expert likes to be regarded as such and finds it nearly impossible to refuse your modest request for counsel. If this sort of approach still sounds too frightening, read on.

## Start with the Friendly Natives

Psychologists have a concept for helping people overcome fears, particularly fears that intensify to the level of phobias. They call the methods *systematic desensitization*, which means exposing the afflicted person to small doses of the feared stimulus until he or she can deal with it, and then increasing the intensity of the stimulus by small increments until the feared object can be confronted successfully. In simpler terms, you can systematically desensitize yourself to personal approaches by practicing every work search inquiry on the people most friendly to you, perhaps the folks who live on your block at home or companions at your school. When you are ready for people a little less familiar, move on to complete strangers.

If you really don't want to talk to anyone at all yet, a good way to begin the work search is by tagging around with others who are making work information inquiries. Watch what they do; offer gentle participation as you feel more comfortable with the process. Let the others coach you in what they are doing.

Another way to prepare for the more difficult steps of meeting target employers face to face is to request innocuous bits of information over the phone.

> Call the information operator and ask for the telephone numbers of people you want to call. . . .
>
> Call a local department store and check on the price of something advertised.
>
> Call a radio talk show to say you like the programming and then ask a question.
>
> Call a local movie theater and ask for show times.
>
> Call the sports desk at the local newspaper and ask for the scores of the last hometown baseball, basketball, or football game.
>
> Call the library and ask the reference librarian what the population of the United States is.[41]

## Identify the Conditions That Scare You Most

As you work with systematic desensitization by building up slowly to the main event, you are starting with friendly natives and other nonthreatening people so you can have *successes* to build on. These early successes spur you on, encouraging you to go a bit further and try a little more difficult target.

You can get a sharper definition of your most feared situations by analyzing the *specific conditions* that accompany your great fear of talking. Is it a large office building that puts you off? Do you have a real aversion to men over forty who wear three-piece suits? Is the blind phone call your particular bugaboo? Perhaps you feel most edgy when you are faced with a person who talks fast and seems always in a hurry. Whatever your most feared interview conditions, it will help you to recognize them. Don't be ashamed of your special fear, just work up to it slowly by arranging the conditions so that your more comfortable settings are tackled first. If you like talking to younger people in nonoffice environments, then by all means that is the way you should begin.

## Try a Census-Type Part-Time Job

If you are weary of trying to arrange conversations with people or still feel uneasy in requesting such meetings, an alternative method is to arrange a part-time job that gives you an *excuse* for contacting target people in the world of work without having to admit you are seeking job information. Examples of this sort of job include marketing research survey work ("What brand of dish soap do you use, sir?"), census takers for the federal government, survey takers for local government offices, mail delivery people, and many others. Even if the people who answer your queries do not have sufficient time to allow you to press them about their work, this sort of experience enables you to become more familiar with the mechanics of interviewing people and allows you to demystify some of the horrors you expect to occur.

## Practice Being an Employer

A good alternative method for the faint-hearted is to get experience with being on the other side of the fence—being in the position of having to talk with another individual as though *you* were the one doing the hiring. To put this strategy into play, create a situation in which you *are* actually evaluating people for a hiring decision. Suppose you need a person to do some cleaning or yard work at your house. Place an advertisement and force yourself to interview several people for the job, even if you like the first one who comes through the door. Be alert for your feelings as the interviewer and observe carefully the behavior of the people you interview. After this sort of firsthand exposure, an information-seeking encounter or job interview may not seem so frightful the next time you are faced with it. You can deepen this experience by seeking part-time work with an employment agency if you really want to view the passing parade of job seekers in all its glory.

# Immersion Experiences

If a judicious plan of small successes does not suit you, it is likely that you are either in a hurry to arrive at the main event, so you can learn how to deal with it once and for all, or not satisfied that the early successes will lead smoothly to an eventual conquering of your aversion to live targets. In such situations, you can consider an immersion experience, one in which you expose yourself to the full strength of the stimulus you fear the most. The rationale for this approach is that you can deal most effectively if you face the beast head-on instead of trying to sneak up slowly and catch it unawares.

One such immersion experience might be a crash program. Give yourself no more than three days to meet a certain number of target people in your field of career interest. Identify before the three days begin the names and addresses of the individuals you most want to meet, and stick to your plan.

Another immersion experience you can try is to name the one person in your career field who frightens you the most, the person you believe would be the most difficult to talk to, and resolve to meet this person face to face to ask the questions that are most crucial to you. Immersion theorists say that if you survive this experience with some measure of success, you can lick anything from that point on.

A third technique is to deposit yourself in a town where you don't know anyone and have very little money, so that you must make contact with key individuals in order to obtain employment. Don't give yourself any breaks. Let the conditions of necessity force you to break the logjam of making work contacts.

# Props as Conversation Starters

Every actor or actress makes effective use of props—physical items that call attention to one's areas of interest and relate to what one is trying to say. Use props whenever you can to serve as evidence of your intentions, clues to your background, or simply objects to focus upon when warming up a conversation.

Carry a book that is relevant to your career or suggestive of your intended career field, for instance. Or carry a notebook that identifies your college or your employer, so that people recognize where you are from. Have an example of your work with you—a graphic design you have done, a computer flow chart, a product you have made—and keep it in view if that is possible to do without being obvious. You could have with you a piece of literature from the organization that interests you, and use it during your conversation ("I read here in your newsletter that . . .").

# Why Interviewers Will Treat You Right

When you seek conversation with someone for an information interview, remember that you always have three advantages that will encourage him to pay attention to you. First, he has been dying to see a fresh face. Until you have worked in an office or other environment where the same twenty faces keep popping up every morning, noon, and night, you cannot fully appreciate the delight of seeing someone new, who introduces an element of surprise, even mystery, into the same old workday. Your never having been there before is an advantage. Most people appreciate a new viewpoint and look forward to meeting a new personality.

A second advantage is that you are nonthreatening. You are probably a "safer" character than most others seen by the interviewer in the course of the day. You make no heavy demands, do not have to be courted for future favors, and have no hidden motivations. Often he will talk openly to you about problems of the organization because he knows you are not likely to spread that word around.

Third, you may have new information of interest to the person you interview. Since you have been visiting other employers of a similar kind, you probably bring news about what the competition is doing. This will endear you even if nothing else does, because most of us are more insulated than we want to be in our offices and welcome any new insights about what the others are doing.

Almost any person who has personal biases about work, strong feelings about how it should be done, and stories about what has happened in past years—that is to say, all of us—will probably regard your appearance as the most enjoyable interlude of the day. Do him a favor. Don't deprive him of the pleasure of talking about himself.

# · chapter twenty-five ·

# Zen of the Work Search

*Copernicus had no motive for misleading his fellow men as to the place of the sun in the solar system. He looked for it as honestly as a shepherd seeks a path in the mist.*
> • George Bernard Shaw
> *Man and Superman*

Our culture is predominantly a scientific one. In our eagerness to validate the power of the scientific method, we have assumed that a career field is no different from a wheat crop, an engineering problem, or the solution to an algebraic equation: it can be observed, measured, and brought under control. We then apply our optimism to the individual and compound the scientific arrogance by proposing that his or her career journey can be charted, planned, and understood in advance. Fortunately, we are learning from experience that a career is far more subtle and complicated than we had imagined.

It is too easy to graft the mentality of the Western Hemisphere onto the processes of the work search. All the convenient props for rational thinking are available. A Western mind would have us think about alternatives, weigh the pros and cons, assess probabilities, and predict outcomes. In short, Western thinkers do everything possible to impose crystalline logic and rational thought on a set of decisions and processes that may be highly illogical, unpredictable, and perhaps even impervious to rational inquiry.

Rational thinking has been so successful in solving modern-day problems—how to place human beings on the moon, how to control inventories of billions of units—that we assume such thinking can accomplish anything. We conveniently forget that rational thinking succeeds best only when the relevant variables are under our control, observable, and objective in the sense that any two observers agree about what they are seeing. We must recognize that the work search is not a highly predictable process, many of its variables are not known or observable, and certainly many of them are not subject to the individual's complete control. Hence, scientific, rational methods of inquiry may be of dubious value.

The problems of the work search are closer to the subtle, unfathomable realm of human relations than they are to the scientific realm of rational inquiry. Though we admit that scientific problems and human relations problems are different in character, we continue to believe that scientific methods can be applied to nonscientific matters.

All our efforts to impose reason on the individual ignore that life choices—career, marriage, and the like—are essentially irrational, perhaps even unconscious, acts. By attempting to introduce order into a disorderly process, we disturb a highly effective but murky process by which an individual makes life decisions.

When we talk about an interpersonal process that is as highly complicated as the work search, the intellect has severe limitations. Powers of reason have to yield ground to other forms of inquiry. In short, until we can demonstrate that Western rationality explains work search behavior in a way that illuminates our career decisions, we must allow for the possibility that Eastern modes of thought have something to teach us. This is what the Zen master D. T. Suzuki has to say about the intellect:

> Let the intellect alone, it has usefulness in its proper sphere, but let it not interfere with the flowing of the life-stream. . . . The fact of flowing must under no circumstances be arrested or meddled with, for the moment your hands are dipped into it, its transparency is disturbed, it ceases to reflect your image which you have had from the very beginning and will continue to have to the end of time.[42]

Suzuki tells the story of a son who asks his father to teach him how to be an expert burglar. The father says nothing until one night he takes the son to a house to be burgled, goes to the attic, locks the unsuspecting son in a trunk, and then leaves the house. The son devises a way to escape the trunk and the house, returns, and asks the father breathlessly why he did that. The father replies: "Be not offended, my son. Just tell me how you got out of it." When the son describes his adventures in the house, the father says: "There you are, you have learned the art of burglary."[43] "The idea of the [burglary] story is to demonstrate the futility of verbal instruction and conceptual presentation," Suzuki says. If we apply this idea to our views about the work search, we may conclude that conceptualization and the intellect have no place in our learning. In fact, this entire book would seem to disturb "the flowing of the life-stream." It is true that this book deals heavily in the description of concepts. Nevertheless, I feel that the skills approach to the work search is compatible with Eastern views because these skills are offered to illuminate the search process rather than proscribe it, to give you ways of approaching it rather than telling you a specific set of rules that must be obeyed.

These skills liberate you from the bonds of immediate decision making by showing you ways of gathering data that render decision making unnecessary. As you use the skills, you may discover that tentative and even more enduring decisions occur naturally in the context of your activity. This is the Zen way.

The skills approach departs from scientific thinking and rational models in its refusal to encourage closure or resolution. Rational models of career choice encourage measurements, tests, or other quantitative data that permit an individual to assess work aspirations in numerical terms and to make decisions based upon measured outcomes; "realistic" choice making based on probabilities of career success derived from supply-and-demand data and predictors of future performance; and judgments made on the basis of summing a person's past experience ("You have twelve years of experience in this line of work; therefore you should . . .").

Throughout this book, rational models of career choice are rejected in favor of personal insights and feelings, however irrational they may seem on the surface; I have stressed the discovery of meaning in your unconscious behavior, the events toward which your life stream flows, and focused on your responses to individual experiences and the identification of new insights about these experiences.

> Zen proposes its solution by directly appealing to facts of personal experience and not to book knowledge. The nature of one's own being where apparently rages the struggle between the finite and the infinite is to be grasped by a higher faculty than the intellect . . .
>
> By personal experience it is meant to get at the fact at first hand, and not through any intermediary, whatever this may be. Its favourite analogy is: to point at the moon, a finger is needed, but woe to those who take the finger for the moon.[44]

The purpose of this book is to describe skills you can use to maximize *experience* in the work search and minimize the need for intellectual and analytical thinking. You are more likely to understand yourself and what you want by direct experience (and a review of your past experiences) than by making arbitrary choices based on criteria external to your own feelings.

By anyone's external standards, my friend Julie would never make it as a dancer. She was a little overweight, didn't practice more than an hour or two a day, and did not possess the natural grace that Balanchine or any other master choreographer was looking for. Her parents urged a shift to the health sciences, her boyfriend tried to interest her in business, and her friends just gave up. Julie continued to hang around dance studios, took lessons even when she could not afford them comfortably, and read books about dance in her many idle hours. One day it dawned on Julie that dancers could help people who could never become dancers themselves, that it could serve as a form of therapy in addition to being an art form. Julie flowed with the idea, discovered a tiny band of people who were just beginning to call what they were doing "dance therapy," and today is one of the first hundred registered professionals in this emerging field. Julie followed her instincts, not what people advised for her.

Suzuki encourages a semiconscious or unconscious flow toward those people and activities that feel comfortable for you. He encourages a "let it happen" mentality and suggests strongly that there is greater wisdom in trusting your inner instincts than in *thinking* about what you should do. "The master [Tennō Dōgo] said, 'If you want to see, see right at once. When you begin to think you miss the point.' "45

## Direction by Indirection

As nearly as I can determine from applying Zen concepts to what is essentially a Western process—the formalized search for better work—Suzuki and other Zen masters would advise us to focus our efforts by not focusing them, to work at the task by not working at it, to organize our energies by not organizing them. Are these senseless riddles that only confuse you? I believe Zen ideas have some promise for us, and that they can be translated into our work search language as follows.

First, let go of judgments. Begin by forcing yourself not to assign external ratings to the work possibilities you explore. If a job pays $20,000 and all your friends say it is a good opportunity, forget that. Explore without making judgments or assigning ratings. Let yourself experience how you feel about the work. Tim Gallwey's brilliant book about the applications of Zen principles to teaching tennis urges a close consideration of the word *abandon*:

> "Abandon" is a good word to describe what happens to a tennis player who feels he has nothing to lose. He stops caring about the outcome and plays all out. This is the true meaning of detachment. . . . It is caring, yet not caring; it is *effortless effort*. It happens when one lets go of attachment to the results of one's actions and allows the increased energy to come to bear on the action itself. In the language of karma yoga, this is called action without attachment to the fruits of action, and ironically when this state is achieved the results are the best possible.[46]

You will note this principle of deferred judgment is echoed in the section that explains how to use creative brainstorming (see Chapter 4). Osborn's view that the best things happen when the mind surrenders its power to evaluate is essentially a Zen idea.

Second, try by not trying too hard. Zen assumes that the best things occur when you turn off your conscious mind and let the unconscious take over. Hard effort is usually associated with hard thought; Zen masters insist that such effort intrudes upon the life stream and inhibits the ability to act.

> As soon as we reflect, deliberate, and conceptualize, the original unconscious is lost and a thought interferes. . . . The arrow is off the string but does not fly straight to the target, nor does the target stand where it is. Calculation, which is miscalculation, sets in.[47]

> Perhaps this is why it is said that great poetry is born in silence. Great music and art are said to arise from the quiet depths of the unconscious.[48]

All this means that your collective unconscious has stored considerable knowledge about what you want in your work, and much of your work search effort should be arranged so that you let the unconscious have its way. Grafting mechanical procedures or formulas onto your instinctive (unconscious) pursuit of compatible work will probably disrupt the process.

A Zen master once asked an audience of Westerners what they thought was the most important word in the English language. After giving his listeners a chance to think about such favorite words as love, faith, and so on, he said, "No, it's a three-letter word; it's the word 'let.'" Let it be. Let it happen. Though sometimes employed to mean a kind of passiveness, these phrases actually refer to a deep acceptance of the fundamental process inherent in life. . . . In the more general sense it means faith in the fundamental order and goodness of life, both human and natural. . . . [Let] problems be solved in the unconscious mind as well as by straining with conscious effort.[49]

Third, remember that insights occur at the times you least expect them. It was Pasteur who said: "Chance favors the prepared mind." The more you have been trying to decide what to do about your work, the more likely you are to find a solution when you are least prepared for it, if you let your unconscious roam freely.

I was struggling with my preparation for a talk to a group of counselors and made little progress when I sat down to think about it. Time overcame me, and I had to depart by car for the conference site four hundred miles away. En route, I parked in New York City, had my car towed away, spent several exhausting hours tracking it down, learned that I didn't have sufficient cash to rescue the car, and had to trundle my belongings to a late-night bus bound for the conference site. By the time I plopped into a bus seat, I was physically drained and, I reasoned, mentally exhausted as well. During the four-hour bus ride, I discovered my thoughts falling into a most coherent pattern and was prepared to talk the next morning at half-past eight.

The unconscious picks its own times and places. Some time ago a group of research chemists were asked where and how they got their scientific ideas. Here are some of their answers:

"While dodging automobiles across Park Row and Broadway, New York."

"Sunday in church as the preacher was announcing the text."

"At three o'clock in the morning . . ."

"In the morning when shaving . . ."

"Just before and just after an attack of gout . . ."

"Invariably at night after retiring for sleep . . ."

"While resting and loafing on the beach . . ."

"While sitting at my desk doing nothing, thinking about other matters..."

"After a month's vacation, as I was dressing after a bath in the sea."[50]

So, prepare your mind for the task at hand by reading about the skills described in this book and then let your unconscious take over; it will orchestrate the process, put the pieces together, and provide the insights you are seeking in the moments you are least prepared for them.

Fourth, notice clues in your tiny experiences. As you flow into your work search, assume that every event has meaning for you, perhaps especially events that seem to have no meaning at all. When you review your broad areas of experience—major field of academic study, the job you have now, the project you completed last year—you will have a marked tendency to overlook the small events, the tiny ones that contain the clues with deeper meaning.

An acquaintance of mine spent many years after his graduation from college trying to figure out what to do with himself. He ignored his engineering major because it didn't excite him enough; he refused his father's offer to enter the family business for a similar reason; he turned down graduate school offers because he had no idea what to study. His frustration came out indirectly with his family; he fell into the habit of criticizing their speech, grammar, and spelling in family letters. All concerned dismissed his behavior as the angry rantings of an unemployed, unmotivated loafer, until finally it dawned on Jim that he unconsciously focused upon *words* in all his idle interactions; these tiny events in which he released frustration revealed an important clue to his future work—he became a copy editor at a publishing house and is prospering in that work today.

What are the tiniest experiences you can focus upon in your daily life? Can you discover any meaning in them? Do you like to plant the garden a certain way? (How do you arrange tasks?) Do you have a preference for the color green? (Do you like working with money, outdoor life?) Do you accomplish your best thinking standing up? (What occupations does this suggest for you? Teacher?) Do you frequently read maps incorrectly? (Do you prefer a sense of adventure, of not knowing where you are going?)

# How to Apply Zen Principles

The foregoing discussion suggests that you cannot apply Zen ideas to your work search except by trying *not* to apply them, that you will be penalized for any conscious effort, that thinking is disqualified. Certainly Zen principles caution you to minimize the extent to which conscious thought interferes with the flow of your life stream. However, I believe that certain conscious processes are implied and that you can reorient your mental activity to take better advantage of your unconscious knowledge of yourself, in the following ways.

**Think of Pictures •** Instead of focusing on words (job titles, job descriptions) or numbers (salary, number of people supervised), use your imagination to envision scenes and situations where you would like to work. Pictures are more powerful than words and can tell you a great deal about what you desire. When you picture yourself at the peak of your capabilities, what do you see? Do you see yourself wandering around your room alone, thinking of solutions to difficult problems? Do you see yourself standing in front of a crowd, persuading your audience of an idea? Are you surrounded by children, teaching them, nurturing them? Are you orchestrating a process even though no one can see you? Do you imagine yourself drinking great draughts of ale, laughing into the night?

**Defer Judgment •** Every authority on creative thinking (Osborn, DeBono, Crawford, and others) insists that the best ideas occur when a person is not inhibited by evaluation or judgment of goodness or badness. Thus, Zen insists that the mind roam freely, without concern about popular opinion, judgments of relatives, or the wisdom of one's meanderings. Creative ideas about work possibilities occur more frequently in an environment of *acceptance*.

**Focus on the Present •** Decisions made for tomorrow require that you pay close attention to how you feel today. Perversely, you may think too much about the past ("What have I done before, and how should this relate to what I do next?") or the future ("If I do this, what will happen five years from now?"). Such backward and forward thinking can help you avoid pitfalls, but it can also seriously inhibit your sense of risk taking, your willingness to respond to what you feel is right for you now. Zen masters would persuade us that the present is our only reality.

**Consult Your Senses** • The intellect has its particular way of judging the worth of a career plan; the body and its visceral senses have other ways of viewing the situation. The next time that you explore a career possibility, ask your body whether it feels comfortable. Do you tighten up when you are at the work site? Do you feel in the hands, abdomen, and back of the neck that this place and these people are right for you? The senses have a lot of information for you, if you will allow it to be presented.

**Work and Play Together** • A powerful test of compatibility between you and your career is the extent to which you can view it as *both* work and play. You can view *work* as all effort that you expend toward a set of desirable outcomes, while *play* is an inherently enjoyable activity, done for its own sake, without concern about outcomes. The most intrinsically rewarding work has elements of play within it, so that you can look forward to what you are doing on a moment-to-moment basis in addition to anticipating the ultimate rewards.

What educator Bill Harper has to say about play expresses the attitude I have tried to communicate about how people should work and try to get better work:

> Play, I think, is very close to being an innate characteristic of man, and for that reason as long as man is man, it is never going to be forgotten or abolished. But there are times when we get very grim and serious, and the whole style of society tends to make it harder for people to play. When this happens—and we are in that kind of period—people languish, become spiritually spindly as they might physically if they did not have sufficient or proper food. I think play is an essential element for spiritual well-being.[51]

# Notes

**1)** Louis E. Raths, Merrill Harmin, and Sidney Simon, *Values and Teaching* (Columbus, Ohio: Merrill, 1966), p. 6.

**2)** Howard E. Figler, *PATH: A Career Workbook for Liberal Arts Students* (Cranston, R.I.: Carroll Press, 1975), pp. 77-79.

**3)** Sidney B. Simon, Howard Kirschenbaum, and Leland Howe, *Values Clarification* (New York: Hart, 1972).

**4)** Ralph Mattson and Arthur Miller (eds.), *The Truth About You* (Old Tappan, N.J.: Revell Press, 1977), pp. 34-46.

**5)** Merrill Harmin, Howard Kirschenbaum, and Sidney B. Simon, *Clarifying Values Through Subject Matter* (Minneapolis: Winston Press, 1973), pp. 32-34.

**6)** Sherod Miller, Elam W. Nunnally, and Daniel B. Wackman, *Alive and Aware* (Minneapolis: Interpersonal Communication Programs, 1975), p. 39.

**7)** Joseph Luft, *Of Human Interaction* (Palo Alto: National Press Books, 1969), p. 13. The Johari Window gets its name from the first names of its inventors, Joseph Luft and Harry Ingham.

**8)** Sidney A. Fine, "Nature of Skill: Implications for Education and Training," *Proceedings*, 75th Annual Convention, American Psychological Association, 1967.

**9)** Ibid., pp. 365-366.

**10)** Edward DeBono, *Lateral Thinking* (New York: Harper & Row, 1970), p. 14.

**11)** Alex F. Osborn, *Your Creative Power* (New York: Scribner, 1972), p. 269.

**12)** Alex F. Osborn, *Applied Imagination* (New York: Scribner, 1953), p. 284.

**13)** Adapted from DeBono, *Lateral Thinking*, pp. 91-99, 131-140, 167-174, 193-205; and from Osborn, *Applied Imagination*, p. 212-214, 217, 261-262.

**14)** *The New York Times*, May 17, 1977.

**15)** Ernst Jacobi, *Writing at Work* (Rochelle Park, N.J.: Hayden, 1976), p. 20.

**16)** John C. Crystal and Richard N. Bolles, *Where Do I Go from Here with My Life?* (New York: Seabury Press, 1974), p. 188.

**17)** Stanley Milgram, "The Small-World Problem," *Psychology Today*, May 1967, pp. 290-299.

**18)** Mark Granovetter, *Getting a Job* (Cambridge, Mass.: Harvard University Press, 1974), p. 33.

**19)** Ibid.

**20)** Austin Marshall, *How to Get a Better Job* (New York: Hawthorn Books, 1964), p. 55.

**21)** Lee Ash and Denis Lorenz (eds.), *Subject Collections: A Guide to Special Book Collections in Libraries* (New York: Bowker, 1967).

**22)** Marshall, *How to Get a Better Job*, p. 49.

**23)** Theodor Reik, *Listening with the Third Ear* (Moonachie, N.J.: Pyramid Publications, 1972).

**24)** Lawrence M. Brammer, *The Helping Relationship* (Englewood Cliffs, N.J.: Prentice-Hall, 1973), pp. 81-82.

**25)** Gerard Egan, *The Skilled Helper* (Monterey, Calif.: Brooks/Cole, 1975), pp. 65-66.

**26)** Ibid., p. 69.

**27)** Paul J. Moses, *The Voice of Neurosis* (New York: Grune & Stratton, 1957).

**28)** Alfred Benjamin, *The Helping Interview* (Boston: Houghton-Mifflin, 1974), p. 67.

**29)** Ibid., p. 69.

**30)** Ibid., p. 80.

**31)** Gordon Bower and Sharon Bower, *Asserting Yourself* (Reading, Mass.: Addison-Wesley, 1976), p. 60.

**32)** Philip G. Zimbardo, *Shyness: What It Is and What to Do About It* (Reading, Mass.: Addison-Wesley, 1977), pp. 13-14.

**33)** Ibid., p. 5.

**34)** Jacobi, *Writing at Work*, p. 4.

**35)** J. Mitchell Morse, "The Age of 'Logophobia,'" *Chronicle of Higher Education*, May 16, 1977, p. 40.

**36)** Thomas S. Franco, "In Answer to Your Ad ..." *Public Relations Journal*, February 1977, p. 24.

**37)** Osborn, *Your Creative Power*, p. 269.

**38)** "Drop that Match," *National Lampoon*, June 1977.

**39)** Richard N. Bolles, *Newletter About Life/Work Planning*, March 1977.

**40)** Adapted from Figler, *PATH*, pp. 145-146.

**41)** Zimbardo, *Shyness*, p. 175.

**42)** Daisetz T. Suzuki, *Essays in Zen Buddhism* (New York: Grove Press, 1949), p. 19.

**43)** Daisetz T. Suzuki, *Zen and Japanese Culture* (New York: Pantheon Books, 1959), pp. 9-10.

**44)** Suzuki, *Essays in Zen Buddhism*, pp. 1-19.

**45)** Suzuki, *Zen and Japanese Culture*, p. 13.

**46)** W. Timothy Gallwey, *The Inner Game of Tennis* (New York: Random House, 1974), p. 138.

**47)** Daisetz T. Suzuki, *in foreword* to Eugen Herrigel, *Zen and the Art of Archery* (New York: Random House, 1971).

**48)** Gallwey, *Inner Game of Tennis*, p. 31.

**49)** Ibid., p. 135.

**50)** Rudolf Flesch, *The Art of Clear Thinking* (New York: Barnes & Noble, 1951), p. 146.

**51)** Bill Harper, quoted in Bill Gilbert, "Play," *Sports Illustrated*, October 13, 1975, p. 90.

# Selected Annotated Bibliography

## Chapter 1
### Values

Figler, Howard E. *PATH: A Career Workbook for Liberal Arts Students—Revised.* Cranston, R.I.: Carroll Press, 1979.
Offers an integrated sequence of exercises for assessing your work-related values, attitudes toward work, and ways that play correlates with work.

Miller, Arthur, and Mattson, Ralph. *The Truth About You.* Old Tappan, N.J.: Roselle Park Press, 1977.
States the importance of key motivators in your career and explains how they can be detected through close scrutiny of your life experiences.

Simon, Sidney B.; Kirschenbaum, Howard; and Howe, Leland. *Values Clarification.* New York: Hart, 1972.
Presents a diverse collection of exercises and strategies for tapping your values, preferences, areas of enjoyment, and feelings about what is worth doing in your life.

## Chapter 2
### Feelings

Miller, Sherod; Nunnally, Elam W.; and Wackman, Daniel B. *Alive and Aware.* Minneapolis: Interpersonal Communication Programs, 1975.
Outlines ways you can better understand your relationships with other people. These insights will help you to clarify your career expectations, since many of your career goals derive from how you feel in the company of certain kinds of individuals.

# Chapter 3
## Skills

Bolles, Richard N. *What Color Is Your Parachute?* Berkeley, Calif.: Ten Speed Press, 1976.
Describes a clear philosophy for the self-initiated career search, in which you learn that your chief skills are a central element in this strategy; the better you know and can talk about your skills, the more effective your search will be.

Lathrop, Richard. *Who's Hiring Who.* Reston, Va.: Reston Press, 1976.
Explains how your chief skills can be summarized for a prospective employer in a "qualification brief" once you have researched the employer and know what skills he or she needs.

# Chapter 4
## Creativity

Adams, James L. *Conceptual Blockbusting.* San Francisco: Freeman, 1974.
A guide to thinking more creatively by breaking conceptual habits. Focuses on perceptual, cultural, emotional, and intellectual blocks.

Biondi, Angelo. *The Creative Process.* Buffalo: DOK Publishers, 1972.
Reviews the major elements of creative thought processes and suggests ways your creative powers can be enhanced.

Figler, Howard E. *PATH: A Career Workbook for Liberal Arts Students—Revised.* Cranston, R.I.: Carroll Press, 1978.
Explains and gives many examples of how your values and skills can be combined creatively into several careers you probably had never imagined before.

Osborn, Alex F. *Applied Imagination*, 3rd rev. ed. New York: Scribner, 1963.
Gives hundreds of examples of creative thinkers and how they got their ideas; also includes an outline of the nine fundamental creative processes and demonstrates how you can nurture them.

## Chapter 5
## Risking

Coleman, John R. *Blue Collar Journal.* Philadelphia: Lippincott, 1974.
Tells the story of a college president who worked for a year as a construction laborer, sandwich maker, and garbageman. The tale illustrates the necessity of looking outside your expected role when you are considering a change of career.

## Chapter 8
## Prospect List

Jackson, Tom; and Mayleas, Davidyne. *The Hidden Job Market.* New York: Quadrangle, 1976.
Explains how your simplest forms of job market research involve combing numerous publications that are widely available to anyone.

## Chapter 9
## Personal Referral Network

Bolles, Richard N. *What Color Is Your Parachute?* Berkeley, Calif.: Ten Speed Press, 1976.
Tells clearly why you will benefit more from your own personal referral network than from traditional sources of help in the career search.

Crystal, John C., and Bolles, Richard N. *Where Do I Go from Here with My Life?* New York: Seabury Press, 1974.
Gives a detailed plan for building and expanding your network of personal contacts through use of systematic targeting. Your geographical preferences, personal goals, and chief skills dictate which targets to include on your list.

## Chapter 11
## Printed Material

Marshall, Austin. *How to Get a Better Job.* New York: Hawthorn Books, 1964.

Details the major sources of printed information you can use to research a job or career and tells how to use them to the greatest advantage.

Todd, Alden. *Finding Facts Fast.* New York: Morrow, 1972.
Shows methods and materials used by librarians, scholars, reporters, and detectives to get information with relative ease. Tells how you can use printed sources to research your target employer before you are interviewed.

## Chapter 12
## Inquiring Reporter

Bolles, Richard N. *What Color Is Your Parachute?* Berkeley, Calif.: Ten Speed Press, 1976.
Gives a detailed rationale for using the field survey method in career search. Tells you how to use the field surveys during all stages of your search.

Figler, Howard E. *PATH: A Career Workbook for Liberal Arts Students—Revised.* Cranston, R.I.: Carroll Press, 1978.
Includes a format of questions to ask when you are researching a target employer.

## Chapter 15
## Listening

Egan, Gerard. *The Skilled Helper.* Monterey, Calif.: Brooks/ Cole, 1975.
Clarifies the essential qualities of a good listener—the verbal, nonverbal, and emotional components of fully attending to the messages of another person. You can use these listening skills to improve your communication in any formal or informal career-related interview.

## Chapter 16
## Questioning

Benjamin, Alfred. *The Helping Interview*, 2nd ed. Boston: Houghton-Mifflin, 1974.
Explains ways asking a question can be used effectively and ways questions can be misused. You can learn ways to use questioning to maximum advantage in your career search, types of questioning, and common errors.

## Chapter 17
### Assertiveness

Alberti, Robert E.; and Emmons, Michael L. *Your Perfect Right.* San Francisco: Impact Publishers, 1974.
Distinguishes assertiveness from aggressiveness and explains how you can build assertive responses into your everyday life. It shows that you need not be especially gregarious or have a dominant personality in order to be assertive.

Zimbardo, Philip G. *Shyness: What It Is and What to Do About It.* Reading, Mass.: Addison-Wesley, 1977.
Reveals the roots of your shyness and gives many methods for overcoming it. You can use these ideas to become fully assertive with contacts, employers, and others in your career search.

## Chapter 18
### Self-Disclosure

Zimbardo, Philip G. *Shyness: What It Is and What to Do About It.* Reading, Mass.: Addison-Wesley, 1977.
Explains the factors that may inhibit you from talking about yourself and recommends many ways to overcome being self-conscious. These methods will help you to talk easily about your skills, values, and relevant life experiences during career interviews.

## Chapter 19
### Writing

Jacobi, Ernst. *Writing at Work.* Rochelle Park, N.J.: Hayden, 1976.
Outlines and explains the numerous subskills and self-attitudes that characterize clear and readable writing. You can apply the many principles and examples to your communication with prospective employers.

Strunk, William, Jr., and White, E.B. *The Elements of Style,* New York: Macmillan, 1972.
Offers the last word on the written word and gives rules and advice regarding syntax, grammar, composition, style, us-

age, form. You should habitually consult this reference when you are unsure about what you have just written.

## Chapter 23
### Interim Jobs

Terkel, Studs. *Working.* New York: Pantheon Books, 1974. Gives personal interviews with the entire panorama of the working world, revealing glimpses of people and how they feel about their jobs. As you tour this book, you will generate ideas for interim jobs that can afford you broad access to career alternatives.

# Index

Academic coursework and partici-
    pant observation, 155
Advertising space salesperson, 245
Age and career search, 33–34
Aggression versus assertiveness,
    189, 190–91
*Alive and Aware* (Miller et al.), 56
Alumni directories, 117
*American Men and Women of Sci-
    ence*, 142
Annual reports, 138, 141
Applications, job, 207, 208
Apprenticeship, 246
Arbitrating skills, 234
*Asserting Yourself* (Bower and
    Bower), 189
Assertiveness, 166, 188–97
    explanation of, 13, 188–90
    on the job, 196–97
    passivity, aggressiveness, and,
        190–91
    rules of, 193–94
    self-putdowns, 194–95
    shy people showing, 195–96
    in the work search, 191–92
Assignment change, desire for, 19
Attack posture at an interview, 166,
    181–82

Ball parks, hanging around, 127

Bars, hanging around, 126
Bartenders, 128, 244
Beauticians, 128
Biographical directories, 142
*Blue Collar Journal*, 247
Body movements, listening and,
    174, 175, 176, 191
Bolles, Richard, 3, 122, 240
*Books in Print*, 140
Boredom with your work, 17
    risk versus, 93, 94, 96
    security traded for, 42
Bower, Gordon, 189
Bower, Sharon, 189
Bradley, Bill, 75
Bragging, 203
Brainstorming session, 226–27
Budget management, 233
Bus drivers, 128
*Business Week*, 140
Bus tokens for support group, 224

Cab drivers, 128, 244
Career ailment, *see* Diagnosing
        your career ailment
Career search:
    assertiveness in the, 191–92
    attitude toward, 223–24
    blessings of, 6–8
    career skills and, *see* Career skills

Career search (*cont'd*)
 conclusion, 37–38
 as a continuous process, 9, 26–28
 as detective work, 25
 as exploring, not hunting, 23–24
 as fun, 23, 27
 as hard work, 5–6
 key assumptions of, 23–26
 luck and, 27–28
 multiple skills as important in, 24–25
 personal style and strengths and, 28–33
 self-directed, 2–3
 stop resisting the, 33–37
 take-charge philosophies, 2
 with time on your side, 25–26
 zen of, 257–65
Career seminars and courses, 232
Career skills, 3–5, 8–23
 chart, 11
 defining of, 9
 diagnosing your career ailment and, 15–23
 everyone's need for, 3–5
 list and explanation of, 11–14
 *see also specific skills*
Census taker, 244, 254
Challenge, need for greater, 17
Chambers of Commerce, 238
Chatterer at an interview, 165
Church committees, hanging around, 127
*Clarifying Values Through Subject Matter* (Harmin et al.), 48
Clerk, retail store, 244
Coleman, John R., 247
Communication skills, 10, 13, 70, 161–217, 234
 assertiveness, 13, 188–97
 chart of, 11
 listening, 13, 170–79
 questioning, 13, 180–87

 self-disclosure, 13, 198–205
 writing, 13, 206–17, 234
 *see also* Interviews
Compulsiveness, 29, 66, 67
 risking versus, 96
Conductor, commuter train, 244
Confronting personality, 66, 67
Consultants, 246
Conventions, professional, 135, 136
Contacts, personal, *see* Personal referral network
Cook, short-order, 245
Coordinating skills, 234
Counterpuncher at an interview, 165
Courthouses and courtrooms, hanging around, 126
Creativity, 80–91
 as divergent thinking, 83–86
 explanation of, 12, 81–83
 questions to ask to stimulate ideas, 87–89
 -stimulating exercises, 89–91
 values and skills brought together by, 81
 wrongheaded thinking and, 83–86
Crystal, John C., 122
Curiosity, 159

Data blabbermouth at an interview, 166
Deadlines:
 ability to cope with, 233
 goal setting and, 99–100
DeBono, Edward, 85, 264
Detail, being persnickety about, 66, 67
Detective skills, 10, 12, 29–30, 105–59
 chart of, 11
 employer's perspective, seeing it from, 110–12

personal referral network, 12, 120–30
prospect list, 12, 113–19
work detective:
  advantages of, over crime detective, 107–108
  getting started, 109–10
Diagnosing your career ailment, 15–23
  "I don't want to change my job, just my assignment," 19
  "I have been in school and have little work experience," 18–19
  "I have tried everything," 21–22
  "I'll want to move eventually," 16–17
  "I'm a late entry returning to the work force," 20
  "I'm bored, I need a challenge," 17
  "I'm panicked," 15–16
  "I'm trapped," 22–23
Diplomat at an interview, the inoffensive, 166
Directories:
  alumni, 117
  biographical, 142
  employer, 116–17, 138
  Polk's city, 242
  of professional organizations, 139, 142
Directory of Professional and Trade Associations, 117, 139
Displays as evidence of skills, 236

Egan, Gerard, 174
Employment agency interviewer, 245
Employer's perspective, taking the, 110–12, 163–64, 254, 256
Encouragement, lack of, 37
Eventual job change, 16–17

Excuses for avoiding the career search, 33–37
  age, 33–34
  alternative work might be worse, 37
  being a complainer, 35–36
  belief in fate, 35
  fear of rejection, 35
  fear of shaking things up, 36–37
  it doesn't hurt enough, 36
  lack of encouragement, 37
  lack of skills, 34
  lack of time, 34–35
  nothing may turn up, 37
  security in present job, 34
Extracurricular activities, 231–32

Fate, belief in, 35
Feelings, 55–59, 174
  affect of, on career search, 57–58
  as barometers of values, 57
  explanation of, 12
  -identification exercises, 58–59
  images and, 56
  range of, 56
  versus content, 55
Fine, Sidney A., 68–69
Follow-up letters, 239
Food for support group, 224
Forecasting abilities, 30–31
Friends, see Personal referral network; Support group
Frost, Robert, 93

Gallwey, Tim, 261
Geographical area, selecting a, 116, 237–38
  see also Remote control
Goals and goal setting, 98–103
  deadlines, 99–100
  explanation of, 12
  getting perspective, 98–99, 115
  goal statement, 99, 101, 237
  intermediate, 100–101

Goals and goal setting (*cont'd*)
  intermediate behavior, 102
  measuring results, 102–103
  outlandish, 86
  resources needed, 102
  sequence of behavior to reach,
    101–103
  strategy and, 101–102
  timetable for, 102
Golf caddie, 245
Grammar, 213
Granovetter, Mark, 124–25
Gregariousness, 29
Group job hunting, 227–29

Handyman, 245
Harmin, Merrill, 42, 48
Harper, Bill, 265
Hawthorne, Nathaniel, 199
Hidden job market, 2, 112, 114, 147
Historical societies, 142
Howe, Leland, 45
Human relations skills, 70

Ideas:
  outlandish, 86
  questions to ask to stimulate,
    87–89
Imaginativeness, 31–32
  *see also* Creativity
Information interview, *see* Inquiring
    reporter, information inter-
    view
In-house newspapers and maga-
    zines, 141
In-person contact, long-distance
    career search and, 238, 240
Inquiring reporter, 143–53
  explanation of, 12–13
  information interview, 144–53,
    157
    agenda for, 149
    for background research, 145–
      47
    guidelines for, 149–50

how to obtain, 146, 150–52
logistics of, 148
to meet target employers,
  147–49
time and setting for, 153
types of questions to ask at,
  149–50
other people of interest to interview, 152
Interim job, 243–48
  career-related, 245–46
  criteria of, 243
  explanation of, 14, 243
  how long to stay at, 247
  unrelated to career goals,
    244–45
  in your work history, 247
Intermediate contacts, 122–24
Intermediate goals, 100
Interview skills, 7, 70, 234
  *see also* Communication skills;
    Inquiring reporter; Interviews
Interviews:
  formal job, 143–44, 145, 146,
    163-69
    demystifying the, 164
    hidden questions, 168–69
    interviewee's questions at, *see*
      Questions and questioning
    from interviewer's viewpoint,
      163–64, 254, 256
    listening at, *see* Listening
    personal chemistry and,
      166–67, 168–69
    practicing for, in everyday situ-
      ations, 164–65
    questions typically asked at,
      167–68
    self-disclosure at, *see* Self-dis-
      closure
    styles that don't work at,
      165–66
  information, 144–53
    agenda for, 149

for background research,
145–47
guidelines for, 149–50
how to obtain, 150–52
logistics of, 148
to meet target employers,
147–49
time and setting for, 153
types of questions to ask at,
149–50
Investment clubs, hanging around,
127
Irrelevant data, 85
*I* statements, 177

Johari Window, 64

Kirschenbaum, Howard, 45, 48

Language of career matters, rigidity
of, 84
Late entry into work force, 20
Lateral thinking, 85
*Lateral Thinking* (DeBono), 85
Letters:
business, 207, 214–15
follow-up, 239
long-distance job search and,
238–39
personal, 207–17
fantasy, 210
to friends, 209–10
getting personal, 208–209
note from admirer, 211
portfolio, 211
sample, 215–17
thank-you notes, 211
to yourself, 210
Librarians, 129, 138–39
Libraries, 116, 138–39, 141
*Life on the Run* (Bradley), 75
*Life/Work Planning* (Bolles), 3
Listening, 32, 170–79
allowing silence, 177
checking for meaning, 178

distinguishing content from feeling, 176
effectively, ways of, 176–78
exercises, 178–79
explanation of, 13, 170–71,
172–73
fake, 172
giving encouragement, 177
levels of, 173–74
nonverbal communication and,
174, 175, 176, 191
noticing body movements, 174,
175, 176, 191
paraphrasing, 177
using *I* statements, 177
to the voice, 174, 176
*Literary Market Place*, 117
Local newspapers, 141–42
Local societies, information from,
140
Long-distance work search, *see* Remote control
Loudness, 66, 67

Magazines, 140
regional, 242
Mail carrier, 245
Managing skills, 234
Market analysis, 232–33
Marketing research interviewer, 244
Materials for support group, 224
Mattson, Ralph, 46
Methodical worker, 66, 67
Milgram, Stanley, 123
Miller, Arthur, 46
Miller, Sherod, 56
Modesty, 60–61, 65, 198
Modulation, voice, 187
*Money* magazine, 140
Morse, J. Mitchell, 212
Moses, Paul J., 176
Moving to target area, 241
Museum guard, 245

Negotiating skills, 234
Newspapers:
  business, 140
  in-house, 141
  local, 141–42
  subscriptions, 241–42
  out-of-town, 241–42
*New York Times Index*, 140, 141
Nonverbal communication, 174, 175, 176, 191
Nosiness, 66, 67
Nunnally, Elam W., 56

Objectives, setting, 227
Observativeness, 32–33
Offbeat personality, 66, 68
On-site visit to organization, 135, 155
Opinion poll interviewer, 244
Organization chart, 141
Organizing skills, 234
Osborn, Alex F., 86, 226, 261, 264
Outlandish goals, 86

Paige, Satchel, 98
Panic, feeling of, 15–16
Paraphrasing, listening and, 177
Participant observation, 136, 154–59
  explanation of, 13, 135
  how it aids career search, 157–58
  how to be skillful at, 159
  levels of, 155–57
Part-time jobs, 156–57, 158
Passivity, aggression, and assertiveness, 190–91
Pasteur, Louis, 262
Periodicals, 140
  regional, 242
Personal chemistry at an interview, 166–67, 168–69
Personal letters, *see* Letters, personal
Personal projects, 155

Personal referral network, 6, 114, 120–30, 133, 135
  best places to hang around, 126–27
  categories of people you should befriend, 127–29
  explanation of, 12
  exercises for developing, 129–30
  how to acquire a, 125–26
  "I don't know anybody" blues, 121–22
  intermediate contacts, 122–24
  to obtain information interview, 150–52
  organizing your "luck," 122
  people in high places, 124–25
  proceeding slowly, 127
  taking full advantage of, 124
  unexpected contacts, 122
Personal style and strengths, 28–33, 66–68
  compulsiveness, 29, 66, 67
  forecasting abilities, 30–31
  gregariousness, 29
  imaginativeness, 31–32
  at an interview, 165–66
  observativeness, 32–33
  persuasiveness, 30
  systematicness, 31
  verbal abilities, 33
  *see also* Self-disclosures; Skills
Personnel experts, 26
Person-on-the-street role, assuming the, 159
Persuasiveness, 30
Photographer's helper, 245
Planning skills, 70
Playing dumb, 159
Poise at interview, 169
Policemen, 128
Polk's city directories, 242
Portfolios, 211, 236
Printed materials, 134, 137–42, 157

benefits of studying, 138
explanation of, 12
in libraries, 138–39, 141
long-distance search and, 239, 240, 241–42
on occupational field, 139–40
on specific organization, 134, 141–42
on specific people, 142
Products as evidence of skills, 236
Professional organizations:
directory of, 117, 139
information from, 139–40
joining, 140
Programs, 236
Prospect list, 113–119, 241
explanation of, 12
geographical area, selecting a, 116
hidden job market, 2, 112, 114, 147
-identification exercise, 118–19
jobs created on your initiative, 113
kinds of organizations, identifying the, 116
obvious and less obvious prospects, 114–15
reasons not to limit, 113–14
sampling widely, importance of, 117–18
specific organizations:
finding information about, 116–17
narrowing down to, 116
strategy for, 115–116
Public opinion as information source, 134
Public relations office of specific employer:
information from, 117, 141
making requests from, 194
Public relations skills, 233

Public Relations Society of America, 212
Public speaking skills, 234
Questions and questioning, 180–87
answerable, 183
to ask at information interview, 149–50
curiosity, 185
double, 185
explanation of, 13
hidden, at formal interview, 168–69
indirect, 184
intellectuality, 186
by interviewee at formal interview, 166, 180–87
effective, 182–84
poor, 184–86
speech pattern, 186–87
as reflection of you, 187
when to ask, 182
loaded, 185
machine-gun style, 185–86
nonthreatening, 184
open versus closed, 183
probing, 186
purposes of, 180–82
to clarify, 181
to elicit feelings, 181
to gather information, 180–81
self-disclosure, 200, 202–203
that shift the subject, 186
typically asked at formal interview, 167–68
well-informed, 184
*why*, 185

Race tracks, hanging around, 126
Raths, Louis, 42
*Reader's Guide to Periodical Literature*, 140, 141
Real-estate offices, hanging around, 127

Reality testing, 156
Receptionists, 245
  friendships with, 129
  making requests of, 191, 194
Reference sources, printed, *see* Printed materials
Referrals, jobs found through, 12, 114, 120–30
Reik, Theodore, 173
Rejection, fear of, 35
Relocating to target area, 241
Remote control, 237–42
  advantages of, 238
  explanation of, 14
  in-person contact, 240
  telephoning, 239–40
  when and where to begin search, 241–42
  when to move to target area, 241
  writing, 238–39
Research and research skills, 10, 12–13, 70, 131–59
  chart of, 11
  getting started, 134, 135
  inquiring reporter, 12–13, 133, 143–53, 157
  participant observation, 13, 135, 136, 154–59
  printed materials, 12, 116–17, 134, 137–42, 157
  public opinion as information source, 134
  reasons people avoid, 133
Resumes, 111, 207, 208, 239
Retailers, 129
Returning to work force, 20
Reversal thinking, 85–86
Risking, 92–97, 159
  boredom versus, 93, 94, 96
  exercise, 96–97
  explanation of, 12, 93–94
  for maximum possible gain, 95
  for maximum probability of success, 95

  for minimum failure, 95
  for probable gain, 95
  risk of not, 94
  risk styles, 94–95
  security versus, 92–93
  when it is necessary, 95–96
Role playing, 227
Rubinstein, Artur, 76

Sales positions, 246
School, returning to, 246
Secretaries:
  friendships with, 129
  making requests to, 191, 194
Security, need for, 34, 36–37, 42
  *see also* Risking
Security guard, 245
Self-assessment skills, 10, 11–12, 39–103, 188
  chart of, 11
  creativity, 12, 80–91
  feelings, 12, 55–59
  goal setting, 12, 98–103
  risking, 12, 92–97
  skills, 12, 60–79
  values, 11, 43–54
Self-directed career search, 2–3
Self-disclosure, 7, 198–205
  being specific about your abilities, 198–99
  exercise, 205
  explanation of, 13, 198–201
  how to practice, 202–204
  modesty, 60–61, 65, 198, 199
  other forms of, 204–205
  private matters, 201
  revealing weaknesses, 204
  timing of, 201–202
Self-marketing, 148–49, 230–36
  applying for job you don't want, 236
  explanation of, 13–14, 230
  how to cultivate skill of, 231–33

career and seminar activity, 232

extracurricular activities, 231–32

market analysis, 232–33

volunteer work, 231

making your pitch, 235

presenting physical evidence, 235–36

ten hottest transferable skills, 233–35

Self-presentation, *see* Self-disclosure

Self-putdowns, 194–95

Service industry employees, 128

Shaw, George Bernard, 86

*Shyness: What It Is and What to Do About It* (Zimbardo), 195, 251

Shy people, 199, 251–56

assertiveness by, 195–96

census-type part-time job for, 254

emphasizing non-verbal work search skills, 251–52

going to the experts, 252

identifying fear-causing conditions 253–54

immersion experiences, 255

practice being an employer, 254

props as conversation starters, 255–56

starting with non-threatening situations, 252–53

why interviewers will treat you right, 256

Silence, allowing, 165, 177

Simon, Sidney, 42, 45, 48

*Skilled Helper, The* (Egan), 174

Skills, 60–79

acquiring new, 71–72

adaptive, 68, 69

communication, *see* Communication skills

creativity and, 81

curse of single outstanding talent, 74–75

developed late in life, 65

explanation of, 2, 63n.

functional, 68–69

human relations, 70

identifying:

exercises for, 77–79

five ways of, 73–74

rules for, 72–74

interviewing, 70

inventory, 62–63, 74

Johari window, 64

maximizing "low-status," 66–68

modesty about your, 60–61, 65, 198, 199

multiple, 76–77

planning, 70

recognizing, 61

research, *see* Research and researching

rules for identifying, 72–73

self-disclosure of, *see* Self-disclosure

self praise, 61, 65

specific content, 68, 69, 70

thinking, 70

transferable, 34, 68–70

trivializing, avoiding, 64–65

valuing, 70

vocabulary, 64

what good are?, 64–65

*see also* Career skills;

Slowness, 66, 68

"Small-World Problem, The," 123

Speech pattern, 186–87

Spelling, 213

Stockbrokerage offices, hanging around, 126

Stock reports, 141

*Subject Collections: A Guide to Special Book Collections in Libraries*, 139

Supervising skills, 233
Support group, 221–26
  assignment of roles to, 225–26
  explanation of, 13, 221–22
  group job hunting, 227–29
  materials for, 224
  methods, 226–27
  roles of, 222–23
  sources of support, 222–23
  your attitude and, 223–24
Suzuki, D. T., 258, 260
Systematic desensitization, 252, 253
Systematicness, 31

Take-charge philosophies, 2
Talkativeness, 66, 67
Taverns, hanging around, 126
Teaching skills, 234–35
Telephone books, 116, 224
Telephone contacts, 117
  long-distance work search and, 238, 239–40
Temporary office worker, 245
Thank-you notes, 211
Thinking:
  lateral, 85
  rational, 257–59
  reversal, 85–86
  skills, 70
  visually, 84, 264
  ways to stimulate creative, 87–89
  wrongheaded, 83–86
Time to find job, lack of, 34–35
Tone of voice, 187
Transferable skills, 34, 68–70
Transition skills, 10, 13–14, 219–47
  chart of, 11
  interim job, 14, 243–47
  remote control, 14, 237–42
  self-marketing, 13–14, 230–36
  support group, 13, 221–29
Trapped feeling, 22–23

Travel agencies, hanging around, 126
Travel agent, 245
*Truth About You, The* (Mattson and Miller), 46
Truth session, 226

*U.S. News and World Report*, 140
United Way, 238

Values, 43–54, 70, 174
  -clarification exercises, 49–54
  creativity and, 81
  explanation of, 11, 41–45
  feelings as barometer of, 57
  identifying, 45–48
    by future desires, 45–46, 47
    by key themes, 46
    by past experience, 45, 46
    subprocesses to aid in, 48, 50–51
  rewards and, 44–45
    conditions, 44
    enjoyment, 44
    value to others, 44–45
  of significant others, 48–49
  work, 42–44
*Values and Teaching* (Raths et al.), 42
*Values Clarification* (Simon et al.), 45
Verbal abilities, 33
  *see also* Interviews; Communication skill
Verbs, using strong, 213
Visual thinking, 84, 264
Vocabulary used in letter writing, 214
Vocal flatness, 187
Voice, the, emotions conveyed by, 174, 176
*Voice of Neurosis, The* (Moses), 176
Volunteer work, 136, 156, 231

Wackman, Daniel B., 56
Walk-in interview, 150, 151–52
*Wall Street Journal*, 140
*Wall Street Journal Index*, 140, 141
*What Color Is Your Parachute?*
    (Bolles), 3
*Where Do I Go from Here with My
    Life?* (Crystal and Bolles),
    122
White Pages, 116, 224
*Who's Who in America*, 142
*Who's Who in the East*, 142
*Who's Who in the West*, 142
Words:
    personal letter writing and,
        213–14
    rigidity of, 84
Work experience:
    interim job, *see* Interim job
    lack of, 18–19
Writing, 206–17, 234
    business letters, 207, 214–15
    explanation of, 13

guidelines for effective, 213–14
how it can work against you, 212
long-distance work search and,
    238–39
personal letters, 207–17
    behind-the-scenes writing,
        209–10
    how to get personal, 208–209
    note from admirer, 211
    portfolio, 211
    sample, 215–17
    thank-you notes, 211
Written information, *see* Printed
    materials

Yellow Pages, 116
*Your Creative Power* (Osborn), 86,
    226

Zen of the work search, 257–65
    how to apply zen principles,
        264–65
Zimbardo, Philip, 195, 251